BISON
BOOKS

MW00559677

STEVE FRIESEN

GALLOPING GOURMET

EATING AND DRINKING WITH BUFFALO BILL

University of Nebraska Press | Lincoln

The University of Nebraska Press is part of a land-grant institution with campuses and programs on the past, present, and future homelands of the Pawnee, Ponca, Otoe-Missouria, Omaha, Dakota, Lakota, Kaw, Cheyenne, and Arapaho Peoples, as well as those of the relocated Ho-Chunk, Sac and Fox, and Iowa Peoples.

Library of Congress Cataloging-in-Publication Data
Names: Friesen, Steve, 1953–, author.
Title: Galloping gourmet: eating and drinking with Buffalo Bill / Steve Friesen, University of Nebraska Press.
Description: Lincoln: University of Nebraska Press, 2023. | Includes bibliographical references and index.
Identifiers: LCCN 2023012609
ISBN 9781496236807 (paperback)
ISBN 9781496238122 (epub)
ISBN 9781496238139 (pdf)
Subjects: LCSH: Cooking, American—Western style—History—19th century. | Buffalo Bill, 1846–1917—Homes and haunts. | Food habits—West (U.S.)—History—19th century. | Frontier and pioneer life—West (U.S.) | Pioneers—West (U.S.)—Social life and customs. | Entertainers—United States—Social life and customs—19th century. | BISAC: HISTORY / United States / State & Local / West (AK, CA, CO, HI, ID, MT, NV, UT, WY) | COOKING / History | LCGFT: Cookbooks.
Classification: LCC TX715.2.W47 F75 2023 |
DDC 641.5978—dc23/eng/20230331
LC record available at https://lccn.loc.gov/2023012609

Set in New Baskerville by K. Andresen.
Designed by L. Welch.

CONTENTS

Part 3. The Last Stands

ILLUSTRATIONS

ACKNOWLEDGMENTS

Special thanks to the staffs at the institutions where I did most of my research: the McCracken Library at the Buffalo Bill Center of the West, the Western History Division of the Denver Public Library, the Beinecke and Sterling Libraries at Yale, the archives at the American Heritage Center in Laramie, and the Buffalo Bill Museum and Grave. Particularly critical to my work was The Papers of William F. Cody project at the Buffalo Bill Center of the West, which provides ongoing research assistance and leadership in the exploration of all things Buffalo Bill and maintains codyarchive.org, a valuable online resource.

Over the five years I worked on this project, I received advice and guidance from many more people than I can name here. But I must single out four who helped me immensely and whom I am also pleased to call my friends: Jeremy Johnston, Tom Cunningham, Bill Carle, and Jacqui Ainlay-Conley. And my final thanks go to Monta Lee Dakin, my advisor, editor, travel companion, wife, and best friend.

INTRODUCTION

A *Culinary Biography*

While you are at luncheon in the tent back of Colonel Cody's you will get your first lesson—and a particularly delightful one. It is that Colonel Cody's table with the Wild West isn't Buffalo Bill's camp fire on the plains or in the mountains, when scouting among hostile Indians. With Colonel Cody, Mr. Salsbury, his partner; Major Burke and other "pale-face" chiefs, you find you are in a jolly company at a lavish feast.

New York Sunday Tribune, 1894

"Galloping Gourmet." For some of us, these words evoke memories of a television program hosted by Graham Kerr. As a teenager, I spent hours watching that program, entertained and informed by the host's cooking skills and antics. Kerr influenced my own interest in gourmet eating and cooking, as he did for countless others. But I have come to realize that he was not America's first "galloping gourmet." That title belongs to a man who graduated from meals on the Great Plains to dinners at the Waldorf, all while promoting America's Wild West to the world—William F. "Buffalo Bill" Cody.

Buffalo Bill certainly galloped through the American West as a frontiersman, buffalo hunter, scout, and ultimately showman. He was many other things as well: actor, businessman, writer, art aficionado, hotelier, even town founder. But a gourmet?

Not long after I wrote my first book on Buffalo Bill, I was introduced to Guillermo Arrellano by our mutual friend Patty Calhoun. Through them I learned that Buffalo Bill had opened the first Mexican restaurant east of the Mississippi. After running across several other intriguing tidbits of information about food innovations in Buffalo Bill's Wild West, I decided to explore further. I found that he often wrote about food and drink in his various autobiographies. And period newspapers abounded with stories about his dining with other celebrities of his day. These were more than tidbits in the historical records; there were literally hundreds of references to his enjoyment of food, drink, and all that surrounds the consumption of each. That consumption assisted Cody's ascendency to celebrity. Annie Oakley once said, "I have seen him the life of the party at dinner with the late King Edward at Sandrinham [*sic*] Palace just as much at home as he was in the saddle." My research uncovered more about eating and drinking with Buffalo Bill than I ever expected, enough to convince me that he was indeed a man as comfortable with dining of every kind as he was on horseback. In short, he was a galloping gourmet.[1]

This book is the result of my investigations. In it I not only explore the role of eating and drinking in Buffalo Bill's life but put that role within the context of his times, his other experiences and enterprises, and the time he spent with other influencers of his day. One is struck by the variety and abundance of foods in those meals, from formal banquets he attended to the daily diet of performers in his show. He lived at a time when there was a burgeoning of food options. It was the dawn of a bountiful consumption that continued into the twentieth century. A wide range of foods, and large quantities of them, previously available to royalty and aristocracy were now accessible to America's and Europe's middle and upper classes.

Not only did Buffalo Bill have marvelous and bountiful dining experiences, he ensured that everyone around him did as well. One newspaper reporter observed, "Colonel Cody displays no more care about anything than the proper feeding of horse and man." His concern for those who worked for him was greater than that of many bosses of his time. This certainly extended to providing fine food, and plenty of it. He also became a "missionary" for western foods in the eastern United States and for American cookery in general as the show traveled overseas. His friend John Burke observed that Cody helped introduce new foods to England and the rest of Europe, noting that "frequently English people would come to the tents to get recipes."[2]

In 1936 Mrs. Betty Isham, who had worked for Buffalo Bill at his home in Cody, Wyoming, remembered that "he was quite hearty and liked good things to eat." She said that among his favorite dishes were fried chicken, soft-boiled eggs with toast, fried kidneys, and custard pie. These were his comfort foods, harking back to the days of his youth in Kansas. They were the sorts of dishes one eats when one is at home. But Bill Cody was rarely at home. Most of the time he was traveling, enjoying everything from sage hen roasted over an open fire to fillet of sole in anchovy sauce to some of the finest steaks served in the United States.[3]

Cody's friend Dexter Fellows recalled, "Those were the days when men seldom took a hand in the kitchen, but they knew how good food should be prepared." Buffalo Bill was a gourmet but not a gourmet cook. During his early days on the frontier, he did cook fish, sage hen, buffalo, and other wild game over a campfire. This love of campfire meals continued throughout his life, and when he camped on hunting trips, he often enjoyed cooking for his guests. But after he crossed the Hudson River for the first time, he relied on professionals to prepare his gourmet fare.[4]

Here are a few notes about names and terminologies used in this book. Buffalo Bill's real name was William F. Cody. While these two names were often used interchangeably, they reflected two different personas. One was Buffalo Bill, a frontiersman and entertainer. The other was William F. Cody, an influencer and captain of industry. The two roles allowed him to both maintain his show business presence and interact freely with the movers and shakers of his day. He was also referred to as Colonel Cody, General Cody, W. F. Cody, Bill Cody, Will Cody, or as his sisters called him, Willie. Throughout the book, the narrative and period quotations refer to him by these various names and titles.

On his first trip east, Buffalo Bill soon found that eastern dining differed greatly from western, not just in what was served but also in when the meals took place and even what they were called. One of his first invitations was to breakfast. He later remembered, "I fixed myself up in the best I had in those days and started out to attend the breakfast." He arrived at 7:00 a.m., a customary time for breakfast in the West, only to discover that it was not served until 1:00 p.m. The next day he was invited to dinner, which was usually served around noon in the West, so he dressed for it at 11:00 a.m. and arrived at 12:30 p.m. However, it turned out that dinner was not until 7:00 p.m., a customary time in the East. This was his first discovery that terms like *breakfast, lunch, dinner,* and *supper* were interpreted differently based on geographic location. Even the times at which each of those occurred could vary. But Cody was flexible, and by 1880 he might eat breakfast, lunch, or dinner at 1:00 p.m., depending on where he happened to be at the time. The terms were used interchangeably in menus, invitations, and other publications throughout the rest of his life and appear in this book in the same manner.[5]

This culinary biography begins with chapters that describe William Cody's early life in chronological order. He was developing as a gourmet during this time, and thus "Acquiring a Taste for the Good Life" is the title of part 1. John Burke, who worked as the Wild West's publicist, did not like the term *show.* In the early years he even threatened employees with being fired if he heard them use that word to refer to Buffalo Bill's Wild West. Yes, it was entertainment, but it was also intended to be an educational exhibition. "Culinary Themes from an Exhibition" is therefore the title of part 2, which includes a series of thematic chapters that tell stories of eating and drinking with Buffalo Bill during the thirty golden years of his Wild West. The narrative concludes with part 3, "The Last Stands," covering Buffalo Bill's drinking and divorce trial, the death of the Wild West, his own death, and his legacy.

The period recipes for many of the dishes Buffalo Bill enjoyed are too interesting not to include. Rather than interrupt the flow of the narrative, I have included an appendix with recipes for some of the foods and drinks in which Cody indulged, along with historical information about each. The appendix is intended to be a source for adventurous cooks who wish to sample the tastes of the past.

Eating and drinking are among the most basic functions necessary to life. They can also bring us some of our greatest joy, whether it is from savoring a particularly tasty dish, recalling vivid memories of good times past, or enjoying a hearty meal with friends old and new. This book is a deep dive into the different roles food and drink played in William Cody's life. It is my hope that it not only provides a new perspective on Buffalo Bill but also entertains . . . and makes the reader more than a little hungry.

Galloping Gourmet

Part 1

Acquiring a Taste for the Good Life

1

Apples, Yellow-Legged Chickens, and Whiskey

Mr. Cody is very popular here and leaves nearly every performance to change his suit of buckskin for a dress suit and attend a dinner or reception. His name appears among the noted guests of every great entertainment in Paris.

Capper's Weekly, 1889

When William F. "Buffalo Bill" Cody strode into any of New York City's finest restaurants, he could confidently take his seat, feeling completely at home. In just over forty years he had become the most desirable dinner guest on two continents, progressing from eating hardtack with fellow scouts on the Great Plains to banqueting with princes in Europe. He was as comfortable dining at Delmonico's as he was sitting by a campfire in the Rockies. His dining companions across two continents included the likes of Thomas Edison, Theodore Roosevelt, Oscar Wilde, and other celebrities. As his friend Annie Oakley observed, "He was probably the guest of more people in diverse circumstances than any man alive."[1]

Cody certainly encountered diverse circumstances during his life, circumstances that molded him into one of the best-known people of his day and a representative of America's West. He worked as a teamster, trapper, gold seeker, and Civil War soldier. He earned his nickname as a buffalo hunter and was awarded a Medal of Honor as a scout. He then parlayed his knowledge of the West, growing celebrity, and charisma into a career as an actor, showman, entrepreneur, and innovator. Throughout it all, Buffalo Bill ate and drank with the gusto of a gourmet. Yet his love of food and drink, as well as the food innovations he introduced, are little-known dimensions of a remarkable life.

The remarkable life of William Cody began on a farm near LeClaire, Iowa, on February 26, 1846. His lifelong journey through the wonders of eating and drinking began with apples and yellow-legged chickens. Among his few memories from that time was stealing apples and melons from a farm nearby, a common form of mischief into which youths of his day often wandered. A large dog guarding the orchard nearly caught him one day when he was climbing over a fence with a hatful of apples. Will got away with the apples but lost his pants, which were firmly gripped in the dog's teeth.[2]

Antoine LeClaire, an early settler in the area for whom the town of LeClaire was later named, planted the first apple orchard in the 1830s. By the time Will commenced his short career in apple stealing, as many as seventy-two apple varieties were being planted in Iowa, including Baldwin, Jonathan, Northern Spy, Winesap, and Spitzenburg, reportedly Thomas Jefferson's favorite. Young Cody could have pilfered any of these.[3]

Several years later, when the Cody family was no longer living in Iowa, Will had a youthful encounter with apples in their liquid—and fermented—form. While visiting a friend's home, he got into a barrel of hard apple cider, drinking a large quantity. His sister Helen later remembered that Will was "in deplorable condition," singing and shouting mightily. Will's heavy consumption had its inevitable aftermath, and he never touched hard cider again. However, this first experience with alcohol did not discourage him from later indulging in its other forms.[4]

The family left Iowa for Missouri in early 1854, anticipating the opening of Kansas Territory. Along the way, they stayed in hotels and "cross-road taverns," taking provisions from them or from farms they passed. For much of the journey, the family relied on corn bread, of which they all became quite tired. When they were within twenty miles of Weston, their objective, they spotted a large brick house. Will's father, Isaac, decided that was evidence the inhabitants were wealthy and remarked, "They probably have white bread there." They were and they did. It turned out that the owners knew Isaac's brother Elijah, a merchant in Weston. They invited the Codys to spend the night and provided them with plenty of white bread, which young Will declared a "luxurious treat."[5]

Fig 1. Weston MO in 1853, the year before the Cody family arrived. Engraving by Hermann Meyer. Author's collection.

Weston was no hardscrabble frontier town. It was a booming community, first settled in 1837 and well populated with five thousand residents, who included not only established businessmen, like Isaac's brother Elijah, but also rough frontiersmen who made forays into the Great Plains and the Rockies beyond. They were there with their sights turned to the West. Weston and other communities along the Missouri River were port cities, stops for riverboats laden with goods being transported throughout the West. Weston alone had over 250 steamboats arriving each year and was one of the largest ports on the Missouri (fig. 1).

Great wagon trains filled with freight traveled from the towns of Weston, Saint Joseph, and Westport (now Kansas City) to Santa Fe, Salt Lake City, and the West Coast. In addition to the commerce, there were also settlers seeking to make new lives in places like Oregon and fortune seekers on their way to the California goldfields. The *Kansas Weekly Herald* reported in 1854 that "the vast emigrations to California, Oregon and the Salt Lake have as yet supplied themselves with stock, provisions, groceries, clothing, etc., at the Towns of Missouri. All the goods consumed by the fifty thousand Mormons of Utah, are taken overland from this frontier and chiefly by the merchants of Weston and St. Joseph."[6]

For Will Cody and his siblings, Weston was an exciting place to be. Their family was poised to enter the vast Kansas Territory in just a few weeks, and they saw other families like their own departing for points even farther into the West. Both Will and his sister later recalled the hundreds of covered wagons they saw upon their arrival in Weston. The wagons were aimed at the unknown, which, for an eight-year-old boy, promised untold adventure. Will decided at that point that he, too, wanted to move westward when he got older.

Just before the territory opened, Will's father took him on brief forays across the river to scout out land. Isaac's plan was to farm and open a trading post with the Indians. Finally, on May 30, 1854, the territory was opened to settlement. Isaac's preparations paid off: when the Cody family finally crossed the Missouri for good, they were among the first settlers in the new territory. They built their farm in the Salt Creek Valley on the west side of the Missouri, just a few miles from Weston.[7]

The Codys were followed by many others who had also been awaiting their opportunity. Will's sister Helen wrote, "Across the curtain of the night ran a broad ribbon of dancing camp-fires, stretching for miles along the bank of the river." There along the Missouri were hundreds of settlers, awaiting their opportunity to cross the river and get new land. Once the territory opened, steam ferries in Weston were busy every day, shuttling wagons filled with household goods and other supplies necessary to settling the new land. A local newspaper observed, "Our young Territory is filling up with a rapidity unparalleled except in the case of California."[8]

Will later remembered, "Thousands and thousands of people, seeking new homes, flocked thither, a large number of the immigrants coming over from adjoining states. The Missourians, some of them, would come laden with bottles of whiskey and, after drinking the liquor would drive them into the ground to mark their land claims." Whiskey flowed freely in the frontier borderlands. Benjamin Holladay established a "dram shop and tavern" in Weston in 1839. With the flood of new immigrants, Benjamin and his brother David opened a distillery outside of Weston in 1856, giving Missourians easy access to bottles filled with whiskey and hopes for new land in Kansas Territory.[9]

Isaac Cody had no opposition to whiskey and other forms of alcohol. In fact, when a temperance society was formed in LeClaire, he made no secret of his disdain for the movement; it was reported that at a public meeting, he "sailed into the temperance folks at a lively rate." Plenty of alcohol was available to the elder Cody as the family crossed the state of Missouri. Whiskey was distilled in St. Louis and could be purchased for thirty-nine cents per gallon at towns like Glasgow, on the Missouri River midway between St. Louis and Weston. Once the Codys arrived in Weston, plentiful amounts of whiskey could be had at Holladay's and other shops, delivered by the riverboats that plied their trade along the Missouri.[10]

The Salt Creek Valley was well situated and considered to be "one of the prettiest valleys in the Territory." The growing community of Leavenworth, anchored by Fort Leavenworth, was just eight miles away, and Weston lay across the Missouri River. The valley had rich soil and was well watered by Salt Creek, which meandered through the land before emptying into the Missouri. Most of the valley was quickly claimed, and a year later improved claims like that owned by the Codys were selling for $1,000 to $3,000. The land's value undoubtedly increased because a great deal of acreage to the north belonged to the Kickapoo Indians and was off-limits to settlement.[11]

The Kickapoos were the first American Indians encountered by Will Cody. He met them during one of his forays across the Missouri with his father before the territory opened. The Indians were friendly, but his efforts to talk with them were largely unsuccessful. In the months after the family moved into the territory, he visited the Kickapoo village many times. Cody wrote that some of them "were living in lodges but the majority occupied log cabins." Two Kickapoo boys also attended a school begun by the Cody family, where they and Will became fast friends. These early positive experiences with the Kickapoos had a marked impact on young Will Cody, who later spoke about the American Indians with admiration and respect. Just as he had made friends among the Kickapoos as a boy, he forged friendships among the Lakotas as a man.[12]

While the Kickapoos were the largest tribe living near the Salt Creek Valley, there were also Delaware and Cherokee tribes in the area. Wishing to maintain a good relationship with their Indian neighbors, the Codys and some of the other settlers threw a Fourth of July barbecue for the three tribes. It was quite the party, with two hundred Indians and settlers in attendance. Isaac's brother Elijah even brought some of his employees and friends from Weston. Isaac supplied two beef cattle for the feast. One was roasted by the settlers; the other was dressed and cooked "Indian style" by the Kickapoos, as Will later put it. The Indians did not waste any part of the cow, even washing out the intestines and cooking them on iron rods over the fire. The settlers in attendance furnished home-baked bread and ample amounts of coffee and sugar. Entertainment was provided by the Indians, who engaged in horse races, demonstrated some of their games, and concluded the celebration with dances. Will's sister Julia declared it "the most wonderful picnic I ever seen." The impact on young Will may have been even greater. Years later Fourth of July feasts figured prominently at Buffalo Bill's Wild West, while dignitaries visiting the show were treated to "Indian style" rib roasts.[13]

A main source of supplies was Rively's store, located two miles away from the farm. M. P. Rively opened a trading post with the Indians around 1853 and was already doing a lively business in the Salt Creek Valley before the territory was opened to settlement. Will remembered visiting the log store on one of his early trips into the territory with his father: "We stopped at this establishment for a while, and found perhaps a hundred men, women and children gathered there, engaged in trading and gossiping. The men had huge pistols and knives in their belts; their pantaloons were tucked in their boots; and they wore large broad-brimmed hats."[14]

Like their neighbors on both sides of the Missouri, the Cody family planted crops, cultivated a garden, and raised livestock. One of the first crops planted was corn, which grew well in the fertile soil of the Salt Creek Valley. When the corn was harvested, it was made into hominy to preserve it. The garden was large, with melons, cucumbers, squash, pumpkins, and potatoes. The family had a cellar where they could keep the potatoes, squash, and pumpkins through the winter season. They also had a small herd of cattle to supply milk and cream for butter. Julia wrote that Will helped with all the chores but milking. "He said he was not going to ever learn to milk, and he kept his word."[15]

The spring and summer of 1856 were particularly bountiful; Julia wrote that the corn reached as high as eight feet, and the garden was filled with vegetables. Summertime in the Salt Creek Valley also offered wild fruit. As the season progressed, the family picked strawberries, then gooseberries, raspberries, and finally blackberries. That fall they had wild plums, crab apples, and grapes. Julia remembered that in the fall of 1858, Will hitched a pony team to their wagon and they gathered wild fruits and nuts.[16]

The valley offered more than fruits and nuts. Julia and Will hunted small game for the family's larder, supplying squirrels, prairie chickens, and quail. According to Julia, they usually caught the quail with traps, "as there was lots of them and we enjoyed getting them." Rabbits were also plentiful and made "fine eating."[17]

The abundance of quail notwithstanding, domestic poultry was central to the family's diet. At the time, people rarely referred to specific breeds of chickens but instead described the colors of their legs. Yellow-legged chickens were commonly raised in the United States in the nineteenth century. They were larger than the blue-, black-, and white-legged chickens. Yellow-legged types familiar later in the century, like the Plymouth Rock and Wyandotte, were not bred until after the 1860s. The Leghorn, a yellow-legged chicken from Italy, was present in a few states in the East but not as far west as Kansas Territory. The yellow-legged chickens most commonly raised at the time were Dominiques, a breed introduced to America in the eighteenth century (fig. 2). Hardy and self-sufficient, they foraged for themselves and were well protected with heavy plumage. A report from the commissioner of agriculture in 1862 stated the Dominique was "the only common fowl in the country that has enough distinct characteristics to entitle it to name." But as far as the Cody family was concerned, they raised yellow-legged chickens.[18]

These chickens were often served to company, circuit-riding ministers in particular. The practice was so common that people

DOMINIQUES,
BRED FROM IMPORTED STOCK BY T. D. GALPIN, ESQ.

Fig 2. Dominique chickens. Yellow-legged Dominique chickens were commonly raised and eaten in Kansas in the 1850s. *Cassell's Book of Poultry,* ca. 1880. Author's collection.

often joked about Methodist ministers and yellow-legged chickens. As one writer noted, "There are certain jokes on the subject of yellow-legged chickens and camp-meetings, which are older than the Constitution of the United States." One Kansas newspaper even quipped that a local ministers' and laymen's institute was actually a society for "the propagation of yellow legged chickens." Some people considered the flesh to be too dry and stringy, comparing these chickens unfavorably to those with other leg colors. Despite that criticism, another writer suggested "that a yellow-legged chicken, when properly cooked, furnishes an essential joy not especially antagonistic to orthodox religion."[19]

Will's sister Helen remembered that their log house was the largest in the Salt Creek Valley and that, since her mother was a Methodist, it was often a destination for circuit-riding ministers, who were served yellow-legged chickens. These chickens "were our best ones and the only thing we had for the ministers to eat." Will, who was not very fond of church meetings, would scatter the chickens with the aid of his dog. He hoped none would be captured and the hungry minister would leave without giving a sermon.[20]

Their crops and animals supplied many of the Cody family's needs, but they also took advantage of goods available at Rively's store, where they could obtain groceries, dry goods, hardware, crockery, clothing, and other supplies. With the arrival of new settlers in 1854, the store's role as a community center expanded. Rively filled the needs of area settlers as well as pioneers embarking for Oregon and California, advertising that his store was "on the Oregon road near Salt Creek" and that "teamsters and others who intend crossing the Plains" could obtain supplies there.[21]

Weston was across the river from the Salt Creek Valley but involved a ferry crossing. It was just as convenient for the family to shop in Leavenworth, only eight miles away. Leavenworth was the first city founded in Kansas after the opening of the territory. Its settlement was facilitated by the presence of Fort Leavenworth, built as a U.S. Army post in 1827. The fort was home not only to members of the military but also to the farmers, blacksmiths, and other civilian personnel who provided services to them. Once the territory was opened, the community grew rapidly as a service center for the many farms and smaller communities that sprang up nearby.

A satirical column in a Leavenworth newspaper wrote in 1856 that anyone heading into the territory should have their stomach "lined with waterproof cement, so as to be able to digest corn bread, bacon and whiskey, for this is all we have to eat." This may have been the experience of some settlers, but the Missouri riverboats that frequented the area brought all sorts of goods to Leavenworth: coffee, sugar, tea, cheese, butter, rice, crackers, oysters, sardines, molasses, flour, salt, yeast powders, spices, sugar-cured ham, bacon, canned fruits and vegetables, nuts, dried fruits, and a variety of wines and liquors. All were available in the booming river town to those who, like the Cody family, could afford them.[22]

Henry Rosenfeld, a Leavenworth dealer in preserves, fruits, cigars, wines, and liquors, advertised that "orders from the country" would be promptly filled. Merrill Smith offered a broad range of provisions that included dried and canned fruits, whitefish, salmon, and mackerel, as well as basic supplies like flour, rice, eggs, meats, and butter. The store also sold imported and domestic liquors in addition to whiskey. With riverboats carrying new supplies arriving almost daily, competition among these purveyors was fierce, and N. McCracken stated that he could "offer such inducements to the farms, and particularly to country merchants as cannot be found in any other house above St. Louis, on the Missouri River."[23]

Isaac Cody traded with the Kickapoo Indians for a short time after the family's arrival in the Salt Creek Valley. But he soon became involved in another venture. Not long after setting up the family farm, he was instrumental in founding the town of Grasshopper Falls, about thirty-four miles west of the valley, where he was an investor in a gristmill and a sawmill. Isaac and other members of his family frequently traveled between the Salt Creek Valley and Grasshopper Falls.[24]

Though it never grew to the size of Weston or Leavenworth, Grasshopper Falls became a successful community. In 1857 the town had nearly twenty houses, and by 1873 it was a thriving community of over twelve thousand. A few years later it was renamed Valley Falls. But Isaac Cody did not live to see the town's success.[25]

A few months after the family settled in the Salt Creek Valley, Isaac was invited to speak at a public meeting at Rively's store. He had been involved in politics in Iowa and agreed with free-state advocates, who opposed the introduction of slavery to Kansas. But his position on the matter was both controversial and dangerous here. When he spoke out against allowing slavery in Kansas, a proslavery advocate in the crowd attacked him, stabbing him near the heart and seriously wounding him. While his wound did not kill him, it left him in a weakened condition.[26]

Buffalo Bill was proud of his father for taking a stand against slavery, but the choice to speak up at Rively's store may have been imprudent, since it was a gathering place for slavery proponents. Even Rively supported allowing slavery in the territory, one of the reasons people who advocated slavery gathered there. Many in the crowd viewed Isaac as a "noisy abolitionist" and looked for opportunities to finish the job begun by his attacker. This menacing situation was likely why the Cody family started taking their business to Leavenworth.[27]

Isaac's speech at Rively's initiated a period of persecution against the Codys. Not only did Isaac receive death threats, but proslavery advocates often stopped at the Cody home hoping to catch him unawares and follow through on the threats. He frequently took to the family's cornfield to hide. He stayed in Grasshopper Falls rather than the Salt Creek Valley during the winter of 1856, which may have been prompted by the threats. Those threats also motivated him to take most of the family's small herd of cattle with him since his adversaries occasionally plundered the farm. Will remembered, "They helped themselves to anything they saw fit, and frequently compelled my mother and sisters to cook for them." The persecution only strengthened Isaac's resolve, and he participated in early efforts to create a legislature in Kansas, all the while advocating against allowing slavery. He even traveled to Ohio on one occasion to meet with abolitionist organizers.[28]

The proslavery men finally got their wish on March 10, 1857, when Isaac succumbed to a fever as a result of his weakened condition. He had lived in Kansas Territory for three years, settled his family on a comfortable farm in the Salt Creek Valley, and helped found the town of Grasshopper Springs. After his death, his brother Joseph moved from Ohio to Grasshopper Falls to manage Isaac's properties. Joseph also started a newspaper, *The Grasshopper*. The paper reported in 1858 that the town had nearly fifty buildings, including several mills, grocery stores, and a church. Grasshopper Falls prospered, but the Cody family did not. By the end of the year the newspaper had closed, and Joseph Cody appears to have left the area. Thus ended the Cody family's involvement with that community. With Isaac and his investments in Grasshopper Falls gone, life became more difficult for the family back in the Salt Creek Valley.[29]

Upon his father's death, eleven-year-old Will became the man of the house and found employment with the firm of Alexander Majors and William Russell, a leading purveyor of retail goods in Leavenworth. The firm obtained a contract with the government in 1855 to transport military supplies west of the Missouri, and when the gold rush to Colorado began in late 1858, they provided supplies to gold seekers. Young Will Cody did a variety of odd jobs for Majors and Russell, ranging from messenger boy to cattle herder, until he was hired by them and their partner William Waddell to work on a wagon train following the Oregon Trail. It was his first opportunity to venture into the West, which had so fascinated him only a few years earlier. From that point on, the American West, with its landscapes, animals, peoples, and adventures, was the central theme of his life.[30]

2

Hardtack and Wagon Trains

On the way down we stopped at Fort Laramie, and there met
a supply train bound westward. Of course we all had a square
meal once more, consisting of hard tack, bacon, coffee, and
beans. I can honestly say that I thought it was the best meal
I had ever eaten.

Buffalo Bill, 1879

As the main breadwinner for his family, eleven-year-old Will Cody
had to grow up quickly. His first job as a teamster for Russell, Majors,
and Waddell was on a freight wagon train to Fort Kearney, in south-
central Nebraska along the Oregon Trail. That trip introduced him
to the foods needed for survival on the frontier.

Will encountered his first buffalo on that trip, writing, "This
country was alive with buffaloes. Vast herds of these monarchs of
the plains were roaming all around us, and we laid over one day for
a grand hunt." A single buffalo provided ample meat, furnishing
ninety pounds of fat and dried meat for pemmican, a common
survival food on the frontier. Eaten fresh, its meat was described
in 1833 as "very juicy and well-flavored, much resembling that of
well-fed beef." It was a meat with which Cody would become quite
familiar.[1]

Later in 1857 Russell, Majors, and Waddell assigned Will to a
wagon train headed for Salt Lake. It consisted of twenty-five wagons, each loaded with six thousand pounds of freight. The train
also carried thirty-one men, who all reported to a wagon master.
The men were separated into messes of seven, each with specific
responsibilities for preparing meals. The supplies were on their
way to U.S. troops stationed near Salt Lake City to stop a potential
Mormon rebellion. The wagon train never reached Salt Lake; it

was ambushed in Wyoming by a group of Mormons who did not want the supplies to reach the soldiers. The Mormon leader said he would leave the men enough provisions to last until they reached Fort Bridger, near the Wyoming-Utah border. Twenty-four of the wagons were burned, along with much of the food that the men had been counting on eating. Cody and the rest of the group were left with just one wagon and six yokes of oxen to pull it.[2]

It was late fall of 1857 when the men reached Fort Bridger, where they were forced to spend the winter. There they joined other employees of Russell, Majors, and Waddell, whose wagons had also been confiscated, and soldiers who were stationed at the fort. With so many mouths, food was scarce, and by late winter they were down to quarter rations. Soon they were killing and eating not only the remaining oxen but also the government mules. That spring Cody and the other teamsters set out for Fort Laramie and the best meal young Will had eaten for a long time: a feast of hardtack, bacon, coffee, and beans.[3]

The Cody home in Salt Creek Valley was large enough to provide lodging for travelers, and the extra rooms were full nearly every night. To bring in more income after Isaac's passing, Mrs. Cody built a hotel and boardinghouse. On a hill near the Cody home, the new Valley Grove House afforded a view of the valley below. Wagons accessing the western trails had to surmount this hill, and the hotel had no shortage of business feeding hungry teamsters. It was later described as a place "where the weary footsore traveler could find comfortable accommodations and motherly attention."[4]

The Valley Grove House was ready to open for business when Will, James Butler "Wild Bill" Hickok, and other teamsters from Russell, Majors, and Waddell returned from one of their trips across the plains. Will was eager to promote the hotel to Hickok and the other friends he had made. His older sister, Julia, who helped her mother manage the hotel in addition to serving as cook, told him she could provide room and board for six persons as boarders. The other teamsters eventually moved on, but Wild Bill stayed with the Codys for several weeks.[5]

A decade later, after the Civil War, Will attempted to follow in his mother's footsteps, moving into the hotel and renaming it the

Golden Rule House. That effort was a failure, but hotels—and hotel food—played an important role throughout most of his life. He lived in them, often one night at a time, for months on end during his early show business career. Later, after he achieved show business success, he also invested in and opened several hotels in Wyoming.[6]

Despite the relative comforts of home, Will continued to be drawn back to the frontier. As he said later, "My restless, roaming spirit would not allow me to remain at home very long." The fall of 1858 brought news of gold discoveries in the foothills of the Rockies, generally described as the Pikes Peak region. Despite reports from other Russell, Majors, and Waddell drivers that food provisions were scarce in that region, the following year Will joined a group of prospectors and headed for the goldfields. Unlike his other trips, this trip the wagons were not loaded with freight, nor were they filled with farm implements like the wagons traveling the trails to Oregon and California. Instead, they transported shovels and picks.

Knowing that supplies would be expensive in the Rockies, the prospectors also filled their wagons with flour, sugar, coffee, canned vegetables, dried fruit, and hardtack, often called hard bread (fig. 3). At the time, flour cost $30 for one hundred pounds, and coffee seventy-five cents a pound, As on previous trips, the men included bacon as a supplement to the game they planned on hunting. Given Will's history with the firm, the group probably purchased their supplies from the Russell, Majors, and Waddell store in Leavenworth. The store advertised, "Now is Your Time! Gold! Gold! Gold! Pike's Peak is Raging And the Best and Only Place to Get Your Outfit is at Russell, Majors and Waddell's." But Pike's Peak wasn't "raging" for Will's group of hopefuls. After two months of prospecting near Central City, he returned home with nothing to show for it. He was unsuccessful on that expedition, but he had been bitten by the gold bug; years later he once again searched for gold, this time in the Arizona mountains.[7]

Will Cody's long-standing relationship with Russell, Majors, and Waddell began with the Cody family purchasing supplies from their stores in Leavenworth and continued through employment

Fig 3. A greatly romanticized late nineteenth-century vision of cooking a meal while on the Oregon Trail. The family is guided and protected by two frontiersmen, one of whom bears a close resemblance to Buffalo Bill. Author's collection.

of young Will as a driver on the firm's wagon trains. According to Alexander Majors, other riders, and Cody himself, when the firm founded the Pony Express in 1860, Will was hired as a rider.[8]

Will's account of his time with the Pony Express provides a picture of what the riders ate in between their whirlwind rides from station to station connecting St. Louis and the Pacific coast. Each station had provisions for both the station agents and the riders, which the men typically supplemented with meals of wild game. During his spare time while stationed at the Horseshoe Station (near today's Glendo, Wyoming), he went bear hunting near Laramie Peak. He never found any bears but did shoot a sage hen, which he cleaned, seasoned with some salt and pepper, then broiled over a fire. After this "genuine square meal" for lunch, he shot two more sage hens, which he intended to have for his evening meal and breakfast. Before setting up camp that evening, he ran into a group of outlaws. He was able to escape from them but rode back to the station through the night without having a chance to eat the other two hens.[9]

J. G. Kelley, a former Pony Express rider, wrote that Russell, Majors, and Waddell treated their riders and wagon drivers well. "They were different in many respects from all the other freighters on the plains, who, as a class, were boisterous, blasphemous, and good patrons of the bottle, while Russell, Majors and Waddell were God-fearing, religious and temperate themselves." The firm also expected their employees to maintain that standard of morality and even presented each employee with a Bible. This temperance choice was noted in the *Nebraska Advertiser*: "We further learn that Russell, Majors & Waddell, the Government contractors, require of every man they hire that 'he shall not taste, touch or handle strong drink.'" This may be one reason why Mrs. Cody permitted eleven-year old Will to travel across the Great Plains for the first time on one of the firm's freight wagon trains. But it was probably during his employment with the company that he acquired a taste for liquor.[10]

Outside of the early incident with hard cider, it is difficult to determine exactly when strong drink entered Will's life. His father spoke out against temperance efforts before the family moved from Iowa and probably drank with some regularity. Alcohol was omnipresent on the American frontier. It was easily acquired in a variety of forms, ranging from wines to whiskey and liquors, available at stores in Weston and Leavenworth, and even at Rively's store near the Cody home. Whiskey was particularly plentiful. By 1860 Kansas had one distillery and Missouri had twenty-two, including the Holladay brothers' establishment in nearby Weston.[11]

Russell, Majors, and Waddell's requirement for abstinence would have been difficult to enforce, given the love for alcohol among many frontiersmen. Since they had to hire as many as three thousand teamsters and wagon masters to meet their government contract, it was probably impossible. While some teamsters and Pony Express riders doubtless made an effort to remain temperate, others clearly violated the requirement. Sir Richard Burton noted that during a visit in 1860, he rarely saw a sober driver among the Russell, Majors, and Waddell employees.[12]

Will Cody counted these teamsters and wagon masters, many of whom undoubtedly drank, among his friends and associates.

In late 1858 he was employed by a Russell, Majors, and Waddell wagon train to Fort Laramie. Once he reached Fort Laramie, he went trapping in the country to the west of the fort. After two unprofitable months, he returned to the fort and joined two men on a trip back to the settlements in eastern Kansas. On the trip, the trio stopped for a night at Oak Grove ranch, located along the Oregon Trail in Nebraska. It was snowing heavily and they were glad for the shelter. There was plenty of food, and the whiskey flowed freely. Will's companions were great lovers of "tanglefoot" and went on a "glorious drunk" for the next three days. "Tanglefoot" was a slang word for cheap whiskey and a word that Cody used quite frequently. Will's account makes no mention of whether he joined them in consuming the tanglefoot.[13]

In February 1859 he arrived home, where he stayed until drawn to the goldfields of Colorado. Between these trips into the vast expanse of the Great Plains, Will Cody briefly experienced a childhood that was rapidly receding into the past. At home he helped around the farm, attended school at various intervals, and spent time with his family. He also enjoyed the foods that came from their farm; the fare was much better than he usually experienced while traveling across the plains. Food on the trail was largely hardtack, beans, bacon, and whatever game the men had the opportunity to hunt. But at home he could enjoy fresh vegetables from the garden, milk and butter from the cows, and meat from the yellow-legged chickens and the wild game that was plentiful in forests around the Salt Creek Valley. His eldest sister, Julia, cooked not only for hotel guests but also for the family.

After Isaac died in 1857, the family was no longer persecuted by the proslavery advocates, and home was finally a peaceful place. But the slavery issue had not gone away. Like the Codys, many other settlers were from northern states that had already outlawed slavery and opposed its introduction into Kansas. Some, however, like those who hung out at Rively's store, favored slavery. The town of Leavenworth was largely antislavery, while Kickapoo, just northeast of the Salt Creek Valley, was proslavery. The settlers in Kickapoo, many from slave states, allied themselves with proslavery advocates in Missouri. When local elections were held, Missourians were encouraged to cross the river to vote and support the proslavery politicians. During one election in 1855, a riverboat had been chartered from Missouri to Kickapoo, offering free transportation and "all kinds of refreshments." The result was over 800 votes in a precinct with only 175 registered residents.[14]

When the vote as to whether Kansas would allow slavery finally occurred on December 21, 1857, proslavery advocates once again traveled from Missouri. A whiskey bar was open near the polling place, and the proslavery advocates formed a ring that connected both locations. Each voter stopped for a drink, cast his ballot, had another drink, returned to cast a second ballot, had a drink, and then voted again. Some voted as many as six times to receive their liquid rewards. Similarly fraudulent ballots were cast elsewhere in the territory. After the fraudulent ballots were discovered and eliminated, the count revealed that the antislavery faction had won. That decision did not settle the matter, however, as the proslavery forces did not accept the count. Kansas was bleeding from internal strife, and a civil war was on the horizon.[15]

In 1859 the decision was finally made; Kansas would not allow slavery. Defeated, the proslavery forces withdrew, and when Kansas became a state on January 29, 1861, the transition was peaceable. But the story was different elsewhere in the nation. On April 12, 1861, Confederate forces attacked Fort Sumter, and the Civil War began. Kansas was now solidly with the Union, but Missouri was divided between secessionists and unionists. Before the war, Will Cody's anger over his father's death and his family's treatment at the hands of the proslavery advocates led him to join a group of Jayhawkers who crossed the river on raids into Missouri. When his mother learned of this, she insisted he leave the group, which she considered little more than a bunch of common horse thieves. Will returned to western Kansas to work as a scout, dispatch carrier, and guide for the army, but he stayed out of the war when it broke out (fig. 4).[16]

After leading a group of merchants to Denver in the fall of 1863, Will received notice that his mother was dying and returned to the Cody home as quickly as possible. His mother Mary died on November 22. Will was devastated. He began to spend more

Fig 4. Will Cody at age eighteen. By this time, he had already crossed the Great Plains several times, surviving on wild game, hardtack, beans, and coffee. Object ID#71.0205, Buffalo Bill Museum and Grave, Golden CO.

time with the very kinds of desperate characters his mother had warned him against. By this time he was all too acquainted with tanglefoot and continued this lifestyle for several months. But as he later wrote, "One day after having been under the influence of bad whisky, I awoke to find myself a soldier in the Seventh Kansas." Will Cody was going to war.[17]

3

Becoming a Gourmet

We had a splendid dinner as can be seen from the following:

Bill of Fare

    Soup: Buffalo Tail
    Fish: Cisco broiled, fried Dace
    Entrees: Salmi of Prairie Dog, Stewed Rabbit, Fillet of
      Buffalo, Aux Champignons
    Roast: Elk, Antelope, Black-tailed Deer, Wild Turkey
    Broiled: Teal, Mallard, Antelope Chops, Buffalo-Calf
      Steaks, Young Wild Turkey
    Vegetables: Sweet Potatoes, Mashed Potatoes, Green Peas
    Dessert: Tapioca Pudding
    Wines: Champagne Frappe, Champagne au Naturel,
      Claret, Whiskey, Brandy, Bass' Ale
    Coffee:

This I considered a pretty square meal for a party of hunters,
and everybody did ample justice to it.

Buffalo Bill, 1879

Will Cody, now in his twenties, discovered gourmet dining on a
"grand hunt" with General Philip H. Sheridan and his friends in
1871. The friends included other generals, members of Sheridan's
staff, several businessmen, and editors of Chicago and New York
City newspapers. The entourage had sixteen wagons carrying tents,
baggage, general supplies, cookware, and enough groceries, including plenty of alcohol, for eleven days of roughing it on the high
plains. Three smaller wagons carried the firearms and ammuni-
tion the hunting party would be using. While Cody had eaten his
share of wild game, he was not prepared to dine in such high style.
The hunt began at Fort McPherson, Nebraska, and ended at Fort

Hays, Kansas. The main objective of the expedition was buffalo hunting, but no creature escaped unscathed: elk, deer, coyotes, turkeys, even prairie dogs fell before the hunters' onslaught. Will was along to act as hunting guide and entertainer. In addition to locating buffalo and other prey for the hunters, he shared stories of his exploits on the frontier as the group sat around a fire each evening. Cody's own culinary adventures were just beginning as he enjoyed such delicacies as buffalo steaks prepared with mushrooms by that same fire.

In the eight years following his mother's death in 1863, Will Cody had made a name and a reputation for himself. It began with his service during the Civil War, a period of just over one and a half years. The record of his enlistment with the Seventh Kansas Cavalry shows he signed up on February 19, 1864, just one week short of his eighteenth birthday. His occupation was listed as teamster, reflecting the years he had put in traveling across the plains with wagon trains.[1]

Cody's Civil War experiences included participation in several battles, carrying dispatches, and scouting. These took place in Missouri, Mississippi, Arkansas, and Tennessee. While he was a part of several battles, he did not particularly distinguish himself in any. His diet during that time was standard army fare, with three exceptions. At one point, he was scouting and ran across Wild Bill Hickok, who was working as a Union spy. They shared a meal of bread and milk. A few days later he diverted Union troops from sacking the farm of a Southern lady and her daughters. Out of gratitude, they invited him for dinner. He noted, "I was pretty hungry about that time, as our rations had been rather slim of late, and a good dinner was a temptation I could not withstand." His experiences during the war, while undistinguished, did give him a connection with veterans of the war throughout the rest of his life.[2]

Will Cody was discharged on September 29, 1865, four months after he met Louisa Frederici in St. Louis. They were soon engaged, but before they were married, he returned to the Great Plains as a scout for William Tecumseh Sherman. He also worked as a stagecoach driver for Ben Holladay. By that time Holladay had gotten out of the liquor business, selling his portion of the Holladay Distillery in Weston and opening the Overland Stage Line. It was a successful enterprise for Holladay, but Cody's heart was not in it. He wrote, "My thoughts turned continually towards my promised bride, until I at last determined to abandon staging forever, and marry and settle down."[3]

Will and Louisa were married in St. Louis on March 6, 1866. They immediately boarded a riverboat for a floating honeymoon on their way back to the Salt Creek Valley, where he intended to follow his parents' lead and settle down. His mother's hotel, the Valley Grove House, was now owned by Dr. J. J. Crook, who had served with Cody in the Seventh Kansas Cavalry. Will rented the place and, following in his mother's footsteps, reopened it as the Golden Rule House. Settling down, however, was not in Will Cody's nature. He operated the hotel for four months, then returned to the western plains of Kansas.[4]

Having been a teamster for Russell, Majors, and Waddell, Will decided he might be able to make his fortune running wagons from Leavenworth into the frontier. According to his sister Helen, he acquired a team and wagon from a friend of the family, then stocked up with supplies from M. E. Albright, a friend who had a wholesale grocery in Leavenworth. This entrepreneurial effort came to a quick end when Indians stole his wagon, livestock, and supplies just beyond Junction City.[5]

His effort to begin a wagon business having failed, Will spent the fall and winter of 1866–67 scouting out of Fort Ellsworth at the suggestion of his friend Wild Bill Hickok. His work also took him to Fort Larned and Fort Fletcher, where he was soon stationed. That spring at Fort Fletcher, he had his first meeting with George Armstrong Custer, for whom he scouted later that summer.[6]

Despite his success as a scout, Will Cody's scouting contract with the U.S. Army came to an abrupt end on August 11, 1867. By that time Fort Fletcher had been abandoned because of spring flooding, and a new fort, Fort Hays, was erected. The Kansas Pacific Railroad had also begun building to the west of Fort Ellsworth, heading in the direction of Fort Hays. Cody and a partner, William Rose, hatched a plot to open a town on the bank of Big Creek, near the fort. They started building, and settlers began moving to the budding community. Cody even built a store in the town. Within one month the town of Rome, as they named it, had two hundred dwellings, stores, a hotel, and saloons. The abundance of whiskey in the town became a concern to the Fort Hays commander, who felt that the availability of liquor was injurious to the health of the soldiers at the post. Stating that the sellers of liquor were unlicensed, and therefore operating illegally, he sent troops to confiscate all alcohol on August 11. Many cases, kegs, and bottles were seized from one J. G. Duncan, who probably operated the tavern in town. The lieutenant who oversaw the seizures also noted that one keg holding four gallons of whiskey, another holding three gallons of bitters, yet another holding one and a half gallons of blackberry brandy, and two cases of assorted liquors were confiscated from one W. F. Cody. At this point Cody began a hiatus from scouting; perhaps he was no longer in the good graces of the fort commander.[7]

The liquor raid was just the beginning of trouble for Cody and his town of Rome. Cody and Rose were soon approached by a Dr. W. E. Webb, who asked to buy into their enterprise. He told them he was an agent of the Kansas Pacific Railroad and was helping the company locate towns along the proposed rail route. The two partners rejected his offer, stating that they would do fine without him. He left and, with the railroad's support, started the town of Hays City, which is one of the largest towns in western Kansas today. Rome was eclipsed and the partners' dreams of wealth were thwarted. Kansas's Rome was built in a month, but its future was destroyed in a conversation.[8]

Will's first daughter, Arta, was born on December 16, 1866, while he was scouting out of Fort Ellsworth. In anticipation of Rome's success, Will had brought Louisa and Arta from Leavenworth, putting them up in the back of his store. With the demise of Rome, they moved back to Louisa's home in St. Louis, while Will sought other sources of income. That income was in the form of a contract from the Kansas Pacific to do grading of the railroad bed over a five-mile stretch between Rome and Hays. One day he took a break from the work to hunt buffalo for meat. While hunting, he had a chance to demonstrate his skills to several army officers who were riding by. Mounted on his horse, Brigham, which was as skilled at hunting buffalo as he, Cody brought down eleven buffalo with twelve shots. He presented the army officers with the tongues and pieces of tenderloin, then loaded the rest of the carcasses onto a wagon to take back for consumption by the grading crew.[9]

Will Cody was clearly adept at hunting, particularly buffalo. His reputation spread, and he soon got a contract as a hunter supplying meat to the Kansas Pacific Railroad workers. Beginning in fall of 1867 and over the course of seventeen months, he killed 4,280 buffalo. In January 1868, a Kansas newspaper reported that in four days, he had shot nineteen buffalo, totaling four thousand pounds of meat.[10]

When the railroad contract ended, Cody confined his buffalo hunting to leading private parties and occasionally providing meat to the army as part of his scouting services. He never worked as a hide hunter and did his hunting while the buffalo still numbered in the millions. On a buffalo hunt with Cody in 1870, Cavalry lieutenant E. C. Edgerton saw several thousand near Fort McPherson in Nebraska. Cody told the lieutenant that he once had to ride thirty miles around a herd that numbered in the millions. But the hide hunters did their damage within ten years. As the buffalo dwindled in numbers, Will was appalled, writing in an editorial in the *New York Sun* in 1883 that "their slaughter has been criminally large and useless, and no hand is raised to stop the utter extinction which threatens them."[11]

Will Cody's skill at buffalo hunting was such that he earned the nickname of "Buffalo Bill" during his months as a hunter for the railroad. He later said it was the railroad workers who bestowed the name on him. The title was well deserved. Lieutenant Edgerton wrote, "'Buffalo Bill' rides along side, but he shoots them before they can turn on him. Ordinary hunters ride a little further out." Cody had to defend his title when challenged by another hunter and scout by the name of Bill Comstock. In a daylong hunt, Cody bested Comstock by killing fifteen more buffalo than his rival. The hunt began with champagne, brought by Cody's friends from St. Louis, and when the two took a break for lunch, they washed it down with champagne. The hunt concluded later that day, and "amid volleys of flying corks, toasts were drunk to the buffalo heroes."

Cody later noted that champagne was "a good drink on a Kansas prairie." This story, which helped solidify his Buffalo Bill nickname, has been challenged, but it has been corroborated by the discovery of champagne bottles at the site of the hunt.[12]

By the time Cody's contract with the railroad ended, he was back in the good graces of the U.S. Army and began scouting once again, but now with a new name and reputation. From 1868 until 1872 that reputation continued to grow as Buffalo Bill Cody became a trusted scout for Generals Sheridan, Forsyth, and Carr. Between 1868 and 1869 alone he took part in nine battles, the most noted of which was the Battle of Summit Springs in July 1869. Buffalo Bill later reenacted the battle, which took place in northeastern Colorado, in his Wild West show.[13]

The food available to a scout depended on what the army provided. At the military posts and forts, the fare could be quite good. It was delivered by suppliers such as Russell, Majors, and Waddell or on newly constructed rail lines. But in the field, rations might be limited to bacon, beans, coffee, and hardtack. At times the men didn't even have that. In 1870 a detachment of soldiers, led by Buffalo Bill as scout, traveled from Fort McPherson in pursuit of a party of Indians who had taken some horses. They left without breakfast or any rations, traveled sixty miles until they caught the Indians, and then returned to the fort without having eaten anything for two days.[14]

Scouts did have some advantage, since they were often miles ahead of the soldiers and could supplement their diet with wild game. On one occasion Buffalo Bill and four men ventured from an encampment during a snowstorm. After finding the desired destination, they settled down in a sheltered area to broil venison from a deer they'd shot earlier over their campfire. It was a substantial meal for Buffalo Bill, who then made the long ride back to the encampment to guide the soldiers along the route.[15]

Sometimes the soldiers also had an opportunity to enjoy wild game. During that expedition, the command of nearly three hundred soldiers happened upon a grove filled with wild turkeys. The soldiers joined the scouts in killing four or five hundred turkeys with whatever weapons they could employ: guns, clubs, even stones.

Cody wrote, "We had turkey in every style after this hunt—roast turkey, boiled turkey, fried turkey, 'turkey on toast,' and so on; and we appropriately called this place Camp Turkey."[16]

Being a scout afforded Cody other opportunities not available to the enlisted men. As free agents, scouts were not always subject to the same rules as the soldiers, and when the rules did apply, they sometimes bent them. Captain Charles King said that scouts were a rather motley group and were "hard riding, hard swearing, hard drinking." Despite that, he said, Buffalo Bill was well respected. That did not keep Cody from doing some mischief, particularly when it came to alcohol. While scouting for General Carr, he and Wild Bill Hickok became aware of a shipment of beer headed for another outfit. Since they were closer than the other outfit, they persuaded the shippers to sell it to them instead. Cody later recalled, "It was sold to our boys in pint cups, and as the weather was very cold we warmed the beer by putting the ends of our picket-pins heated red-hot into the cups. The result was one of the biggest beer jollifications I ever had the misfortune to attend."[17]

Some time later, Cody and Hickok were called before General Carr regarding a fight they had gotten involved with at a local sutler's store, after an evening imbibing a bit too freely. While satisfied with their explanation that they had not instigated the fight, Carr nevertheless was annoyed. Perhaps thinking it would keep Buffalo Bill out of mischief, the general commanded him to spend his time hunting antelope instead. Turning to the task, Cody bagged fifteen to twenty antelope a day, supplying fresh meat to the men until they moved on.[18]

In another incident, Buffalo Bill was sent with a companion into North Platte to buy food for the Fifth Cavalry's cook at Fort McPherson. Deciding there was no reason to spend good money on food, they purchased the supplies they felt were appropriate and put them in the cook's wagon. The next day the cook confronted them about the provisions. When they innocently asked what he meant, he replied that the wagon held only "a five gallon demi-john of brandy and two cases of Old-Tom-Cat gin." The two expressed surprise at the situation and apparently got away with it, as well as smuggling in some whiskey the cook was not aware of.

They found that the officers at Fort McPherson had plenty of food, and as Cody later said, "[We] got more provisions for our whiskey than the same money, which we paid for the liquor, would have brought." Old-Tom-Cat gin was probably Old Tom gin, so called because the bottles often had a black tomcat on the label. Old Tom gin was sweeter than other gins and was believed to be a useful medicine for kidney disease. At that time the gin, usually imported from England, sold for anywhere from $1.40 to $5 per bottle.[19]

That was not the only time Buffalo Bill went to North Platte during the early years after its 1868 founding. He was friends with Dave Perry, who operated the California Exchange Keg House, a saloon offering liquors of all kinds, including gin, brandy, wine, and whiskey. Cody frequented the Keg House many times over the years and presented Perry with a rifle in 1878. While he engaged in drinking during his off hours, there is no record of his ever having been drunk while on duty.[20]

As a scout, Cody was on call. If his services were not needed, he was not paid. For that reason, he took every opportunity to make additional income. Cody put his entrepreneurial spirit to work on at least one expedition with the Fifth Cavalry. On that occasion, he hired a man to drive a team pulling a wagonful of groceries, including canned fruit and vegetables. As a scout, Cody was not required to stay within the camp, so he parked the wagon with his tent nearby so he could sell the soldiers food to supplement their rations.[21]

Fort McPherson was well set up with supplies and had the space to feed everyone stationed there. It was only eighteen miles from the growing community of North Platte, a major stop on the Union Pacific Railroad. The fort had a large quartermaster's warehouse and a commissary storehouse. Each of the barracks also had a cooking room, while several twenty-four-by-fifteen-foot kitchens supplied food for the officers' quarters. The hospital building also had a kitchen and a dining room. A log building with a large oven served as the fort bakery. The Cody family went to three sutlers' stores at the fort once a month for groceries and other supplies. Buffalo Bill made arrangements so Mrs. Cody could regularly pick up groceries at two of the stores, belonging to sutlers McDonald and Bower, when he was away. The family also bought meat at Maggie Cohn's butcher shop in the fort. Sometimes they shopped in North Platte and even as far away as Omaha and Cheyenne. Cody said they had everything in their home in the way of "provisions and delicacies as any of the officers had at the fort."[22]

The wives and other women at the fort held formal dinners and teas, taking advantage of the supplies that regularly arrived on the railroad. Louisa had moved to Hays City with Arta when Will got the contract to supply buffalo for the railroad. She moved again with him to Fort McPherson, where their second child, son Kit Carson Cody, was born. He was named after the famous scout, whom Will admired. While Will Cody did his scouting at Fort McPherson, his family had their own house, a two-room cabin at edge of the fort's boundaries. They lived close enough to the fort to be in little danger from hostile Indians, but at times the Pawnee Indians, who were allies, dropped by. On one such occasion, Louisa Cody had prepared a dinner of sage hen, antelope meat, cakes, and pies for her husband and six officers from the fort. After receiving her husband and visitors, Mrs. Cody went into the kitchen to discover several Pawnees consuming the food she had intended for her guests.[23]

In his youth and as a young man, Will Cody enjoyed food prepared by his mother, his sister, and his wife. He ate food made by U.S. Army cooks and survived on rations as necessary. He also learned to cook wild game while a teamster on wagon trains and as a scout. During that time, his fellow teamsters introduced him to whiskey, gin, and other forms of tanglefoot. In 1871 twenty-five-year-old Will Cody, now Buffalo Bill, was introduced to the finer forms of eating and drinking. The basics were not unfamiliar to him; they were often wild game, vegetables, and alcohol in its various forms. What set them apart was the time and thought given to their preparation and presentation. They were not just food; they were gourmet fare provided by those he guided on hunts.

As a scout, Cody supported his family with additional income he earned as a guide. In this capacity, he took part in hunts with celebrities who were visiting the West. His desirability as a guide was enhanced by the publication of *Buffalo Bill: The King of Border Men*, Ned Buntline's greatly fictionalized novel, which was serialized in the *New York Weekly* from late 1869 to early 1870 (fig. 5). Using Cody's recently earned nickname, it put Buffalo Bill on the national stage. The men he guided were eager to meet him, and he in turn was eager to learn about their world and their lives.

The menu presented at the beginning of this chapter represented a new plateau of dining for Buffalo Bill. It was one of several gourmet dinners prepared for General Sheridan and his guests when Cody guided them through the Great Plains. He wrote, "There were none of the discomforts of roughing it during that expedition. A course dinner of the most delicious viands was served every evening by waiters in evening dress, and prepared by French cooks brought from New York." The hunting expedition had twenty-five wagons, three of which contained ice to keep the meat and wine cold. Others carried linens, glass, china, fine porcelain, and a commodious dining tent.[24]

While Buffalo Bill found the meal eaten with Sheridan and his guests impressive, one of the others, General Henry E. Davies, described it as "simple, hardy food." He noted that after the hard day of hunting, they all relished the "hunter's fare," and remarked that even the prairie dog entrée was palatable eating, much like squirrel. The hunters were as impressed with Cody as he was with the food and its presentation, and they named one campsite Camp Cody in his honor. Davies described him as a striking figure who "realized to perfection the bold hunter and gallant sportsman of the plains." The expedition celebrated its last evening on the trail with "an immense reservoir of champagne punch."[25]

Buffalo Bill's next celebrity hunt added even more to his reputation and also included gourmet dining. Grand Duke Alexis of Russia traveled the United States in a much-publicized visit. Like many visitors, he wanted to experience a buffalo hunt. Much satisfied with his previous year's hunt, General Sheridan arranged for Buffalo Bill to assist with setting up the expedition and guide the group. Alexis began his hunt on January 12, 1872, with a train trip to North Platte. The expedition then traveled north about fifty miles to an area where Cody knew they would find plenty of buffalo. Along the way, they stopped for "a light lunch of sandwiches and champagne." Joining them at camp was George Armstrong

Fig 5. *New York Weekly* from December 23, 1869, with the first installment of Ned Buntline's dime novel *Buffalo Bill: The King of Border Men,* serialized in the newspaper. Object ID#2012.0002.1, Buffalo Bill Museum and Grave, Golden CO.

Custer, who had shot a prairie chicken through the head, leaving its meat undisturbed. Alexis was delighted and accordingly was served the bird for dinner that evening as part of a "sumptuous feast" of wild game meat. One witness wrote, "The meal included different varieties of game to be found on the Western prairies. Choice wines were served with different courses."[26]

The Alexis expedition was even more extravagant than Cody's previous experience with General Sheridan, with thirteen tents, including two large ones that were placed side by side to create a dining area. An additional thirty to forty smaller tents served as quarters for the military escort and the duke's attendants. The grand duke's tent was luxuriously appointed with carpet flooring. Nearby were the tepees of one hundred Lakota warriors, whom Cody had asked to join in the hunt and provide dances for evening entertainment. No expense had been spared when it came to food and drink, which included a variety of liquors, flour, sugar, potatoes, canned vegetables, and other provisions for preparation shipped from Chicago. The party did not carry any domestic meat, intending to live off the wild game the men shot. And they shot plenty of it, furnishing elk, antelope, deer, turkey, ducks, and buffalo for their meals. When Alexis killed his first buffalo, the steaks from it were broiled as the main attraction at dinner that evening.[27]

At the end of the hunt, General Sheridan reminded Buffalo Bill of an invitation to New York from the gentlemen who had been with them on the hunt the year before. He said that he would ensure that Cody got a leave of absence from Fort McPherson and a pass for the railroad. Will had never ventured much farther east than the Mississippi River, so he decided to accept the invitation. The following month Buffalo Bill departed for Chicago, his first major stop on the trip and the beginning of a new career.[28]

4

Dining at Delmonico's

On arriving at New York I was met at the depot by Mr. J. G.
Hecksher, who had been appointed as "a committee of one"
to escort me to the Union Club . . . where I was to make my
headquarters during my visit in the great metropolis. I had
an elegant dinner at the club rooms, with the gentlemen who
had been out on the September hunt, and other members
of the club.

Buffalo Bill, 1879

Buffalo Bill's trip east to New York in 1872 was prompted in part by
his growing public reputation. He was the right person in the right
place at the right time. When Ned Buntline wrote *Buffalo Bill: The
King of Border Men* in 1869, Wild Bill Hickok was better known. But
unlike his friend Hickok, Cody liked people and was very gregarious,
so Buntline chose to focus on him, although Hickok was also in the
story. The choice was a good one: Cody loved the spotlight, and it
loved him. While Buntline's dime novel enhanced Buffalo Bill's
reputation on the national scene, Cody's hunting trips with General Sheridan in 1871 and early 1872 awakened his inner gourmet.

General Sheridan and the men who had gotten to know Cody
on those hunting trips were familiar with his outgoing personality
and saw his growing public reputation. They intended to introduce
him to their society friends. Within weeks of the Grand Duke Alexis
hunt, Buffalo Bill headed east. His hosts as he traveled through
Chicago and on to New York included *Chicago Daily Journal* owner
Charles Wilson, *New York Herald* publisher James Gordon Bennett
Jr., New York financier Leonard Jerome, and of course, General
Sheridan and his attachés. Not only did they introduce him to their

society friends, they also took him to dinner at some of the finest establishments in their cities.[1]

The trip to New York was much simpler than a few years earlier. The Union Pacific railroad reached the town of Cheyenne, Wyoming, in December 1867, crossing all of Nebraska from Omaha. The transcontinental railroad was completed in 1869, changing everything in the West. While a trip across the Great Plains to the West Coast once had taken months, by 1872 a nonstop trip from New York to San Francisco could be completed in seven days. Trains on the routes between Omaha and New York even had dining cars. So when Cody took his trip, crossing the country was nothing like it had been ten years earlier, when canvas-covered wagons slowly followed the Oregon Trail along the Platte River.

The arrival of the railroad meant an end to surviving on hardtack and beans on a Great Plains journey. Eating wild game was an option, not a necessity. By 1872 many lines were providing Pullman dining cars. An advertisement for the line between Kansas City and Chicago stated that it offered "dining-room cars attached on which can be had all the luxuries of the season." A passenger on another line observed, "You may have your choice in the wilderness—eating at the rate of twenty-two miles per hour—of buffalo, elk, antelope, beef steak, mutton chops, or grouse." The towns through which the railroad traveled had plenty of hotels and restaurants. In fact, the railroads even provided eating establishments at the various station stops. In 1876 a pamphlet on rail travel stated, "The trains of the Union Pacific Railroad are arranged so as to stop at excellent stations, at convenient hours, for meals." Passengers could order wild game, steaks, fish, biscuits, and hot coffee. Cody's lunches were probably taken on the train or at station stops. But his trip was also timed so he could overnight in major towns along the rail line. There he stayed in comfortable hotels, all offering a variety of culinary delights. He was acquiring a taste for the good life.[2]

The first stop of his trip was in Omaha, a town already familiar to him, where he posed in his buckskin outfit at a local photo studio for portraits to be sent to the Grand Duke. The photos depicted a handsome twenty-six-year old, later described in a Chicago news-

Fig 6. *Scouting among the Civilians.* Buffalo Bill donned fancy dress for the first time when he danced and dined on his trip east to Chicago and New York City in 1872. This image appeared in *William F. Cody, Story of the Wild West and Campfire Chats* (Richmond: B. F. Johnson, 1888), 630. Author's collection.

paper as "tall, slim, with a frank countenance, piercing gray eyes, and long curly hair."[3]

The next stop of the journey was Chicago, where Cody was welcomed by members of the 1871 hunting trip. There he attended a number of "swell" dinners and went to a ball with General Sheridan (fig. 6). Cody later wrote, "It was more difficult for me to face the throng of beautiful ladies, than it would have been to confront a hundred hostile Indians." Though he was often asked to wear his buckskins, on that occasion he wore formal evening attire, which, like the ball, was not something he was acquainted with.[4]

Leaving Chicago, he made a luncheon stop in Cleveland at a "depot dining hall." An imaginative report from the dining hall, which was shared with newspapers across the country, had him leaping seventeen feet in the air and scalping a wooden cigar store Indian. It also said he ate raw beef and cut his bread with a bowie knife.[5]

His next stop was Buffalo, New York. While there, he made a visit to Niagara Falls, already a popular tourist destination. Dinner was at the Spencer House, the finest lodging and dining establishment on the American side of the falls (fig. 7). Perhaps Cody had learned of the Spencer House from Grand Duke Alexis, who stayed there less than two months earlier and enjoyed an extravagant banquet that consisted of eleven courses. The offerings included consommé, salmon in a bechamel sauce, "gelatine of turkey" with truffles, lobster salad, leg of lamb, quail on toast, beef fillets with mushrooms, calf's head en tortue, a ragout of rabbit in red wine, and a wide variety of vegetables and relishes. Dessert was an assortment of tarts, pies, cakes, and puddings. The royal gathering drank wine from bottles covered with ribbons representing the Russian colors. No record exists of Cody's dinner, which was undoubtedly less extravagant but might have included comparable menu items.[6]

Following dinner at the Spencer House, Cody returned to Buffalo, where he stayed at the Continental Hotel. The evening of his second day in Buffalo, he took in a performance of *The Black Crook*. Loosely based on Faust, the popular play combined music, ballet, and theater in a tale of mythical creatures, sorcerers, and gypsies. It is sometimes credited with being America's first musical. It must have appealed to Buffalo Bill, because later on the trip, he saw the play again at Niblo's Garden in New York, where it had first premiered.[7]

Buffalo Bill's next stop was Rochester as a guest of Professor Henry Ward. Ward first met Buffalo Bill on the Great Plains when he engaged Cody to acquire specimens for Ward's Natural Science,

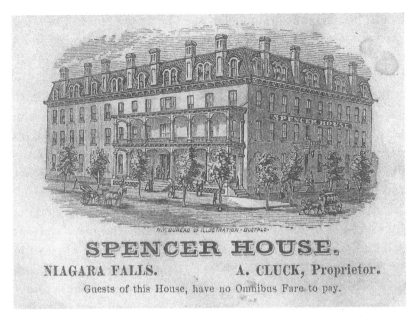

SPENCER HOUSE.

NIAGARA FALLS.   A. CLUCK, Proprietor.

Guests of this House, have no Omnibus Fare to pay.

Fig 7. Trade card illustrating Spencer House in Niagara Falls in 1872. Buffalo Bill dined here on his trip to New York that year. Author's collection.

a company he had founded to provide scientific specimens to high schools and colleges. The two met again when Ward accompanied the Alexis hunt to collect specimens. As Cody's train arrived in Chicago, Ward was there to greet him and traveled with him through Buffalo to Rochester. After showing Cody all around Rochester, Ward then took him to dinner with the mayor that evening.[8]

One of the men who had been on the General Sheridan hunt in 1871, J. G. Hecksher, met Buffalo Bill at the train depot in New York City. Hecksher took him to the Union Club, where they had an elegant dinner with the other gentlemen who had been on the hunt. The Union Club was organized as one of the first and most prestigious men's social clubs in New York City. Since Cody's hosts were members, the club was intended to be his headquarters during his visit to the city. After dinner, Hecksher took Cody to see Ned Buntline at the Brevoort Place Hotel. Buntline insisted that Cody stay with him at his home, while the proprietors of the hotel pressured him to stay as their guest. Cody resolved the situation by dividing his time among all three places: the Union Club, the Brevoort, and Ned Buntline's place. The Brevoort's proprietors took advantage of the situation by publicizing that "Buffalo Bill, the Great Indian Scout" was staying with them.[9]

Buffalo Bill's arrival in New York City prompted a flurry of invitations to dinner and other society events as his hosts kept him busy. The whirl of events so confused Cody that he lost track of his schedule. One evening publisher James Bennett, one of his hosts from the hunt, invited Cody to a banquet in his honor at the New York Yacht Club. Including fine wines, fish, salads, and fruit, the cost per diner was nearly $100 each. Delmonico's even loaned the club some of its finest silver for the occasion. The meal went off well and everyone had a fine time, but there was one hitch—the guest of honor never appeared. When contacted the next morning, Cody replied, "Well, rake me with scalping knives if I didn't forget all about it." He later met Bennett at a dinner in banker August Belmont's mansion. Fortunately, all was forgiven, and Bennett asked Buffalo Bill to accompany him to the Liederkranz masked ball on February 15.[10]

Cody did not forget that invitation. The Liederkranz, which was one of the biggest society events of the year and continues to be prominent in New York City today, is a male singing society that promotes German music. The 1872 ball opened at 11:00 p.m. with a procession of men wearing animal costumes. Then began the dancing, which lasted until morning. Cody recalled that "the merry and motley throng presented a brilliant scene, moving gracefully beneath the bright gaslight to the inspiring music." His buckskins were his costume, and he noted, "[I] took part in the dancing and exhibited some of my backwoods steps." A newspaper reported that "the ball was specially noticeable for the attendance of fashionable society."[11]

In addition to evening social events, Cody kept busy throughout the day seeing the sights of New York. These included City Hall, police headquarters and police court, the shot tower on Centre Street, the Academy of Design, and the Equitable Life Insurance Building, built around 1870 as the world's first skyscraper. He also met Thomas Nast during a visit to the artist's studio. On several evenings Buffalo Bill enjoyed theatrical productions, and he was wined and dined at Delmonico's, one of the finest and best-known restaurants in the city.[12]

The high point of Buffalo Bill's New York City experience occurred on February 19, 1872, at the Bowery Theatre, when the play *Buffalo Bill* had its New York premiere. Cody was in the audience, as Buntline had taken him to the theater. The timing of Buffalo Bill's entire visit to New York City was more than coincidence, something noted by the critic for the *New York Daily Herald*. Once again Cody was the right person in the right place at the right time. And Buntline had a hand in it. When Buffalo Bill was introduced to the audience, the critic reported, he was greeted by "an ovation such as actors at the more aristocratic theaters never received." Buffalo Bill was asked to ascend the stage and give a few remarks. He later recalled that he spoke "almost inaudibly," stunned by the sea of faces in front of him. The play received accolades, and one critic noted that it was "one of the most exciting and thrilling melodramas that was ever placed upon the Bowery boards." He went on to state, "Of the future success of this drama there cannot be the faintest shadow of a doubt."[13]

Afterward, the play's manager offered Buffalo Bill $500 per week to play himself. He turned the manager down, saying, "You might as well make an actor out of a government mule" and later explaining, "I didn't have the requisite cheek to undertake a thing of that sort." Yet Ned Buntline also thought he did, pressing Cody to give up scouting and go into show business. Both men failed, however, to persuade Cody to participate in the play. Still, the manager put Buffalo Bill's visit to good use, taking out an ad in the *New York Daily Herald* repeating the praises from the newspaper critic and stating that the hero of the story was present at the theater and "endorses the life-like picture."[14]

After several weeks, it was time for Buffalo Bill to leave New York. Before his departure for Fort McPherson, he visited relatives in West Chester, outside of Philadelphia. He had never met them, but they all got along quite well during the daylong visit. Buntline accompanied him and doubtless continued trying to get Buffalo Bill onstage. Cody's uncle, General Henry Guss, was the proprietor of the Green Tree Hotel in West Chester. Guss ran the hotel, also licensed as a tavern, from 1855 to 1880. As with Will's mother, who ran the Valley Grove House back in Salt Creek, and Will himself, who ran the Golden Rule House for a brief while, operating places of lodging seemed to run in the family.[15]

Cody returned to Nebraska in the spring and resumed his regular activities of scouting and leading hunting parties. As a scout, he took part in several engagements, including one for which he was awarded the Medal of Honor by Congress. He enjoyed scouting and hunting, but he was a changed man. He had tasted a different life, and it agreed with him. Through summer and into fall he received letters from Ned Buntline urging him to become part of a stage show, playing himself. While he liked being in the spotlight, however briefly, he also remembered the awkwardness of his experience at the Bowery Theatre. He recalled, "I never felt more relieved in my life than when I got out of the view of that immense crowd" and was reluctant to go back onstage.[16]

By the fall of 1872 Buntline had convinced Cody that he should try out the stage as an experiment. If it went well, he would continue doing it, for it paid considerably better than scouting and hunting. If, on the other hand, it was a failure, he could always go back to scouting. Cody's wife, Louisa, said that if he did choose to "tread the boards," it would be an opportunity for her to take their newborn daughter, Orra, to St. Louis to spend time with her parents. About this time, his friend John "Texas Jack" Omohundro, with whom he had been scouting and hunting, said he would like to give stage acting a try as well. Since Texas Jack had also figured in some dime novels by then, the two decided they would see what it would be like to become performers. The party, including Louisa with their three children, Arta, Kit, and Orra, stopped in Omaha, where, according to Buffalo Bill, they dined at the "leading restaurant in town." Then Jack and Bill headed to Chicago, while Louisa and his children proceeded southeast to St. Louis.[17]

Texas Jack and Buffalo Bill were to appear with Ned Buntline in Chicago at Nixon's Amphitheater on December 16 in a new play, *Scouts of the Prairie* (fig. 8). Advertisements for the engagement had already appeared in the Chicago papers, announcing that Cody

Fig 8. Buffalo Bill with fellow scout Texas Jack Omohundro, renowned dancer Giuseppina Morlacchi, and dime novel writer Ned Buntline. They opened the play *Scouts of the Prairie* in December 1872. Object ID#80, Buffalo Bill Museum and Grave, Golden CO.

and Texas Jack would be joined onstage by well-known actress and dancer Mademoiselle Giuseppina Morlacchi. When they arrived on December 12, Morlacchi was ready but Buntline was not. He still hadn't written the script, and outside of the three headliners, most of the company had not even been hired. And there were no Indian chiefs or warriors, as the advertisements promised. Buntline managed to complete a script and hire the necessary personnel, including Chicago locals standing in as Indians. He cast himself as trapper Cale Durg, while Buffalo Bill and Texas Jack played themselves. Bill and Jack spent the next several days memorizing their lines and rehearsing. Cody later recalled, "The first rehearsal was hardly a success and the succeeding ones were not much better."[18]

When the curtain went up, Cody's fears were realized as he gazed upon another immense crowd. He froze and forgot his lines.

Buntline asked him a question as a cue, and Buffalo Bill launched into storytelling, one of his fortes. For the rest of the evening, Buntline gave Cody cues, which set him up to ad lib and tell stories. Over the next few days, the critics were remarkably forgiving. The critic for the *Chicago Tribune* said it was evident that "they had never been on any but the overland stage" and that "one would be almost ready to swear that these gentlemen are not great actors." Another noted that the audiences considered both Texas Jack and Buffalo Bill celebrities and that even a faltering recitation was applauded. Later, during the show's New York appearance, yet another critic wrote, "Everything was so wonderfully bad that it was almost good." Even if the critics were, well, critical, the people loved *Scouts of the Prairie.*[19]

Some critics stated that it would have been better if Cale Durg, Ned Buntline's character, had been killed in the first act, before he could deliver a long temperance speech in the second. Ned Buntline was actually a pen name for Edward Zane Carroll (E. Z. C.) Judson. An opportunist, Judson had seen the growing popularity of the temperance movement. Like Cody, he was a charismatic man and he was a convincing public speaker. He supplemented his writing income by providing temperance lectures and in fact had delivered one such lecture at Nixon's Amphitheater two evenings before *Scouts of the Prairie* opened. The play gave him a new opportunity to orate on the subject, with the action stopping at one point to allow him to do so. His lectures were delivered with great sincerity despite his own, sometimes quite apparent, drunkenness. On one occasion, he delivered his lecture during the play while drinking from a pitcher that everyone supposed contained water. As his speech became more disorganized and his center of gravity wavered, it became clear to everyone that it held whiskey.[20]

Scouts of the Prairie went on to other cities and was a resounding success. When the season ended in June 1873, Buffalo Bill and Texas Jack expected a nice payoff. Buntline pocketed most of the proceeds, however, and the two scouts, the real reason the audiences had been so large, got only around $6,000 each. Disappointed, they returned to Nebraska for several weeks of hunting. During that time, the two decided to organize their own show,

Scouts of the Plains. They recruited their friend Wild Bill Hickok to join them. Hickok stayed with the show from September 1873 through March 1874. While he joined the company to indulge his friends, he thought they were making fools of themselves. Like most frontiersmen, he enjoyed his whiskey. During one evening performance, while the three were sitting around a fake campfire spinning yarns and passing a jug of whiskey, he took a long drink, then spat it out, swearing. "Cold tea don't count—either I get real whiskey or I ain't tellin' no story." From that point on, Buffalo Bill made sure the jug was filled with real whiskey.[21]

Hickok's bad attitude toward the work, constant drinking, and tendency to pick fights with local residents finally led to a confrontation with Cody. They made up, but Hickok said, "I can't stay here where the people make a practice of eating upon tables and sleeping upon beds" and left the show. Hickok wasn't alone in his enjoyment of whiskey. After his departure, Texas Jack and Buffalo Bill received a keg from a friend. Cody wrote that they became so full of the contents that they "could not care." Cody's performances were occasionally affected by "too free indulgence of intoxicants," as a reporter noted after an appearance in Janesville, Wisconsin, in 1882. In this respect, he was not that different from Ned Buntline. Balancing the pleasure he took in strong drink with his show business persona would be a challenge for Cody throughout his career.[22]

After Hickok's departure in early 1874, Buffalo Bill and Texas Jack carried on with the melodramas. In 1876 Texas Jack left to start his own touring company with Mademoiselle Morlacchi; Wild Bill Hickok was killed in Deadwood, Dakota Territory. that same year. Texas Jack Omohundro died of pneumonia in Leadville, Colorado, in 1880, and Ned Buntline died of heart failure in 1886. By then Cody's experiment had proven a success. His theatrical company, the Buffalo Bill Combination, traveled throughout the United States doing plays about the West. All of them featured the famous scout Buffalo Bill. His days of sleeping on the ground and living on hardtack were over. Now he rested his head and dined in some of the fanciest hotels in the country.

5

Buffalo Bill Ate Here

Hotel Arrivals
Purcell House—Cobb Bros., Prop'rs.
October 4— . . . WF Cody, Buffalo Bill; Eddie Burgess,
US Interpreter; Little Warrior, Pawnee Chief; Follow the
Sun, Nez Perce Chief; Eagle That Flies High, Pawnee;
Young Grass That Sprouts in the Spring, Squaw; and
others of Buffalo Bill Troupe.

Wilmington (NC) Morning Star, 1878

With his show business success, Bill Cody no longer spent life on the trail as a scout. But he did spend much of his life on the road, traveling to and staying in hotels. His visits to his home and family became even less frequent than when he was scouting and leading hunting trips on the plains.

After its first engagement in Chicago in late 1872, the next stop for *Scouts of the Prairie* was St. Louis, where Cody's wife, Louisa, and their children were staying with her parents. That St. Louis stop was from December 23 to 28, so he was able to enjoy Christmas with the family. During the following year, even though Buffalo Bill was reenacting life on the frontier, he never got west of the Mississippi. That May he wrote to his sister Julia that he was once again visiting with their uncle Henry Guss and family in West Chester. He talked about all the relatives in the area, saying, "We had a family dinner while in Philadelphia and there were 42 persons to dine, all uncles, aunts, cousins, half cousins and so forth." A home base that was close to relatives and places like Washington DC, Philadelphia, and New York was just what he needed at that point in his career. He finished the letter by noting that by the time she replied, the family would probably be living in West

Chester, "so write me there." Subsequently, he moved the family to West Chester, where he purchased a house near his uncle and extended family.[1]

Buffalo Bill's letter to his sister also mentioned that he had made a trip to Washington DC: "I called on the President and family this morning and am invited to dine with him. That is bout as near as I will come to live in the White House." The invitation from President Ulysses S. Grant provides a sense of how rapidly Cody's star was rising. Grant was the first of several American presidents that he would come to know. As he predicted, Buffalo Bill never lived in the White House, but he did frequent it.[2]

By early 1874 it was clear that Buffalo Bill would be successful in show business. The acting troupe he started with Texas Jack was now known as the Buffalo Bill Combination and was bringing in good income. Over the course of ten months, it also become clear that West Chester was not where the family wanted to put down roots. Perhaps it was a bit too close to Will's relatives. Louisa did not get along well with his sisters, and that friction may have extended to other family members as well. He was frequently on the road, while she was around his relatives all the time. Whatever the motivation, the family decided to leave West Chester. Will had been impressed with Rochester on his visit with Professor Henry Ward, so he purchased a house there, and the family moved in March. Even though he resided in upstate New York, he nevertheless found time to drop by West Chester occasionally for a drink and a chat at his uncle's Green Tree Hotel.[3]

Over the next few years the Buffalo Bill Combination spent most of its time in the East but made occasional forays westward, even venturing to San Francisco on the West Coast. Cody usually spent July and August, between show seasons, on hunting trips in the Great Plains. One such hunting trip occurred in 1874, when he guided Thomas Medley, a wealthy Englishman, for the sum of $1,000 per month. Medley, however, did not want to travel in luxury but preferred to rough it, killing and cooking wild game and sleeping on the ground. This surprised Buffalo Bill, who had been anticipating meals more like those he enjoyed with Grand Duke Alexis. According to Cody, Medley proceeded to do all the necessary chores at each campsite, including "preparing and cooking the meals, never asking me to do a thing."[4]

Buffalo Bill's summer hiatus in 1876 lasted a bit longer than expected. That April his tour was interrupted by the death of Kit Carson Cody from scarlet fever. The loss of his son, who died in his arms, was a terrible tragedy that he never forgot. Cody purchased a family plot in Rochester's Mount Hope Cemetery, where Kit was laid to rest. Then in May, Cody's attention was drawn to tensions in the Black Hills between the U.S. Army and the Lakotas. The Combination closed three weeks earlier than the year before, and Buffalo Bill quickly returned to the plains. As he wrote later, "I was anxious to take part in the Sioux war which was then breaking out."[5]

Upon his arrival in Cheyenne, Buffalo Bill resumed his old duties, joining the army as chief of scouts. Not long after that, his regiment learned of the death of Lieutenant Colonel George A. Custer and his command at the Little Bighorn. Ten days later Cody took the "first scalp for Custer" in an encounter with a group of Cheyennes (allies of the Lakotas). This incident was much publicized, given Cody's celebrity, and was later used by the Combination in a play titled *The Red Right Hand, or Buffalo Bill's First Scalp for Custer.*

Buffalo Bill continued to scout for the army through the rest of the summer. A news correspondent's dispatch dated August 3, 1876, recounted his experiences traveling with Cody through the Laramie Plains region of Wyoming. He complained that there were few buffalo and antelope in the area, which was mainly populated by sage hens and rabbits. Cody and the other scouts did most of the hunting for fresh meat. Good water was scarce, and when the regiment finally got into the foothills of the Rockies, they were able to drink ice-cold water, "which was more appreciated by us after the stuff we had been drinking than if the stream had been flowing champagne." They also enjoyed the delicious trout they caught from the stream, undoubtedly a welcome change from sage hen and rabbit.[6]

The same day that the correspondent sent his dispatch, Jack Crawford arrived with dispatches for General George Crook from General Philip Sheridan. He also had a special gift for Buffalo Bill from a friend in Cheyenne. On learning it was a bottle of good whiskey, Cody shushed him, warning that there were "too many dry men around us" who would try to take the bottle if they knew. In fact, Jack was the only man who could be trusted with the bottle, since he was a teetotaler. Cody invited General Carr, who was also part of the command, to join him in a drink. Because of this and other shared experiences, Carr became a lifelong friend.[7]

Among the dispatches brought by Jack Crawford were orders for Crook's command to join General Alfred Terry's. As much as Buffalo Bill enjoyed fine dining during hunts or in eastern hotels, he did not think it at all appropriate during a military campaign. General Terry seemed focused on making life comfortable, with a train of wagons carrying large tents for sleeping and dining. After Cody completed his scouting duties and returned to Rochester, he told a newspaper, "General Crook slept on his blanket, made his own coffee and broiled his own bacon. General Terry had a bed brought with him, a portable cooking range and an extension table. We could not travel fast enough to catch the Indians, as we would break the dishes."[8]

Buffalo Bill began his next season in the fall of 1876 close to home, in Rochester, with six evening performances. In 1878 he decided to leave Rochester, where Kit was buried in the family plot. Over the next fifty years the plot served as a final resting place for the other Cody children, even though Will and Louisa were interred in Colorado. The family moved to North Platte, near Fort McPherson, which they had called home before he got into show business. There he purchased the first of a series of houses, with North Platte serving as a home base for the rest of his life.

Although the Cody family lived in Rochester and then North Platte, Buffalo Bill spent most of his time in hotels with his traveling company. The Buffalo Bill Combination was a success, bringing a good income, so he could afford the kind of life he had first experienced on his trip to New York. The hotels in which he stayed during those ten years were often the best available in the cities where the Combination played, and their restaurants offered the finest-quality dining.

In 1878 Cody stayed at the Purcell House, the best hotel in Wilmington, North Carolina. It offered gourmet dining, as illustrated by an 1881 breakfast menu that included standard southern fare like eggs, sausage, bacon, ham, toast, and grits. It also offered broiled beefsteak, mutton chops, veal cutlet, fresh fish, stewed kidneys, tripe, and fried liver. Buffalo Bill undoubtedly had breakfast while at the hotel, choosing from a wide range of alternatives. When the show was in Portland, Maine, later that year, Cody's accommodations were at the United States Hotel, which had been recently remodeled. Originally built in 1803, it had also been where President James K. Polk stayed in 1846. One of the finest hotels in Portland, it hosted a special dinner for the governor of Maine and guests three years after Buffalo Bill's visit. It is unknown what he ate at the hotel, but the governor and his guests had escalloped oysters and lobster salad, the seafood undoubtedly having been delivered fresh by local fishermen.[9]

Buffalo Bill would have had convenient lunches while traveling from town to town with the Combination, as the new Pullman dining cars provided comestibles on most rail lines east of the Missouri River. Passing through Kansas City in November 1878, he did not have time to get off the train, so a reporter from the *St. Joseph Gazette* joined Cody for lunch on the Kansas City, St. Joseph, and Council Bluffs Railroad. Seated at a table in the new City of St. Joseph dining car, the reporter and Cody ordered food and talked about the upcoming season.[10]

The Buffalo Bill Combination visited Hartford, Connecticut, nearly every year, where the shows were enthusiastically received. Buffalo Bill's first appearance there was on February 24 and 25, 1873, with Texas Jack and Ned Buntline in *Scouts of the Prairie*. The local paper reported that the men visited the Colt firearms works and made clear that "whenever they shoot anybody they insist upon using Colt's pistols." They stayed in the Allyn House, which was built in 1857 and became the city's premier hotel. The first floor of the hotel housed a variety of retail establishments during its first decades, including a bakery and a drugstore offering ice cream sodas. With rooms for three hundred guests, it was the largest and most elegant of Hartford's hostelries. In 1859 the hotel's dining room offered such options as leg of mutton in caper sauce, oyster fritters, and sautéed kidneys in port sauce. Cody continued to visit the Allyn House during his eleven trips to Hartford with the Combination. He also ate at the Honiss Oyster House, patronized by his friend Mark Twain, who had a home in Hartford. Although 1879 was one of the only times the Combination did not perform in Hartford, Cody still visited the city that year, when his autobiography, *The Life of Hon. William F. Cody, Also Known as Buffalo Bill,* was published by Hartford's Frank E. Bliss.[11]

The Buffalo Bill Combination performed *Knight of the Plains, or Buffalo Bill's Best Trail* at Nashville's Grand Opera House on November 24 and 25, 1879. The house receipts were the highest for that season. The cast stayed at the Maxwell House every night they were in town. The hotel, which first opened in 1869, had just undergone $25,000 in improvements and was considered one of the "best appointed" in the country. Corinthian columns framed the entrance; the elegant lobby had mahogany cabinetry, chandeliers, and gilded mirrors; and the large dining room doubled as a ballroom. Seven presidents stayed at the hotel during its heyday. An elaborate dinner was served every Christmas Day, with the menu for 1879 including an enviable assortment of foods: boar's head, beef, duck, mutton, and rabbit, all prepared with exotic sauces; turtle soup, gumbo, boned turkeys, and boiled Mackinaw trout; and local specialties like leg of Cumberland black bear, Tennessee opossum baked with sweet potatoes, and Kentucky raccoon in "devil's sauce." Desserts ranged from dried and fresh fruits to English plum pudding and assorted pastries. The hotel offered English breakfast tea and French coffee but did not yet serve the beverage through which its name lives on—Maxwell House coffee—developed and offered to the hotel by its creator in 1892. After many annual holiday feasts, the hotel burned down on Christmas night of 1961.[12]

Buffalo Bill's Combination, now including a military brass band, Pawnee Indians, and a demonstration of marksmanship by Cody, concluded its 1880 season with three shows called *Buffalo Bill at Bay* at Buffalo's Academy of Music on May 12. The troupe stayed at the Mansion House. Before leaving town, Buffalo Bill, the Indians, and "Boy Chief of the Pawnee" Eddie Burgess were guests at an "elegant wine supper" at Gerot's Restaurant, an establishment

Fig 9. Envelope from Sturtevant House in 1882 showing that meals were included with the cost of a room. In 1883 Buffalo Bill spent twenty days here while performing in New York City with his Combination. Author's collection.

offering French food. The event included recitations, toasts, and music provided by the academy's orchestra.[13]

By 1883 the Combination, now called Buffalo Bill's Combination of Twenty-Four Artists, was doing well financially. That year Buffalo Bill did twenty evening performances in both Brooklyn and New York City. On January 11 he wrote a business associate that he could be found at the Sturtevant House in the city. The Sturtevant, opened after the Civil War, was particularly popular with members of the military and folks in show business. Given that clientele and its central location on Broadway, it was ideal lodging for Cody. A six-story hotel, the Sturtevant was equipped with elevators, modern conveniences, and a dining room that was open from 5:00 a.m. to midnight. The cost of room and board was $3.00 or $3.50, "according to location" (fig. 9). When Cody checked in, he was presented with a bottle of whiskey, and he received a box of candy every Sunday evening. Great care was afforded the meals, which were served five times each day. A popular item on the Sturtevant's menu was Broiled Pigs' Feet à la P. T. Barnum, the showman's favorite meal and a specialty with a reputation that "extended far and wide." It probably featured in at least one of the meals Cody enjoyed at the Sturtevant during his twenty-day stay.[14]

From New York, the Combination headed northward. The troupe stayed at the DeWitt hotel in Lewiston, Maine, on March 8. Considered one of the best hotels in northern New England, the DeWitt had a dining room on its second floor. The local newspaper noted that the Indians with the Combination ordered a variety of side dishes in the dining room and were "highly civilized and dignified in their conduct."[15]

With his Combination appearing in the major cities of the East, Buffalo Bill was making good money, but he had his eye on bigger things. Once in motion, his plan would take him all over North America and Europe. Dining in the fanciest hotels continued as a theme for the rest of his life, but so would eating in tents. And even as the West that he knew disappeared, he would live it on a daily basis.

Part 2

Culinary Themes from an Exhibition

6

Founding and Feeding the Wild West

In the dining tent the long lines of neatly set tables looked most inviting. The men were just taking their places, and a hungry lot they seemed. Fortunately the necessities of life were not lacking, for the supplies back in the kitchen were great enough to feed a small army. Clothes baskets full of fresh lettuce, barrels full of fresh beef, milk can after milk can of pure milk, a wagon load of bread, and so on was at hand. Six hundred meals are served in this tent three times a day.

Brantford Courier, 1897

After a decade presenting plays, basically dime novel melodramas, on stages across the country, Buffalo Bill decided he wanted something more. He wanted to re-create the West he knew, with its wide open spaces, diversity of peoples, and abundant wildlife. He wanted the crowds that thronged to his shows to see, smell, hear, and even taste the real West—but a stage would not be large enough for what he had in mind. Cody wrote, "Such exhibitions as I had prepared to give could only be shown in large open-air enclosures." And so, Buffalo Bill's Wild West was born in 1883.[1]

Buffalo Bill was once again the right person at the right time. His Wild West started at a time when the West it depicted was waning and would soon disappear altogether. Later, advertising for his show even drew parallels between the peoples of the West and the dinosaurs, creatures from a long dead past being popularly reassembled in museums of the day. It was a time when people were curious about a West they had read about but not experienced. Those who participated in western expansion pronounced the show authentic and found it an opportunity for reminiscence. One woman from Deadwood, South Dakota, encouraged others to visit

Buffalo Bill's Wild West "for the sake of living it over again for one night," noting that they would be "harrowingly homesick for a least a week." One notable patron was Mark Twain, who wrote to Cody that the Wild West was "genuine" and that the "effect[s] produced upon me by its spectacles were identical with those wrought upon me a long time ago by the same spectacles on the frontier." The show even included the smell of campfires and, for the lucky, an opportunity to taste an authentic western rib roast.[2]

Buffalo Bill's first collaborator in creating such a show was Doc Carver, another western sharpshooter. They called it The Wild West: Cody and Carver's Rocky Mountain and Prairie Exhibition (fig. 10). John Burke, who had handled promotion for the Buffalo Bill Combination since 1873, continued in that role. The trio gathered cowboys and cowgirls, Mexican vaqueros, American Indians, and cavalrymen, accompanied by western appurtenances like a stagecoach and a prairie schooner. Elk were brought in from Colorado, and buffalo were gathered from the plains. The troupe rehearsed in Columbus, Nebraska, and the show made its first appearance in Omaha on May 17, 1883. There ten thousand turned out for the first performance and twenty thousand for the second. The stages on which Buffalo Bill had previously appeared would have been too small for such crowds, and in fact, few theaters could have accommodated audiences of this size. The show was greeted with acclaim wherever it traveled over the following months. But as Cody later wrote, "The enterprise was not a complete financial success during the first season, although everywhere our performances were attended by immense audiences." He and Carver were not particularly good money managers and also spent entirely too much time drinking with old friends who dropped by to see the show.[3]

At the end of the first season, financial tensions and other differences led to a split between Cody and Carver, the latter going on to create his own western show. Cody engaged a new business partner, Nate Salsbury, who had a national theatrical reputation as a comedian and impresario. Capitalizing on Buffalo Bill's national fame, they renamed the show Buffalo Bill's Wild West. Cody wrote about Salsbury, "I knew him to be a reliable friend, and withal endowed with a rare business sagacity that gave him the reputation

Fig 10. A rare 1883 program for Buffalo Bill's first outdoor show, The
Wild West: Cody and Carver's Rocky Mountain and Prairie Exhibition.
Object ID#2016.015, Buffalo Bill Museum and Grave, Golden CO.

of being one of the very best, as well as successful, managers in the show business."[4]

One thing Salsbury insisted on was that Buffalo Bill no longer drink on the job, something that had distracted him from work while he was with Carver. Cody promised that he would not drink during the show's active season: "This drinking surely ends today and your pard will be himself, and on deck all the time." With few exceptions, Buffalo Bill kept to that promise. In fact, his abstinence during the season even led some to speculate that he was a supporter of the growing U.S. temperance movement. The drinking issue settled, Salsbury was fully onboard. With Salsbury as business manager, John Burke as promoter, and Cody as the showman, Buffalo Bill's Wild West soon became both a popular and financial success and remained so for the next three decades.[5]

Not entirely assured that the show would be a success, Cody continued to tour with Buffalo Bill's Combination in the winters of 1883–86, while operating Buffalo Bill's Wild West the other three seasons. He did experiment at operating the Wild West as a year-round show during the winter of 1884–85. Anticipating warmer winter weather in the South, he moved it to New Orleans to coincide with the 1884–85 World's Industrial and Cotton Centennial Exposition. The exposition was unsuccessful, however, and Buffalo Bill's Wild West was a disaster. Incessant rains kept visitors away from the outdoor show, and Cody left New Orleans with a debt of $60,000. After that experience, Cody occasionally operated the show in winter but only at indoor venues, like New York's Madison Square Garden. The following summer, with the addition of Annie Oakley and, briefly, Sitting Bull, the show rebounded from its losses. By the spring of 1886 Cody had enough confidence that he dropped the Combination.[6]

Buffalo Bill subsequently spent his winters preparing for the next show season, exploring business investments, meeting with the important personages of his day, and even getting involved in politics. In 1887, just before Cody's first trip to Europe, Governor John Thayer appointed him a colonel in the Nebraska National Guard. Later, in 1890, Thayer upped his rank to general during the Ghost Dance conflict, but Bill preferred to be referred to as

Colonel Cody. It was a rank that proved useful when he hobnobbed with military figures in the United States and Europe.

Over the next thirty years Buffalo Bill's Wild West saw some changes. In 1893 horsemen and horsewomen from all over the world were added for the World's Columbian Exposition in Chicago, and the show's name was expanded to Buffalo Bill's Wild West and Congress of Rough Riders of the World. Rough Riders, a term for those who exhibited excellent horsemanship, was used by Cody five years before Theodore Roosevelt appropriated it for his regiment during the Spanish-American War. In 1909 Buffalo Bill joined forces with Gordon "Pawnee Bill" Lillie, who had been a member of Cody's Wild West in 1883 and had gone on to create his own Wild West show. The combination of the two was known as Buffalo Bill's Wild West and Pawnee Bill's Great Far East. In that combination, "exotic" performers, like acrobats from the Far East, were added to the show. The American Indians on horses were joined by Hindu fakirs on elephants.[7]

With his full participation in Buffalo Bill's Wild West, as well as the changes the show went through, Cody's life also changed. He no longer spent every night in hotels while touring but often stayed in a tent on the show grounds. It was furnished with carpets, curtains, easy chairs, a desk, and even an ice-cooled refrigerator from which he could offer drinks to visitors. Other times he stayed in his private train car, which had a sleeper and dining area. When he did stay in a hotel, particularly in the larger American and European cities, he frequently returned to the show grounds to dine with his employees.

Buffalo Bill sometimes referred to his Wild West troupe as a "mimic army." There is an old saying that "an army marches on its belly." While that quotation has been erroneously attributed to Napoleon (it is not clear just where it originated), it could certainly have applied to Buffalo Bill's mimic army. The large quantities of food consumed by the troupe were often noted by outside observers. Buffalo Bill's army was supplied with ample food, and he ensured that it was food of quality.

The show was typically performed from April through October, and during this time, Cody usually ate with his employees. One newspaper observed, "The followers of Buffalo Bill are blest with the best of appetites, and the general always dines and sups with his men." Cody explained, "Why shouldn't I? I work with them. Besides, I haven't time to go to a hotel. Yes, I sleep here too. I have a tent of my own back there." Most meals were taken in a dining tent that was as large as circus big tops of the day. This occasionally varied, depending on the circumstances. While traveling in England, the show used two tents for meals, one seating 130 people and the other 160. And when the show performed at Madison Square Garden, a southwest corner of the facility acted as their dining room. Sometimes members of the staff, seeking a change of pace, ate in town rather than with the show. Buffalo Bill frequently hosted special dignitaries at meals in his own tent or, like his staff, ate in restaurants in the towns where the show appeared. One editorial said he was "as much at home at Delmonico's as in the Indian tepees." His enjoyment of fine dining proved to be of benefit to his employees, who dined like dignitaries. Annie Oakley later observed, "None could possibly tell the difference between the reception of a band of cowboys and the train of an emperor. Dinner at camp was the same informal hearty humorous story telling affair when we were alone, and when the Duchess of Holstein came visiting in all her glory."[8]

Buffalo Bill didn't give up fine dining when he started the Wild West; he shared it with his employees. One observer noted that show personnel received "just as good meals as the high liver at a first class hotel." Reporters who visited the show wrote that the food was excellent and enjoyed by everyone from the lowest canvasmen (those who erected the tents) to Buffalo Bill himself. During the show's visit to Boston in 1899, a reporter stated that one "could not have found a better meal in Boston, as far as the quality and quantity of the food were concerned." Yet another reporter observed, "It must be said that Mr. Cody looks well after the inner man and his necessities."[9]

Whenever the Wild West arrived in a town, the first tent erected was the dining tent, and the show's cooks immediately started preparing breakfast. With breakfast over, they began lunch and then supper. Wild West employees entering the dining tent encountered a space that was clean and attractive, and some said it "would put to shame many a hotel." The tables were covered with tablecloths and set with napkins, silverware, and china of various kinds. The food tent was "clean and inviting as a restaurant." The staff did not line up mess-hall style to be served; instead, white-clad waiters took their orders and delivered their food. One account described waiters rushing in and out of the tent as they took orders and delivered them: "Soup for two; dry toast for one; roast beef, vegetables, fried potatoes and toast for four."[10]

Annie Oakley, who joined the show in 1885, described breakfast as consisting of "good coffee, bread, butter, preserves, fine steaks broiled over wood coals, with fruits and berries in season." A summer lunch in upstate New York included rice and tomato soup, beef brisket in tomato sauce, cold roast beef and pork, corned beef hash, bread, coffee, milk, and iced tea, while a summer supper in Hamilton, Ontario, included fish (baked, boiled, and fried), roast beef, roast veal and dressing, roast lamb, new potatoes, and new string beans. Beef, a staple on the Wild West's menu, was consumed in various forms. One visitor reported that "a dozen cattle, quartered and ready to cut in stews, roast and soup bones, are piled up together, looking like a mountain of meat, and it represents but one day's meat allowance." The show employed two butchers to look after the large meat supply. Keeping healthy habits in mind, "no less than three kinds of vegetables were served at every dinner." Everything was prepared in large quantities, including one-yard-square meat pies, 350 square tarts "as big as your hand," and for breakfast, 150 pounds of bacon, 120 dozen eggs, 110 quarts of coffee, and 125 quarts of tea. The coffee was cooked in a hundred-gallon pot, described as so large that "six Indian warriors can dance a battle step" inside it. Cody said that the pot would supply so much coffee that his performers would not be thirsty enough to drink "fire water" and thus there would be more discipline in the show.[11]

The year 1896, thirteen years after the opening of Buffalo Bill's Wild West and seventeen years before it closed, is one of the best-documented in terms of culinary operations. In addition to numerous articles in newspapers describing the show's kitchen, a souvenir book was released following the 1896 season that included a "Cook

House" staff list of fifty-six people. Cody did not directly oversee the daily operation of the kitchen but hired a caterer. That year caterer J. E. Robbins, formerly with the P. T. Barnum Circus, was in charge of the food service. William G. Hatch was the head chef, assisted by eight cooks, two of whom focused on pastries. The kitchen personnel also included two butchers, thirty-two members of the waitstaff, three persons in charge of cooking fires, two watermen (who supplied water for cooking, serving, and cleaning), four dishwashers (including a silver washer), and since the Wild West used a lot of dishes, from fine china to graniteware, two full-time dish packers.[12]

One of Robbins's most important roles as head of the food service operations was ensuring that necessary provisions were procured in the towns Buffalo Bill's Wild West show visited. The 1896 souvenir book contained numerous advertisements from the food purveyors used by the show in that year. When in Tiffen, Ohio, on July 23, Robbins acquired groceries and breads, as well as hay for the show's horses, from Lauer Brothers Groceries and Provisions. A week later, in Owosso, Michigan, the show made its purchases from Hall Brothers Grocers, which offered "special prices to all the large shows." Two days later the show was in Ann Arbor, where Robbins obtained groceries "supplied at lowest prices" from Calkins Mercantile. On August 13 the show played Goshen, Indiana, a community surrounded by Amish and Mennonite families. There the caterer bought locally baked goods from George S. Kolb, whose store was in the "German Block." By the end of August the show was in Janesville, where Robbins procured groceries and feed for the horses from the Van Kirk Grocery Company, which advertised that providing for the needs of circuses was one of its specialties. In September Buffalo Bill's Wild West played Winona, Minnesota, where John Winkels and Company provided fresh and salted meats, including wild game and poultry. Robbins also purchased groceries from F. M. Whitney and baked goods from Charles Westman's Boston Bakery and Confectionery. The show patronized Hicks Grocery Company during a two-day stand in Minneapolis, while Young and Monson Grocers supplied their needs in Mankato. More fresh meat was acquired on September 25 in Mason City, Iowa, where Smith Brothers City Meat Market offered "special prices to shows."[13]

The results, and costs, of Robbins's efforts were significant. During a visit to Columbus, Ohio, on July 13, 1896, fourteen hundred meals (breakfast, dinner or lunch, and supper) were served in the dining tent on eight long tables, seating a total of 480 people at a time. Food expenses for the week before, culminating in the Columbus visit, were $1,424.30. By then the show's staff had swollen to six hundred, consuming four hundred loaves of bread each day.[14]

Even the best-laid plans sometimes went awry. Buffalo Bill's Wild West and Congress of Rough Riders of the World arrived in Emporia, Kansas, on October 3, 1900, as part of the Emporia Street Fair, a heavily marketed event. The town was filled with visitors to the fair as well as spectators planning to attend Buffalo Bill's show. The troupe had been delayed and was set to arrive at 1:00 p.m., with no time for the regular sit-down lunch before delivering a matinee performance. Cody telegraphed ahead to his advance man in Emporia, "Have sandwiches and coffee for six hundred." But none of the restaurants would furnish them with either, since they were reserving their food for their customers. Finally, the advance man contacted well-known Emporia newspaperman William Allen White, who worked with a local church group and several other businesses to procure enough sandwiches for the show. The staff got their quick lunch before the show, but the next day White's newspaper observed that this had created a sandwich famine in Emporia, and for a day "sandwiches were scarcer than pearls in oyster cans."[15]

Food preparation was overseen by men who were as colorful as Cody, like John Keanan, who quoted Shakespeare while cooking; chef Billy Hatch, described as jolly and curly-haired; and "Water Hoss" Hoover, who kept the cooks, dishwashers, show personnel, and all the livestock supplied with water. Hoover remarked that keeping everyone fed at the Wild West could be "worse than an Irish famine from sunrise to sunset."[16]

With the turn of the century, neither the quality nor quantity of food changed at the Wild West. A newspaper in Boise, Idaho, observed the staff being fed during an appearance there on August 18, 1902:

> In the restaurant about 500 guests were eating their supper. This traveling cook shop is as clean as hard work can keep it. Flowers were on each table and the napery was fit to pass anywhere. Women and men alike enjoy its comfort, and there is an anti-smoking rule. The bill of fare had on it everything that the city market provided, and quantity was in the same class with quality. Colonel Cody is particular about his men's fare.[17]

The manner in which food was served in the Wild West's one-eighth-acre food tent also stayed the same. One innovation was a flag, run up a pole on top of the tent at mealtimes, indicating that hot food was now ready. When serving time was over, it was taken down from the pole until the next meal. A waitstaff of as many as fifty still delivered food to those seated in the "restaurant," picking it up from a counter above stoves that kept the cooked food hot. In the center of the tent were multiple large tea and coffee urns from which the diners could help themselves; apparently the hundred-gallon coffeepot was no longer in use. The food tent still had long tables with tablecloths and utensils, and the show's staff was seated on blue-painted benches on either side. The only hierarchy evident was in seating and place settings. Buffalo Bill and the leadership of the show were seated together at a table with space for special guests (fig. 11). They ate off china with silver utensils, while the cowboys, Indians, and performers at other tables ate off stoneware plates with pewter utensils. Support personnel, like the canvasmen, had their own tables and ate off graniteware plates with metal spoons. Everyone received the same food, however.[18]

A British columnist visited the Wild West while it was at Madison Square Garden in 1903 and recorded his observations. He heard one of the food contractors complain about the voracious troupe, who consumed "five hundred loaves of bread, five hundred bowls of soup, two thousand cups of tea and coffee, a ton of meat and vegetables" daily. He watched waiters bustling about, delivering food to tables with bright red tablecloths and green, yellow, and

Fig 11. Buffalo Bill eating at the head table in the Wild West food tent, flanked by Nate Salsbury on his right and Johnny Baker on his left. Object ID#70.0302, Buffalo Bill Museum and Grave, Golden CO.

white paper napkins. The Indians with the show seemed to eat twice as much as everyone else, washing down their food with coffee from large bowls rather than using cups like everyone else. The manager of the operation told him, "If they took it in cups, it would require two men to refill them as fast as they could go." The cowboys were downing mutton stew and beef, also accompanied by liberal amounts of coffee. Waiters rushed around the tables with gigantic pots, hollering, "Coffee up!" and "Tea up!" The columnist sympathized with the contractor's frustration, noting, "I never saw so much food and drink swallowed in so short a space of time. It was shoveled up, placed between their lips, and down it went. It was like posting letters."[19]

The Wild West menus varied. Beef and pork were consistently served, frequently shipped to the show by rail from Chicago.

Whether chicken, fish, and various sides appeared depended on the season and what was available.[20]

In 1909, when Buffalo Bill's Wild West combined with Pawnee Bill's Great Far East, a new dessert was added to the regular menu—ice cream. While ice cream had been around for many years and could be made in small quantities at home or in larger quantities at commercial establishments, providing it to a traveling show the size of the Wild West required improvements in manufacturing, storage, and delivery. Although ice cream still was not available to the show in many of the towns visited in 1910, it was a different story in the cities. During performances in Los Angeles, 150 gallons of ice cream were acquired for show personnel each day. And a purchase of 360 gallons of ice cream while in Vancouver, British Columbia, led the local paper to remark that the "Wild West performers are fastidious of taste."[21]

A lot of mouths consumed the ice cream; the troupe ranged in size from 850 to over 1,500 between 1909 and 1913. Keeping the entourage fed occupied the full-time attention of fifteen cooks plus sixty support staff ranging from butchers to waiters. Feeding so many mouths was tough work, and personnel who started in the spring occasionally left midseason. In the late summer of 1912, the show advertised in a Wisconsin newspaper that it needed cooks, butchers, meat cutters, and waiters. A month later, while the show was in Oklahoma, it had filled some of the positions but still needed cooks and waiters.[22]

A typical day of meals for such a large group began with an abundant breakfast that offered a variety of cereals, pork or lamb chops, fish cakes, beefsteak, bacon, eggs, biscuits, rolls, and griddle cakes. Although the show included people from all over the world who were used to different diets, nearly everyone seemed to like griddle cakes, thousands of which were made every morning. Lunch was traditionally the lightest meal of the day. One newspaper reporter observed that the quantity of food at lunch was limited by the imminence of an afternoon matinee, as "men with heavily loaded stomachs cannot very well handle bucking horses." Supper consisted of vegetable soup; roasts of beef, ham, and mutton; boiled or mashed potatoes; vegetable side dishes; and various desserts. All of these could be readily prepared for large numbers of people. Some foods that were difficult to obtain or required more care in preparation, like chicken or fresh fish, were less frequently on the menu than beef, pork, and mutton.[23]

Even though Buffalo Bill ate on china at a separate table, visitors commented on his culinary solidarity with his employees time and again over the three decades of his Wild West show. Breakfast was the only meal he typically did not consume with his staff in the food tent. Instead, he ate in his private train car's dining room, handling correspondence and other business matters. Since the troupe performed a matinee and an evening show, morning was the only time he could spend on such pursuits. He also occasionally met with senior staff and guests over breakfast in the dining room. But he always ate the same foods as his men, delivered by one of the show's waiters.[24]

Buffalo Bill ultimately presided over the Wild West repasts throughout the thirty years. Determining what he preferred to eat while with the show is difficult, since he rarely talked about food during interviews. Instead, he chose to tell tales of the Old West or promote the show's performances. The frequency with which some foods, like beefsteak and fricasseed chicken, or chicken fricassee, appeared on the menu suggests he may have favored them. An 1896 newspaper report suggested that Buffalo Bill and his family were fond of broiled steaks and "other delicacies of the seasons." On a different occasion, a reporter observed him eating a watermelon in his tent. Another time, while expounding over a meal on the joys of life in the show's camp, Cody offered his guest a bowl of bean soup, saying, "You've got to eat bean soup if you live in camp." Perhaps his enthusiasm for the soup harked back to his "best meal" of bacon and beans at Fort Laramie in the spring of 1858.[25]

Buffalo Bill's "camp" bore little resemblance to his early camps while scouting and hunting buffalo, even as his shows were attempting to re-create those days. The West he knew was retreating into the past; soon Buffalo Bill's Wild West and its imitators were the only places where that past could be witnessed. In 1890 the U.S. Census Bureau announced the end of the American frontier. It was a new era in the United States, and innovations in everything from transportation to food preparation at Buffalo Bill's Wild West made that reality abundantly clear.

A DAY OF DINING AT BUFFALO BILL'S WILD WEST

The provision for feeding the troupe is one of interest. William Langan of New York has charge of the catering. Today 280 dozen of eggs were used for breakfast, 1600 pounds of beef, sixty gallons of coffee, five hundred loaves of bread, twenty bushels of potatoes. The dinner tent will seat all of the troupe, Indians, cowboys, Persians, Hindoos and artists. Col. W. F. Cody eats his meals with the troupe and sits at the head table. The food is prepared by a corps of thirty men, four large ranges being used for the cooking. The breakfast this morning was cooked in one hour after the cooking apparatus arrived at the grounds, and consisted of the following: Fried eggs, beefsteak, pork chops, fried bacon, oatmeal and milk, Lyonnaise potatoes, rolls, tea, coffee and milk.

The dinner, which is served at six o'clock this evening, will comprise the following: Macaroni soup, fillet of beef, roast pork, corn fritters, Lyonnaise and baked potatoes, pork chops, pies, puddings, coffee and tea.

The plan of arranging and cooking the food is the same as armies are fed, substantial; at noon a lunch is served.

"At the Grounds," *Portsmouth (NH) Times*, June 7, 1900, NSBY

7

Meals on Wheels

The equipment of the company is the most complete that has
been seen. Dining tents, stables, electric light plant, etc., for
the accommodation of eight hundred men and five hundred
horses is something seldom seen in a company traveling from
city to city and from country to country.

Knoxville (TN) Daily Journal, 1897

Over the course of thirty years, Buffalo Bill's Wild West grew to be
one of the biggest shows on earth. Such an ambitious operation
required careful logistics for everything from transportation to marketing to food preparation. Those logistics stimulated innovations,
particularly when it came to feeding as many as 1,500 performers
and support staff while entertaining 12,500 guests twice a day. The
action in the Wild West arena was what drew everyone, but it was
just one part of an operation that fascinated visitors, reporters,
and even heads of state.[1]

While Buffalo Bill's Wild West sometimes stayed in cities like
Chicago, New York, Glasgow, or London for several months, most
of the time the show was on the road. During the 1896 season the
Wild West traveled 10,787 miles, with 132 stops for performances.
Occasionally the troupe played in one city for as many as four
nights, but more frequently they performed a matinee and an
evening show in one town, then went on to another town the next
day. The show often traveled at night so that the daylight hours
were not wasted. As one newspaper put it, when the train arrived
in Dayton at 5:00 a.m., Buffalo Bill and his staff were "peacefully
sleeping in their curtained couches."[2]

Fortunately, Buffalo Bill's Wild West burst onto the world stage
at the dawn of the golden age of rail travel. Trains were becoming

faster and more powerful, enabling the transport of large shows throughout the United States and Europe. And the Wild West was huge. In 1896 the show occupied three different trains with a total of fifty-two cars. During its European tour of 1905–6, it filled four trains, referred to as sections, each with twelve or thirteen cars. One section could be as long as 756 feet, and the entire grouping, not including the locomotive, could weigh over three hundred tons. In 1898 the train had fifteen stock cars for the animals, carrying up to six hundred horses and mules plus a small herd of buffalo, as well as eight sleeping cars for personnel and sixteen flatcars for rolling stock. Among the rolling stock were two plants to generate electricity, show wagons, two water tanks, a refrigerator wagon, and a huge range wagon used for cooking.[3]

Souvenir guidebooks available from the Wild West emphasized just how many miles the show traveled, noted the number of train cars required, and provided other interesting statistics. For example, in 1902 all the tents used over twenty-three thousand yards of canvas and were secured with nearly twenty miles of rope. That season the show traveled 14,039 miles, and all three sections of show trains had to be ferried across bodies of water, including the Mississippi River and the Straits of Mackinac, a total of six times.[4]

When the show entered a town, the community was anticipating its visit. As many as sixty-three advance men had already arrived in special train cars two and four weeks earlier. They distributed colorful couriers advertising the show to area barbershops and other businesses. Posters were pasted on every available wall in town, sometimes over competitors' advertising. Another vital responsibility of the advance men was arranging fodder for the livestock and food for the performers. They contracted with local butchers for meat, bakers for breadstuffs, and grocers for vegetables and other supplies they could not, or chose not to, transport.[5]

Within one to two hours of the troupe's arrival, "wagons and beasts were in the field, the big cooking apparatus was making the morning meal, canvas was up, and the immense arena framed in." As the show got larger in the early twentieth century, it continued to move with comparable speed. One performer noted in his diary in 1911 that the show arrived in Salem, Massachusetts, at 5:00 a.m.

and everything was up by 6:30 that morning. The cast then had breakfast, and "everyone went fishing for flounder."[6]

Buffalo Bill's Wild West occupied a minimum of eleven acres, with its horseshoe-shaped open-air arena in the center. The seating area was covered by long, continuous tents, open in front for viewing the show and closed in the back. These afforded the audiences shelter from sun, rain, and on rare occasions, snow. The open end of the horseshoe had a backdrop, often painted to resemble mountains, and an entrance for the riders, horses, buffalo, and various performers. Behind the backdrop and the arena seating were a variety of tents for the horses and other livestock, dressing rooms, blacksmiths and farriers, and administrative functions, as well as a large dining area. At the opposite side of the horseshoe from the backdrop were refreshment tents and ticket sales offices. The performers' tents and American Indians' tepees were also arrayed around the outside of the arena. Sideshow entertainments, sometimes called Buffalo Bill's Varieties, were added shortly after the turn of the century and housed in another tent near the entrance. The show was laid out so well that one newspaper observed, "All the arrangements are perfect and the amphitheatre presents points of vantage such as are absent from the average circus."[7]

At night those "points of vantage" were assisted by illumination from seventy-six arc lights, each offering two thousand candle power and making the performance area "as bright as day." The show also employed three movable searchlights with ten thousand candle power each. Eight hundred incandescent lights were spread throughout the entire village of tents, as was electrical power where needed, including enough energy for an electric fan in Buffalo Bill's tent. All the power came from two large portable generators, which they called light plants, one named Buffalo Bill and the other Nate Salsbury.[8]

The nighttime illumination of the Wild West was very innovative for its time. But the innovations that received the most attention were those associated with feeding the show's many performers and support personnel. With so many mouths to feed and a tight performance schedule, food preparation had to be done both quickly and efficiently. Central to it all was the range wagon, which had the capacity to feed a large company, was efficient, and was easily transported. Just as the chuck wagon was an essential invention for preparing food on the long cattle drives of the nineteenth century, the range wagon was an essential invention for Buffalo Bill's Wild West. Buffalo Bill's range wagon was probably first used in 1890, during the show's trip across Europe. A newspaper editor in Florence visited the show and, among his observations, noted a "wooden house" on wheels that served as a kitchen. It had a tall chimney that could be removed during transport so it could pass through railroad tunnels. This was the first version of the show's range wagon, which was modified according to needs over the next twenty-three years.[9]

The range wagon was the sort of contraption that inspired newspapermen to wax eloquent, and they variously described it as a "monster range on wheels," a "gastronomic hub," and an "altar of gastronomic hopes." The fires leaped high within it, and one wrote that it was "a small Vesuvius" from which "belched forth smoke and whence issued savoury dishes heaped with meat and potatoes." Another went so far as to say it was "almost as important a piece of impedimenta to this big band of pilgrims as was the ark to the ancient Israelites." Though this may have been an exaggeration, the range wagon was vital to the Wild West's functioning and was the center of a kitchen operation that occupied half an acre. The area was roped off from the curious public, who could observe the food preparation from outside those barriers. Within the ropes were fires over which stood five massive pots the size of barrels (fig. 12). Some were filled with boiling water for coffee and tea, while others were used for preparing vegetables and soups. Nearby, men peeled potatoes and onions. Just beyond them were dishwashers, using the hot water to hastily clean cooking pans and dishes. Also within the perimeter were a massive refrigerator wagon and a water wagon overseen by "Water Hoss" Hoover. The show paid the towns for the privilege of filling the water wagon at nearby hydrants.[10]

All this activity revolved around the range wagon, which was twenty feet long and looked like one of today's moving vans, although it was transported on a flatcar. Once it was rolled off the car and taken by a team of eight horses to the show grounds, it was

Fig 12. Massive kettles behind the Wild West's food tent. These were used to cook soup and vegetables and to heat water. Object ID#87.0056, Buffalo Bill Museum and Grave, Golden CO.

positioned in the center of its half acre. There the sides were lifted and propped up to reveal a massive cooking range with room for four to eight cooks around its sides. It was actually an assemblage of several ranges, connected together and sharing a large smokestack that vented the massive wood fire burning within (fig. 13). Some years its appearance changed, with the ranges varying in size and another smokestack being added. But it always served similar functions and attracted onlookers. It was on top of this range that the griddle cakes, eggs, chops and steaks, toast, and other fried foods were prepared. The range also had ovens below, where meat was braised, vegetables roasted, and biscuits baked.[11]

Upon the show's arrival in a town in the morning, the range wagon was one of the first items unloaded, and the wood fire was immediately started. The wagon was then taken to the show grounds, where the cooks set to preparing breakfast. The food tent was the first to be erected. Breakfast was served from 7:00 to

Fig 13. The Wild West's range wagon, with four cooking ranges sharing
a common chimney. This innovation, at the center of a large cooking operation, enabled efficient feeding of as many as one thousand
employees. Object ID#87, Buffalo Bill Museum and Grave, Golden CO.

9:00 a.m., before any rehearsals or other activities were held. The
goal was to begin serving within forty-five minutes of arrival. In
1896 chef Billy Hatch bragged that they used the range wagon to
"prepare 800 to 1,000 individual steaks every morning and serve
them for breakfast." Lunch was cooked and served from 11:00
a.m. to 1:00 p.m., before the afternoon matinee. Dinner or supper
was enjoyed by the cast between 4:00 and 6:00 p.m., before the
evening show. Hatch pointed out that the evening meal was "nip
and tuck with breakfast" in terms of both quantity and popularity.
On the day he was interviewed, the evening meal entrée choices
included roast sirloin of beef with mushrooms, roast loin of pork
with apple sauce, roast sugar-cured ham and Madeira sauce, and
corned beef and cabbage, along with green peas and potatoes,
mashed and baked. Such hearty meals were par for the course,
since "they all work hard and this kind of life seems to be good
for the appetite."[12]

Buffalo Bill's Wild West and Rough Riders of the World used the range wagon through the nineteenth and into the twentieth century. When the show toured Europe from 1902 to 1906, it still served as the main device for cooking meals. As had been the practice in the States, the range wagon was first thing off the train, and the cooks used it to prepare as many as three thousand eggs for breakfast each day. England's *Swindon Herald* noted that "a cow-boy regards half a dozen eggs as a mere palate-tickler."[13]

By 1904 the range wagon included a portable boiler. Pipes ran from it to a "distribution center" near the six kitchen ranges on the wagon. From there, fixed and flexible tubes distributed hot water for a variety of uses. Hot water was sprayed below the meat racks to keep the cuts from drying out and was distributed to heaters for other foods. The boiler also supplied hot water to a coffee urn, "an ingenious contrivance capable of producing 1,000 cups of coffee in a few minutes." The efficiency of this system enabled one relatively small fire to provide all the hot water needed to feed the six-hundred-person staff during that season.[14]

Keeping food cold at the Wild West was an equal, if opposite, challenge. When Buffalo Bill's Wild West began in 1883, refrigeration technology already existed that could be used to create ice, but it was not applied to keeping food cold. The ice was used for that purpose in iceboxes at homes and businesses. When beef and other meats were delivered to the show, they either came from local butchers or were packed in ice and transported by rail in refrigerator cars from meat-processing and packing centers like Chicago. Neither an icebox nor a refrigerator car could meet the Wild West's needs, so caterer J. E. Robbins created a special refrigeration wagon after he began with the show in 1896.

Robbins's invention, like the range wagon, attracted a good deal of attention. The show's refrigeration wagon was described as "practically a huge ice wagon in the front of which is a large meat chest furnished with sliding, zinc-lined trays." Underneath the wagon were smaller chests with flavoring extracts and various other perishable items. It was described as having the appearance of "a brewery wagon in disguise, equipped for making one-night stands through Iowa and Kansas." The wagon was loaded off and onto a train flatcar at each stop. About a ton of ice was acquired for the refrigerator wagon every day. Meats, fish, poultry, milk products, and produce could all be kept fresh in the wagon until used. In an interview, Robbins stated, "I can keep thousands of pounds of meat in that now, because it is a regular ice cave."[15]

The innovations associated with the show, particularly those used while preparing the meals, were a point of fascination for visitors. Few had ever witnessed such an enterprise, and onlookers gazed in amazement from the rope barriers at the range wagon, refrigerator wagon, and other trappings associated with eating at the Wild West. "It was a surprise to the big crowd of spectators how the cooks managed to prepare in so short a time such a good meal for so large a number."[16]

At the end of the day, the show hadn't even finished before the canvasmen and other members of the Wild West crew began taking down tents and putting away supplies. By the time the evening performance ended, all the tents were down except for those associated with the show itself. Then those tents were put away, the animals were loaded, and the staff boarded the sleeping cars. Within two hours, less if possible, the show was back on the railroad, heading for its new destination. As one newspaper observed, "In an incredibly short space of time—for every man knows what is required of him—the exhibition will be dismantled and packed up, and where but a day or two before was all noise, bustle, and a huge concourse of people, is now only a grassy field recovering from the effect of the tramping feet of many thousands." It was the show's many innovations, quite novel to visitors but necessary to the efficient operation of the show, that enabled Buffalo Bill's Wild West to set up promptly, feed its personnel, entertain the public, and then rapidly move to its next destination.[17]

8

The World at Buffalo Bill's Table

One of the most interesting places about the big show is the dining hall. Here 1,800 meals are served every day to probably the most cosmopolitan lot of guests ever gathered under one roof.

Kansas City World, 1898

Buffalo Bill's Wild West began as a presentation of life in the American West. While that was always a central theme of the show the scope of the presentation expanded over the years, as the western performers were joined by diverse peoples and acts from all over the world. As these changes were made, the show came to be described as "history, humanity, heroism on horseback" and "a great school of anthropology." This was particularly evident in the dining tent, where it appeared as if, as one Englishmen observed, "the types of humanity depicted in the coloured plates of a good atlas or geograph had suddenly left those pages to take a stroll" into the tent. This diversity of humanity performed, worked, and dined together.[1]

Buffalo Bill's Wild West began in 1883 with a cast of players from the Great Plains, including Pawnees, Lakotas, a few representatives from other plains tribes, white cowboys and cowgirls, African American cowboys, and Mexican vaqueros (fig. 14). By 1890 the American Indian representation in the show consisted primarily of members of the Lakota tribe, chosen by Cody for their outstanding horsemanship, fierceness in battle re-creations, and vibrant culture.

In 1892 the cast was expanded to include Argentine gauchos, English lancers, and Cossacks. When a group of gauchos arrived to join the show while it was in Britain, a Scottish newspaper reported that they were the sixth delegation of what was to eventually become a "Congress of Horsemen of the World." Cody, Salsbury, and Burke

Fig 14. An 1895 courier used to advertise the Wild West. It illustrates the diversity of performers in the show, all having their own dietary traditions and preferences. Object ID#71.0018, Buffalo Bill Museum and Grave CO.

chose London as the organizing point of these delegations in preparation for the 1893 World's Columbian Exposition. When the show opened outside the exposition in Chicago the following year, it did so with a new name: Buffalo Bill's Wild West and Congress of Rough Riders of the World. Over the ensuing years, Rough Rider representation changed to include Hawaiians, Boers, Japanese, and other ethnic groups. They were joined by Syrian swordsmen, Chinese acrobats, and sideshow performers in the "varieties" tent. While some of these groups stayed for only one season, others remained with the show for many years. In 1908, before Pawnee Bill's Far East combined with Buffalo Bill's Wild West, the cast and crew already had so many peoples from around the world that one newspaper described the large lunch tent as being "filled with a gathering that looked like the leaves of an illustrated geography." With the addition of Pawnee Bill's Far East in 1909, including an Aboriginal person from Australia demonstrating boomerang throwing, the show had representatives from every inhabited continent. And everybody had to be fed. A visit to the food tent looked much like a visit to the cafeteria of today's United Nations, with everyone breaking bread together.[2]

Feeding such a wide diversity of ethnicities posed challenges to the show's cooks. Head cook William Langan remarked in 1894 that "people coming from different countries demand different kinds of food, cooked in widely different ways." On special occasions they were allowed to cook some of their ethnic foods for themselves. But ordinarily, everyone had to choose from the foods that were offered, although the cooks did make an effort to satisfy. Some of the more exotic foods simply could not be obtained, but personnel could choose from meats like mutton, pork, poultry, and beef; fish; dairy products; fruit; and a wide variety of vegetables. As Langan noted, the challenge was cooking within those food groups to each ethnicity's satisfaction. The American Indians were usually happy with beefsteaks, bread, and coffee three times a day but didn't care for sweets, while the Mexican vaqueros preferred their food heavily spiced and fatty. The Cossacks, gauchos, and Arabs would eat some foods but avoided others for religious reasons.[3]

Meals were usually taken in one or two large dining tents, although sometimes the Indians were supplied with a tent of their own. Since most show seasons lasted from spring until fall, the venues were outside, with the dining tents and lodging arrayed near the main performance area. When the show did winter performances, they were staged inside large facilities with indoor lodging and dining. In 1886 the popular *New York Sun* reported on "Camp Life in Town," explaining how the show was situated in Madison Square Garden. All the tepees, housing seventy-two Indians, were in an upstairs hallway with a ceiling high enough to accommodate the poles. Families had their own tepees, while single men shared one with as many as nine others. The cowboys, vaqueros, and other personnel were housed in bunk beds in several large rooms. Some also slept in tents in the arena but had to take them down each morning and erect them each evening so as not to interfere with the show. Show personnel ate in several large rooms. While Buffalo Bill often joined them at meals, he also ate at Delmonico's, which he had visited on his first trip to New York in 1882. The finest restaurant in the city, it was across from New York's most elegant hotel, Hoffman

House, which provided lodging for the likes of Sarah Bernhardt, President Grover Cleveland, and of course, Buffalo Bill. It was even more elegant and expensive than the Sturtevant, where Cody had stayed during his stage-performing days. After 1883 the Hoffman House became his go-to hotel when visiting New York City.[4]

In 1886 Buffalo Bill introduced a new type of food to New York City, provided in a temporary restaurant at Madison Square Garden and prepared by the wives of two Mexican vaqueros. A reporter from the *Sun* joined Buffalo Bill and selected guests for a "Mexican breakfast" at the restaurant. His posting to the *Sun* stated that "nothing in it but the chocolate, which was admirable, was recognizable to the taste of the average untravelled New Yorker." He was unimpressed with the repast, noting that the tortillas tasted "for all the world as the paste-soaked circus poster must taste to the ravenous goat." He was also unimpressed by the "henchilada," which he warned looked like a rolled French pancake but was "a very different thing indeed." A reporter from the *New York Times* described the "henchilada" as "the sort of grub the prodigal son subsisted on when he was in the hog business," filled with "some inflammable material that calls for large draughts of iced claret." Claret was not available, however, and those present at the breakfast had to settle for mezcal or Mexican chocolate. Believing all the dishes to be too peppery and not at all tasty, both reporters decided the only item of any value was the chocolate. The reporter for the *Times* did note that the experience was entertaining.[5]

It is possible that other New Yorkers shared the reporters' opinion, and Cody learned from that experience. While lunch stands at the show operated by local cafés occasionally provided foods to visitors over the following years, the Mexican café was the first and last time Buffalo Bill's Wild West offered an ethnic food concession. The Madison Square Garden effort did help introduce tamales to New York City; within eight years tamale carts were found throughout the city, and tamale parties were all the rage. Buffalo Bill did not realize at the time that not only had he introduced a new culinary offering to New Yorkers, but his was the first Mexican restaurant to open east of the Mississippi.[6]

By 1913, when the combination of Buffalo Bill's Wild West and Pawnee Bill's Great Far East returned to Madison Square Garden, even more ethnic groups were associated with the show, and even more care was devoted to meeting their dietary desires. Specific cooks were assigned to prepare foods for the different groups: the Indians received steaks cooked to their satisfaction and with no vegetables; the Cossacks, with their love of pickled foods, were served pickled meat three times a week; the Cingalese, natives of Sri Lanka (then Ceylon), who drank only water, received food heavily spiced with pepper and plenty of rice; and the Arabs ate unleavened bread baked specially for them on certain days of the week.[7]

While all the employees usually dined under a common community tent or in common rooms at indoor venues, they sat separately according to their ethnicities. This would have been more convenient for the waiters, who could become acquainted with each group's unique dietary needs. An 1894 article reported that each table in the dining tent was "set apart for a certain squad." This continued into the new century, when a 1908 article described a scene in which "Cossacks and Bedouins, South Sea islanders, cowboys, French cuirassiers, German hussars and women dare devil riders, in boots and short skirts, filed in, grouping at separate tables." At the last table were the "horny handed, iron muscled canvasmen with red shirts, overall and slouch hats." Despite the separation, the tables were close together, and one observer noted that "one standing in the centre of the room can hear lively conversations in a dozen different languages."[8]

The different groups may have dined separately, eaten food prepared different ways, and even experienced some language barriers, but one reporter mentioned that "painted Indians, blonde Germans, swarthy Arabs and grizzled Cossacks were enjoying their well-served food side by side, and seemed to form a genuine happy family." Outside the dining tent and off the arena, the cast did fraternize. Everyone but the Indians, who usually dressed in their tepees, shared a large tent in which they dressed for performances. It was divided into rooms by cloths hung on ropes strung six feet above the ground. There they talked and horsed around while relaxing between shows.

One reporter witnessed a card game between two English artillery-men, a Cossack, and a Turk, interrupted only as each took a swig from a bottle of ginger ale they were sharing. Frederic Remington observed, "As you walk through camp you see a Mexican, an Ogallala and a 'gaucho' swapping lies and cigarettes." Candid photographs of members of the company show Mexican vaqueros relaxing with Cossacks, members of the U.S. Cavalry chatting with Indians, and cowboys watching a game of table tennis between two Lakotas. Even the French and the Prussians got along, which prompted a reporter to remark on the "brotherly unity" exhibited at the show.[9]

Sometimes fraternization among the performers included drinking. While it was discouraged by Buffalo Bill's Wild West, performers and staff members drank wine, whiskey, and other spirits on occasion. Contracts between the Lakota, agents on the reservations, and Buffalo Bill's Wild West expressly forbade drinking of alcohol. In fact, in the United States at the time, it was unlawful to serve alcohol to American Indians. While management was usually able to control the use of alcohol within the show encampment and on the train, it had little power over consumption in the towns the show visited. On several occasions, performers got a bit wild in local saloons, and Cody had to intervene. In one incident, three Cossacks and six Lakotas were drinking at a local saloon and began "executing a war dance." When Buffalo Bill discovered this, he walked into the saloon, pulled his revolver, and ordered the men to leave. He then reminded the innkeeper that it was illegal to serve alcohol to Indians. In many cases when individual performers got drunk in bars and were arrested, they were let go from the show. If a Lakota warrior became drunk repeatedly, he was shipped back to the reservation, even if it happened in Europe.[10]

Table manners differed among ethnic groups. One newspaper reported that the Cossacks ate like they rode—very quickly. "Mastication cuts no ice with them; they could apparently digest rocks if necessary, after having swallowed them whole." The horsemen billed as Cossacks were actually from the region of Guria in the country of Georgia. Since Georgia was part of Russia at the time, and the Cossacks of Russia were known to be fierce fighters and expert horsemen, the Gurians were publicized as Cossacks. In many ways, the Gurians were more skillful than the Russian Cossacks, with a long tradition of horsemanship and trick riding. The Gurian foodways included a love of wine, pickled vegetables and meats, stews like goulash, poultry, and eggs. That meant most of the foods served to the Wild West performers agreed with them. Like the American Indians, the Gurian Cossacks particularly appreciated steak and black coffee, never adulterating it with sugar or milk.[11]

The American Indians had table manners that diverged from most of the other performers (fig. 15). They did not like the white man's way of eating and preferred tinware to china. One reporter noted that everyone dined with tablecloths but the Indians, who had no use for them. In fact, it was reported that once seated with their food, the Lakotas did not like to be seen while eating and would sometimes hunch over the table, pulling their blankets over their heads and feeding themselves through an opening in the fabric. Yet one observer mentioned that "nobody ate with his knife, and everybody who drew a napkin knew what to do with it."[12]

Perhaps the Lakotas' reluctance to be seen while eating was motivated by a lack of privacy in the Wild West. Visitors, particularly members of the press, would stroll about the grounds with little restriction. On the occasion when curious onlookers wandered into the food tent, the troupe dealt with them in a not particularly subtle way. The first people to spot the interlopers would stop eating and begin rattling their spoons against their plates. They were followed by other diners, until the entire tent was filled with a cacophony of sound. Confronted by the din, the intruders quickly realized they were not welcome and retreated.[13]

While all the performers in the show were well fed, the Lakota Indians received special consideration. They were the single largest ethnic contingent within Buffalo Bill's Wild West, and as far as Buffalo Bill and the audiences were concerned, they were the most important part of the show. The Lakotas were eager to take part in Wild West shows as an opportunity to get away from miserable conditions on the reservations and make some money. But politically powerful reform groups existed that felt the Lakota had to give up their "savage" ways and assimilate into white culture. Their motto was "kill the Indian and save the man." They thought

Fig 15. Indian ordering his meal in the mess tent at Buffalo Bill's Wild West. It is one of a series of drawings done behind the scenes by Frederic Remington for an 1894 *Harper's Weekly*. Author's collection.

that Buffalo Bill's Wild West encouraged the Lakota participants to observe the old ways and hindered their development into "civilized" people. The reformers' efforts to get the government to prohibit involvement in Wild West shows included claims that the Indians were mistreated and underfed, and they aimed most of their fury at Buffalo Bill's Wild West, as the largest and most famous show.

The reformers' efforts came to a head in summer of 1890, when several Lakota performers were sent back to the United States from Europe. The Wild West had a policy whereby the Indians selected policemen from among their ranks. It was their job to enforce the show's rules regarding behavior. The policemen dealt with those Indians who were troublemakers, got into fights, or drank too much. The Indians who returned to the States that summer, at midseason, were sent back because the policemen felt their behavior was no longer tolerable and asked Buffalo Bill to send them home. The returnees immediately began claiming conditions at the show were unacceptable and said they were given "food unfit for a dog." The reformers latched on to these stories, insisting that the Indians should be barred from joining Buffalo Bill's Wild West. John Burke immediately wrote a letter to the newspapers, stating, "Our pride as well as our interest lies in the good food and good health of our people. . . . Would that every white man in the world was as well fed, clothed and looked after as our red tourists on Buffalo Bill's Wild West." Despite Burke's protestations, he and Cody had to return from Europe that fall with the remaining Lakota performers for an inquiry held by the secretary of the interior. After interviewing thirty-six of the performers, the secretary concluded that they were treated fairly, were paid regularly and promptly, and had been furnished "good, wholesome food in abundance."[14]

The testimonies of the thirty-six were corroborated by other performers over the years. The following year, Short Bull, one of the leaders of the Ghost Dance, was released by the government into Buffalo Bill's custody to travel with the show through Europe. He wrote upon his return, "We get good food three times a day," noting, "If our people have any complaints it is fixed at once." Luther Standing Bear, a leader among the Lakota who later traveled to Europe with the show, had vivid memories of dining with the Wild West. He recalled that on arriving in England, they were served mutton with potatoes and vegetables. They ate the meat and sent the rest back to the kitchen with a request for more meat. "We kept those waiters busy bringing in meat and carrying out the vegetables." On another day, he remembered, they were served leftover pancakes from breakfast at dinner. When he complained to Buffalo Bill, Cody called the manager of the dining tent over and told him, "My Indians are the principal feature of this show, and they are the one people I will not allow to be misused or neglected. Hereafter see to it that they get just exactly what they want at meal-time." The manager complied and on another occasion served a breakfast of fried steak with raw kidney fat and sweet onions to all the Indians at Standing Bear's request. They enjoyed the plentiful repasts but still missed some of their traditional foods, like wild peppermint tea, dried meat, and chokecherry soup. Standing Bear noted, "We really had plenty to eat, but it was not cooked 'Indian style.'"[15]

The Lakotas usually were not able to eat food cooked "Indian style" during their excursions at many of the places visited by the Wild West. They saw the sights in Europe while there and also dined on local foods, like the Scottish food at Galloway's in Glasgow or coffee at Caffè Greco in Rome. When they performed at the Wild West show grounds just outside the 1893 World's Columbian Exposition in Chicago, they frequently visited the fair, where they could sample some of the food innovations being introduced. In 1902 the show traveled to the West Coast for the first time. It was also the first time Buffalo Bill had been in the San Francisco area since doing stage shows there with his Combination in 1886. He and the Lakotas with his show took a trip to the beach, where they posed for a panoramic photograph with the elegant Cliff House in the background. Afterward they dined and drank soda water on the hotel's veranda, overhanging the rocky shore beyond the beach.[16]

The American Indians, with their very different approach to food consumption, were fascinating to those observers allowed to visit the dining tent. Most surprising were the prodigious quantities of food they consumed. The *Sun* noted that when the Lakotas first joined the show, they were not used to having such plentiful supplies of food. Though the reformers claimed the Lakotas did not get enough food while with the show, in reality it was back on the reservation that they were nearly starving. The government often failed to deliver promised food rations, and since they could no longer hunt, meat was in short supply. Flat Iron remarked in an interview that at times he had been driven by hunger to chew the soles of his moccasins. Once they discovered they could eat as much as they wanted with the show, the Lakotas often overate to the point of being sick. Crow's Ghost consumed seven large beefsteaks on his first day with the show and was warned such indulgence would make him sick. He replied, "To die from eating too much would surely be a happy death."[17]

Lakota chief Rocky Bear, who breakfasted with a reporter visiting the show, ate four steaks, two pork chops, five plates of corn cakes, six boiled eggs, and half a pie, washing it all down with a bowl of coffee. A different reporter noted that at one breakfast, a different brave ate a half pound each of sausages and beef. He said that the Lakotas didn't care for nicely decorated food, and "dainties are not in their line, but they will not throw pie on the floor if it is placed before them." They also drank three or four cups of coffee at each meal. The Lakotas' favorite meat was steak, which they ate without salt or other seasoning. The cooks also had to make sure the meat was cooked so thoroughly "that not a trace of color can be seen in it." Not every Lakota restricted his diet to steak, however; during his four months with the show in 1885, Sitting Bull acquired a fondness for oyster stew.[18]

The most unusual dietary habit observed among the show's American Indians, usually only once per season, was a "dog feast," one of the times they were allowed to eat "Indian style" in the Wild West. They believed that eating stewed dog meat once a year was good luck; the meal was celebrated as a holiday and represented a break from their ordinary diet. After the dog was killed, two Indian women butchered it and put the meat into a kettle of boiling water. They then fried the liver, eaten by the women as a reward for their work, and the heart, presented to the chief. After the meat was cooked, it was distributed to all in attendance, who ate it solemnly. The event concluded with singing and a "dog dance." At the Wild West, this was not carried out in secret but was open to the public to observe. Occasionally the feast was even shared with outsiders. One newspaperman took part in an "Indian meal" with other members of the press. After he had thoroughly enjoyed the food, one of the Indians turned to him and said, "Dog meat good, huh?" In 1902 the commissioner of Indian affairs ordered that American Indians could no longer have dog feasts, along with other traditional ceremonies, on reservations, but they continued to observe the feasts while with Buffalo Bill's Wild West.[19]

While the different groups occasionally ate their own food or had preferences in the types of food they were served, dining was one occasion when they shared a common experience. The sight of so many different peoples from so many different nations eating together in Buffalo Bill's Wild West prompted one newspaper to observe that it was the "exemplification that in time knowledge and acquaintance will dispel racial prejudices and national hatred, and emphasize the fact of all mankind's kindredship."[20]

FIRST MEXICAN RESTAURANT EAST OF THE MISSISSIPPI

The first course was a sort of meat chowder. It was called "puchero" on the menu cards. There were a great many things in it, among which rice and chile peppers were distinguishable with the eyes closed. This was similar dish long and favorably known in New York boarding houses as hash, but it was not the familiar hash of commerce which has given a certain fascinating air of mystery to so many repasts at home. It was a moist and curious hash, so seasoned with chile peppers as never to become cold in any climate. The tortillas resemble cold buckwheat cakes in size and appearance, but they taste for all the world as the paste-soaked circus poster must taste to the ravenous goat.

"Chile concarne y fringolas" was the piece de resistance of the breakfast. It looked like a dish of beef a la mode surrounded by a curious kind of well-cooked beans, and was not unpalatable, though peppery. Following this came the "henchiladas," a device of the cook, that looked like a dainty French pancake with jelly, and was, in fact a very different thing indeed. A strong man, born to the custom, might learn to like the henchilada. A New Yorker isn't likely ever to contract an incontrollable appetite for this Mexican dainty. "Tamales," which were next served, are still less likely to become popular in New York restaurants, but they are curious, and for once perhaps, might repay study. Corn husks, dough, and chile peppers go to make up tamales. The peppers are hashed and seasoned with brimstone and then rolled in dough until each tamale looks like a peeled banana. This is rolled in the inner husks of corn, such as a prodigal son might eat in an emergency and a preparation like mucilage is poured over the whole. It is then ready to be eaten, and Mr. Cody's guests yesterday noon tried to eat of the dish. There was a lack of gusto in the attempt, however.

A dainty dish at a Mexican breakfast is "Chiles rellenos," which is simply chile peppers hashed, and concealed in a sort of omelet of eggs and unseasoned batter. Nuts and raisins add variety to the peppers.

With the "chocolate Mejicano," which closed the repast, was served a pudding, something like plum duff without plums and called "capirotada." It was slightly sweetened. The chocolate was like any well-made beverage of the kind, and every one drank two cups of it, scalding hot as it was, to cool off the lips and throat, which the peppers had inflamed. Mr. Cody called for Pond's extract to drink.

The last course at the breakfast was in the nature of a digestive, and is called "Mescale." It comes in a black bottle, and is distilled from the juice of a peculiar variety of cactus. In appearance mescale is like gin; in taste, a combination of the flavors of gin, rum, and rhubarb, and in effect, in small quantities, not unpleasant, but in repeated doses it is said to have the power of all other intoxicants combined. It is, in fact, the whiskey of Mexico, and no man can toy with it with impunity.

This was the bill of fare at yesterday's breakfast:
    Puchero Mejicano
    Chileconcarne y Frigolas
    Tortillas
    Henchiladas
    Picadio Con Tortillas
    Chiles Rellenos
    Tamales
    Café a lo Mejicano
    Chocolat Mejicano
    Capirotada Mejicaoo

The Mexican restaurant is now open to visitors, and chocolate and tamales are served as a specialty.

"At a Mexican Breakfast," *New York Sun*, December 19, 1886

9

Rib Roasts, Orphans, and Public Relations

I want to give the people of the East an idea of how easy it is
to prepare a real good feast without the aid of fashionable
restaurants fitted up with all the modern improvements.
Buffalo Bill, 1886

John M. Burke had a natural flair for promotion, combining a cunning understanding of marketing with florid speaking and writing. His frontier nickname, Arizona John, was not given to him by others but was a product of his imagination and a tool for self-promotion. But as much as Burke might have promoted himself, he promoted Buffalo Bill and the Wild West even more. Burke joined the Buffalo Bill Combination in 1872 as the manager of Mademoiselle Morlacchi, the female lead in the cast of *Scouts of the Prairie*. He soon began creating promotional efforts for the Combination, then smoothly moved into being the primary publicist and marketer for Buffalo Bill's Wild West. Burke, whose girth suggested his own love of food, recognized that it was the key to successful promotions for the Wild West and introduced western feasts.[1]

The feasts were extended to special guests of Buffalo Bill's Wild West, ranging from the press to politicians, royalty, and famous people of the day. One of the first big promotional meals coordinated by John Burke was a western banquet in Cincinnati less than a month after the show began in 1883. Cooked on the premises, the food was served on tin plates. The following year a similar western banquet was presented in New York City. It was the Wild West's premiere in the city, and besides providing a unique eating experience, the banquet offered the press a first look at the show.[2]

Buffalo Bill hosted another rustic feast for reporters and other guests at the show's location on New York City's Polo Grounds. Attendees included writer Prentiss Ingraham, who published a number of dime novels featuring Buffalo Bill, as well as a biography of Cody in 1895. After a stagecoach brought the guests from the Sturtevant Hotel, they were ushered into a tent where animal skins were strewn across the ground and benches, stools, and trunks served as seating. They were then presented with a menu of western delicacies such as a "soup" consisting of whiskey with water, a "fish" course of straight whiskey, and an "entrée" of "crackers, pepper, salt and whiskey." The whiskey was probably dispensed from a grouping of bottles arranged around a cask; Buffalo Bill explained that they contained concoctions prepared by "various medicine men." A couple of cowboys also carried a keg of beer around to the guests. In addition to the whiskey, beer, and crackers, guests were served radishes, onions, watermelon, and a main course consisting of chunks of roasted buffalo. The meat was distributed by a "grizzled veteran" carrying it in a large tin pan that "resembled a young bath-tub." The guests had no plates, but each was given a sharp wooden stick with which to impale a piece of meat.[3]

Cody and Burke repeated the "meat on a stick" banquet when the show reached Boston later that year. This one featured roasted beef, prepared on a large spit over a fire. The guests were seated on benches, and a stick sharpened at both ends was stuck into the ground in front each person, with a hunk of beef impaled on it. Guests were expected to pull the stick out of the ground and eat the beef off of it. More meat was passed around on large plates for seconds. If someone wished to pause while eating, the stick was reinserted into the ground. Each diner was also presented with a tin plate and a small glass to be filled with "delectable liquor with which to wash such viands as stuck in his throat." The meal was served "in true Western plains fashion, with all sorts of fresh vegetables, each guest holding his plate on a napkin spread over his knees." One of the attendees remarked that "the food was enjoyed quite as much from its intrinsic merit as a banquet as from its novelty."[4]

Lakota chief Sitting Bull made a four-month appearance with Buffalo Bill's Wild West in 1885. During this time, he joined Cody in hosting the "rib roasts," as they were now known. In Philadelphia one local reporter who attended referred to it as "a genuine Indian banquet tendered to a score of palefaces." The guests were once again presented with pointed sticks in the ground in front of wooden benches, but this time without skewered meat. Sitting Bull and Buffalo Bill sat at the head bench, where Cody demonstrated how to eat the meat, passed around on plates, by pulling his pointed stake out of the ground and impaling a piece. Following the meal, Sitting Bull addressed the group through an interpreter, stating that the war in the Black Hills in 1876, which led to the death of Custer, was caused by miners invading the Lakotas' territory.[5]

After the show's appearances in Philadelphia and Boston, it proceeded northward to Montreal, where another "cowboy's camp dinner," or rib roast, was held for local dignitaries and members of the press. Among the guests were Honoré Beaugrand, the newly elected mayor of Montreal; prominent businessman W. W. Ogilvie; and Peter Mitchell, owner of the *Montreal Herald* and former member of the Canadian Parliament. As this august group ate the chunks of beef off their sticks, they were also provided with crackers, whiskey, and lemonade. The repast concluded with custard pie; no record was provided as to how it was eaten.[6]

In 1886 Buffalo Bill's Wild West encamped for five months over the summer and fall as the sole entertainment at Erastina, a resort on Staten Island. The guest of honor at one meal was Gabriel Dumont, a leader of the resistance against the Canadian government by the Saskatchewan Métis, the mixed-race descendants of American Indians and early settlers during the fur trade era. Buffalo Bill, Nate Salsbury, and the leaders of the Lakotas and Pawnees with the show toasted Dumont, who was in exile in the United States. At the culinary center of the event were two large beef rib roasts, bound together with wire and hanging from two crossed poles over an open fire. Two Lakota women, described as much more beautiful than the average cook, tended the meat by raising and lowering it over the flame with a rope tied to the wire.[7]

Within a special tent erected for dining were rows of three-foot-long stakes driven into the ground. A thick layer of hay was strewn about to absorb any meat juices, grease, and other remnants that fell on the ground. As at previous feasts, the stakes took the place of eating implements, plates, and tables. Large chunks of roast were passed around in large tin basins. A witness reported that "each man speared out a piece with his sharp stick, and proceeded to eat it with his fingers . . . it was considered a breach of etiquette to hold the meat otherwise than in the hands." A platter was passed about with crackers, sliced tomatoes, pepper, and salt. Beer was served in painted buckets and dispensed into cups made of tin and buffalo horn. Dessert consisted of watermelon slices. Demonstrating how to behave, Cody's normally reserved business partner Nate Salsbury sat down on the straw "with a chunk of beef in one hand and a hunk of watermelon in the other," presenting what one writer called "a primitive picture." As such meals occurred with greater frequency, the rib roast feasts came into their own as curiosities nearly as fascinating as the action in the arena. Another newspaperman observed that there seemed to be "no end of novelty at the Wild West Camp of the Hon. William F. Cody," particularly when it came to dining experiences.[8]

While John Burke aimed to use the feasts as a unique form of promotion for the show, Cody's goal was more culinary. He stated that the rib roasts were meant "to give the people of the East an idea of how easy it is to prepare a real good feast without the aid of fashionable restaurants fitted up with all the modern improvements." No matter the motivation, they captured the imagination and piqued the palate of everyone who attended, with the guests having a once-in-a-lifetime dining experience.[9]

When Buffalo Bill and his Wild West went to England in 1887, they took the practice of hosting rib roasts with them, and the meals proved to be as popular there as in the United States. One American press service article remarked, "Buffalo Bill's rib roast appears to have successfully hit the British appetite for a good dinner." One of the most successful and publicized dining experiences during the 1887 sojourn was a breakfast thrown for Gen. Simon Cameron. Now ninety years old, the American statesman who had been secretary of war under Lincoln was visiting England for the first time. The forty attendees also included other dignitaries, with several members of Parliament, a senator from Connecticut, and American and British businessmen. The feast was built around rib roasts cooked over a fire by the Indians, but only they ate their meat with the wooden stakes. Perhaps bowing to British formality, the show set out the repast on long tables from which the guests ate in a more traditional manner. And it included much more than roast beef. Referred to as "Grub Stake Rations," ribs of beef, salmon, roast mutton, ham, tongue, lobster salad, stewed chicken, corn, hominy, and potatoes were all on the menu. The meal concluded with coconut pie, apple pie, and "Wild West pudding."[10]

Not all the feasts used by Burke to promote the Wild West and American cuisine were rib roasts. On one occasion, the show's cowboys and a group of English actors played an early morning baseball game. After the cowboys won the game, everyone retired to a breakfast hosted by Buffalo Bill, consisting of spring chickens fried in cream, corn and corn bread, onions, and hash. One reporter noted that the English guests "came away with respect and a dash of envy for American cookery."[11]

After five months in London and a brief stop in Birmingham, the show moved on to another five-month stand in Manchester in 1887–88. There a local newspaper presented a poem about a rib roast held near the conclusion of the Wild West's stands:

Bean soup first and then fried oysters,
Ribs of Pez-he-kee, the bison,
Served on plates of tin and garnished
With the sweet corn, the Mon-da-min–
Eaten in true savage fashion;
Knife and fork alike forbidden–
Gnaw the bone and suck your fingers,
That's the way to cop the flavor–
Of the noble redskin's rib-roast.
Pork and beans, that Boston's glory,
Buck wheat cakes and thick molasses
Hominy and piccalilli,

Went their way to bright Po-ne-mah
To the Land of the Hereafter.[12]

In May 1888 Buffalo Bill's Wild West returned to the United States, where it performed once again at Erastina for six weeks. This return was marked by more rib roasts. The first was given for a "distinguished party of ladies and gentlemen," numbering around twenty-two people. Among them were the duke of Marlborough and western artist Albert Bierstadt. This comparatively intimate affair, more of a dinner party, employed cutlery rather than sharpened sticks. The roast ribs were accompanied by chicken kidneys "cooked in original style," roasted corn, pickles, and pumpkin pie. Each of the ladies was presented with an Indian apron. The sharpened sticks returned for another dinner a few days later. That meal concluded with "a popping of corks" as extra dry champagne was served to those present. The show traveled to Pennsylvania, Virginia, and Maryland before concluding the 1888 season.[13]

In 1889 Buffalo Bill's Wild West revisited Europe, beginning with a two-month stand in Paris, then traveling across the continent by rail, rarely spending more than two days in one place. Although the rib roasts had been popular, they required a lot of preparation for an operation that was constantly on the move and fed a minimum of 650 employees every day. Now there were no more blazing fires with rib roasts dangling above them, carefully tended by the American Indians with the show. Those had ended, but special meals were still thrown for visiting dignitaries and the press. From that point on, they received foods similar to those consumed by the staff, judged to be quite excellent.

During the Wild West's trips to Europe over its thirty years of operation, it performed for many princes, princesses, shahs, queens, and even kings. Rarely did these dignitaries stay for a meal, although the prince regent of Bavaria and his daughters, both princesses, did drop by for a Wild West breakfast on April 23, 1890. Prince Regent Luitpold was the uncle of Ludwig II, the "mad king" who built Neuschwanstein and the other fairy tale castles of Bavaria. Ludwig had been deposed and then died under mysterious circumstances in 1886. Luitpold was asked to take over the government and ruled

Bavaria until 1912. After having a "distinctly American" breakfast, the prince and princesses posed for photographs with the show's cowboys and Lakota performers. One report recognized the show's successful promotion by Cody and Burke, stating, "Mr. Barnum was a clever advertiser, but he never succeeded in making princes so useful to his enterprise as Buffalo Bill has been able to do."[14]

After concluding the 1892 season in Europe, having met and performed for royalty and commoners alike, Buffalo Bill set his sights on the upcoming World's Columbian Exposition in Chicago. The exposition promised to attract visitors of all kinds, but particularly from America's growing middle class. It was to look back at the progress in America since 1492 and look forward to the next century. Visitors to the exposition could see America's past presented as prologue to a bright future. When his request to set up the show in the exposition's Midway Plaisance was rejected, Cody procured land right outside the entrance to the exposition. Using a new name, Buffalo Bill's Wild West and Congress of Rough Riders of the World, the show opened on April 26, 1893, a month before the exposition.

The Wild West's arena accommodated eighteen thousand people per show and held two performances each day. The grounds were open to the public, who could wander around and meet the performers before and after each show. In 1890 the U.S. Census had declared that the American frontier was officially over. In 1893 Frederick Jackson Turner made his famous speech about the role of the frontier in U.S. history at the American Historical Society annual meeting in Chicago, which occurred simultaneously with the World's Columbian Exposition. The Old West was no more, but for the nostalgic, there was Buffalo Bill's Wild West, presenting the vanished frontier twice daily for six months.

Buffalo Bill's Wild West and Congress of Rough Riders of the World was a hit, with sellout crowds, until it closed in October. Even though the show was not part of the Midway, Cody still had a presence at the exposition. He furnished a significant exhibit in the Nebraska Building, consisting of a Lakota tepee, a collection of Indian artifacts, and two mounted buffalo. His performers were also conspicuous visitors to the fair. Advertisements for Buffalo Bill's show were inserted in official and unofficial publications. Signs at the exposition train station pointed the way to both the fair and the show. A Cody Day was even held at the exposition. These efforts served to promote both Buffalo Bill's Wild West and the World's Columbian Exposition. Buffalo Bill and John Burke continued to extend every sort of hospitality to the press that they could, including invitations to dine, as they marketed the show in Chicago.[15]

Besides the dignitaries welcomed to Buffalo Bill's Wild West and Congress of Rough Riders of the World for lunch and a show, Cody hosted several thousand waifs, orphans, and paupers off the streets of Chicago. When the World's Columbian Exposition turned down requests to host a Waifs' Day with free admission to children from area orphanages and schools, Cody stepped in. He loved children, and it had always been his practice to give free admission tickets for his show to local orphanages. He announced that, in cooperation with Chicago's Waifs Mission, he would hold a Waifs' Day on July 27: "Bring them on, my show is free to them; they shall have every benefit within my power to bestow while they are under the canvas of my show." The mission arranged with the Illinois Central Railroad to transport children from all over the city for free. Bootblacks, newsboys, children from the sweatshops and orphanages, and others flocked to the show for a free meal and free admission. Estimates of attendance ranged as high as eight thousand.[16]

Knowing full well that the children would have trouble enjoying the show with empty bellies, Cody and the Waifs Mission solicited food from Chicago purveyors, many of whom were supplying the Wild West's cooks, to feed the masses of children. When the children arrived, it was lunch first. They were lined up and ushered through a small building, where fifty women filled cardboard boxes with sandwiches, doughnuts, pie, and pickles, which they handed over as quickly as the children entered. Big barrels of lemonade were used to fill tin cups. It was a feast few of the children had experienced, and as one newspaper observed, "The children ate until they were tired." But they were not too tired for the games and contests organized by representatives from the major Chicago newspapers, who volunteered at Cody and Burke's behest. When they heard the announcement that the show was ready to begin, the children rushed to the grandstand and took the best spots, since all eighteen thousand seats had been reserved for them.[17]

Waifs' Day turned out to be a great public relations coup for Cody. One newspaper trumpeted, "Buffalo Bill was a great man today," and Cody received a copper plaque of thanks from the Chicago Waifs Mission Messengers on behalf of the "Waifs of Chicago."[18]

The Wild West's stand in Chicago closed in October, the same month the World's Columbian Exposition closed. In gratitude for their extensive coverage of the show, Cody threw a luncheon for representatives from Chicago's newspapers. Fifty people attended and "joined in the sentiment and song that 'they are jolly good fellows.'" Cody and Burke certainly knew that the way to a reporter's heart was through his or her stomach. The international performers headed back to their homelands, and Cody went back to a hero's welcome in his home base of North Platte, en route to a hunting trip with his friend Gen. Nelson Miles.[19]

His time in Chicago made so much money for Cody that he returned to North Platte a millionaire. He purchased a mansion in town for his family, expanded his ranch outside of town, and began investing in other business pursuits, such as a coffee company he began with his friend Frank Powell. With his greatly increased wealth, he gave to local churches and other causes, acquiring new uniforms for the North Platte town band.[20]

Hoping to realize the same success that he had experienced in Chicago, Buffalo Bill rented land at Ambrose Park in Brooklyn for the season of 1894. The rent and cost of setting up the show was $100,000. The twenty-two-acre grounds included a 312-by-455-foot arena, enclosed by a grandstand housing twenty thousand people. The grandstand surrounded the arena on three sides, with the fourth being a large backdrop made to resemble the landscape at the Little Bighorn, since the show re-created Custer's ill-fated battle. On the grounds were 140 tents, including a main dining tent and a private one for Cody, plus the Lakotas' tepees and a log cabin that served as the press headquarters. The camp was laid out with walks and avenues just like "primitive Western towns," and the show had 758 performers and support personnel, as well as eight hundred horses. It was a large investment but also a good one. The park was well situated for attracting visitors from all around New York City and surrounding metropolitan areas, including Philadelphia, Hartford, and even Boston.[21]

Cody and Burke knew that press coverage would be vital and immediately began inviting reporters to special meals, always paired with complimentary admission to the show. Before Buffalo Bill's Wild West and Congress of Rough Riders of the World opened to the public on May 12, it held several press luncheons. Burke began by hosting a "voluminous dinner" on April 18 while the show was still being built. This was followed by an advance peek at the show and its camp for one hundred members of the press on May 10. Following a morning tour of the grounds, Cody hollered to everyone, "Boys, have you mouths?" and the group headed to the dining tent for lunch. Following lunch and some speeches, the group enjoyed an afternoon rehearsal.[22]

Another large meal was served to twenty newspaperwomen a month later in Buffalo Bill's private dining tent, decorated for the occasion. The walls of the tent were draped in pale pink and cream, while the table was decorated with "a mass of roses, trailing vines and glittering glass." The pink roses were matched with pink carnations at each guest's plate. The meal, consisting of strawberries, chocolate éclairs, ice cream, and "all of those things dear to the feminine palate," along with wine, was described as "daintily served." Behind a discreet curtain, a mandolin and guitar provided a pleasant musical accompaniment. When the dining had ended, both Cody and his business partner, Nate Salsbury, made brief speeches. Cody's speech in particular was a tribute to his mother. One reporter remarked on "what a charming host he is at the head of his own table."[23]

Buffalo Bill and his special guests shared other lunches, dinners, and breakfasts in his private dining tent while the show was at Ambrose Park. These included editors and proprietors of various out-of-town publications like the *Texas Farm and Ranch*, a "coaching party" of fifteen from New Jersey, and New York City mayor Thomas Gilroy with a group of influential friends.[24]

After 1894 Buffalo Bill's Wild West and Congress of Rough Riders of the World rarely remained in one place for more than a week.

Most of the stops were one-night stands. Large public relations feasts, which had worked so well when the show stayed at a location longer, now became too difficult. The show's personnel, and the cooking staff in particular, had to concentrate on unpacking everything, getting everyone fed, and doing two shows, then hitting the road again. One or two local reporters might be treated to a meal in the dining tent at Cody's private table, but they ate the same fare as everyone else. Nevertheless, they never ceased to be amazed at the operation—and at their experiences with Buffalo Bill himself.

From John Burke and William Cody's first meeting during the Buffalo Bill Combination years, their relationship proved to be the right combination when it came to publicizing Buffalo Bill's Wild West. They both realized the importance of eating as a universal experience and food as a way to beguile and attract; it was another facet of show business. Thus they turned the foods of the Wild West into attractions, introducing the public to the innovations used to feed hundreds, ethnic dining in a Mexican restaurant in New York City, and Indian rib roast feasts. Ensuring that the press and dignitaries were well fed was a critical part of marketing Buffalo Bill's Wild West as it traveled throughout the United States and Europe.

10

Buffalo Bill's British Invasion

The repast was none the less enjoyable for being of a frankly
unconventional character, and some of the guests were introduced for the first time to gastronomic delicacies of a distinctly
American type.

Reporter in Bristol, England, 1891

Rib roasts were just some of the gastronomic delicacies introduced
to Europe by Buffalo Bill and John Burke during the Wild West's
travels around the continent, beginning in Great Britain. The
uniquely American exhibition that was Buffalo Bill's Wild West
included many foods and drinks that were unfamiliar to European
palates. Even some foods that were common in the United States,
like corn bread, were novelties on the other side of the Atlantic.

While traveling with the Buffalo Bill Combination, Cody had
contemplated touring Europe with the show but never got around
to it. After Mark Twain saw Buffalo Bill's Wild West in 1884, he
urged Cody to take the show to "the other side of the water,"
where it would have the advantage of being the first distinctively
American exhibition. Then John R. Whitley, a British entrepreneur,
who called the show "a genuine product of American soil," invited
him to bring it to London's 1887 American Exhibition, celebrating
the Golden Jubilee of Queen Victoria's reign. And that is exactly
what Cody did.[1]

Buffalo Bill's Wild West arrived at Gravesend Harbor in England
on the steamship *State of Nebraska* on April 16. In addition to personnel numbering around 220, it also carried 180 horses, 4 donkeys,
8 mules, 5 Texas longhorns, 18 buffalo, 10 elk, and 2 deer. Cody
went ahead to London to check on the progress with the show
grounds while the animals and equipment were cleared for entry.

At the American Exhibition's headquarters, he was welcomed with a "bounteous repast," speeches, and numerous toasts. He later wrote, "My genial hosts' capacity for the liquid refreshments would have made me envy them in the 60s." Despite this opportunity to imbibe, he followed his commitment to Salsbury and drank little, if anything. Soon, however, the concessions associated with the Wild West would introduce the British to an even greater quantity of liquid refreshments.[2]

After everyone and everything was cleared for entry, the *State of Nebraska* steamed into the London docks, where the show was taken by rail to the London neighborhood of Earl's Court. There Whitley had created a show grounds similar to Staten Island's Erastina. Once Buffalo Bill's Wild West arrived at the site, the staff erected tents and tepees to one side of a circular amphitheater, which was still under construction. The American flag was raised to the sound of "The Star-Spangled Banner," played by the show's cowboy band. People from the surrounding neighborhoods cheered the new arrivals. Buffalo Bill later described the scene:

> The first domestic episode (our camp-meal being necessarily eaten in full view of our kindly neighbors, the large dining tents not yet being up), was as novel to them, from our variegated and motley population of Indians, cowboys, scouts, Mexicans, etc. and eminently practical method of "grubbing," as the supply of fresh beef, mutton, corn-bread, ham, etc., *l'Americaine* was grateful to our sea-faring palates. The meal was finished by seven o'clock, and by 9 p.m. the little camp was almost as complete as if it had been there for months.[3]

Over the next several days the amphitheater was completed, a large dining tent raised for the staff, and a log cabin built to act as a kitchen. A smaller dining tent was set up for Buffalo Bill and Nate Salsbury to host guests; it was decorated with hanging plants, mirrors, and pictures. A special waiter was assigned to that tent.[4]

The amphitheater and surrounding grounds occupied by Buffalo Bill's Wild West were in a triangular area surrounded by railways and separated from the large exhibition buildings where the rest of the American Exhibition resided. Those buildings included agricultural and industrial machinery, numerous American products, and a fine arts hall. Whitley, who was in charge of the exhibition and had invited Cody, later bemoaned the fact that many major industrial firms in the eastern United States had decided not to exhibit in London, which weakened the exhibition. He also noted that Buffalo Bill's Wild West "threw the other parts of our picture into the shade." And that it did, with critics pronouncing the American Exhibition weak and even tiresome—with the exception of Buffalo Bill's Wild West. One visitor on opening day, May 9, enjoyed a special luncheon supplied to the press but wrote that the exhibition had "nothing particularly attractive" except Buffalo Bill's Wild West. She went on to praise the realism of the show and noted that Cody's physique and dress were "unmistakably American." While the exhibition was weak, it was probably not weakened by the Wild West, as Whitley suggested. The popularity of Buffalo Bill and his performers drew thousands to the exhibition, when it might otherwise have suffered.[5]

The exhibition's fine arts hall was filled with paintings by American artists, including several massive images of the Rocky Mountains by Thomas Moran and Albert Bierstadt. These paintings, plus many hunting trophies in an adjacent hall, doubtless set the stage for the experience awaiting visitors at Buffalo Bill's Wild West. The fine arts hall faced a large bridge over the West London Railway into the Wild West's compound. In only a matter of yards, visitors could walk from graphic renditions of America's spectacular western landscape into an encounter with the peoples and animals from that very place.[6]

A preview of the American Exhibition in late April was marked by a parade of dignitaries, passing through the various exhibits of American industry and arts to take a sneak peek at Buffalo Bill's Wild West. The assortment of lords and ladies was accompanied by famous British actor Henry Irving and former prime minister William Gladstone. Since the preview only featured excerpts from the show, Gladstone returned on May 9 for the full experience, including a special luncheon thrown for the occasion by Cody, Burke, and Salsbury. At the luncheon, Gladstone pronounced the show "a true and accurate representation of the American world."

Despite utterances by some newspapers that it was not representative of the whole American world, Gladstone and other Europeans were quite content to believe Buffalo Bill's Wild West did represent true American life. Mark Twain had been correct that the show was distinctively American, but neither he nor Cody could have anticipated how lasting that distinction would become. This initial exposure, followed by years of performances in Europe by Buffalo Bill's Wild West, helped establish stereotypes about the American West that continue even today.[7]

Among the exhibit buildings was a large dining saloon offering ordinary fare. Visitors' reactions to the food were tepid at best. According to one, the refreshment contractors were nothing more than "purveyors of expensive dyspepsia" who charged far too much. But just across the bridge was a full American experience, including refreshments from what for many was still a mysterious continent.[8]

Crossing the bridge, visitors first encountered what the official program of the American Exhibition referred to as "the American bars of Buffalo Bill's Wild West." The largest bar was seven hundred feet in length, wrapped around the Wild West amphitheater, and was said to be the biggest in the world (fig. 16). American bartenders were imported to provide the drinks. Visitors to the bar received an "almanac of American drinks," a calendar with a concoction for every day of the year except Sundays. An American visitor noted, "Hard to please indeed must be he whose taste can not be hit off here to a nicety. Noggs, slings, cocktails, cobblers, skins, twists, fizzes, swizzles, flashes of lightning, sours and ticklers—what more do you want in the way of liquoring up?" Other drinks included mint juleps, pineapple punches, Old Chum's Revivers, Bosom Caressers, and claret sangarees (sangrias). Altogether, the bar supposedly offered four hundred different kinds of drinks. While the amphitheater bar was the largest, it was just one of several American bars scattered around the Wild West grounds. Presumably to capture the feel of an American saloon, one of them was a small log cabin near the performers' tents. Like Buffalo Bill's Wild West show, the bars proved to be popular with everyone from ordinary citizens to British royalty.[9]

Fig 16. An 1887 map of the Wild West grounds at Earl's Court in London. The seven-hundred-foot American bar was located within the crescent-shaped grandstand. Object ID#1998.0045, Buffalo Bill Museum and Grave, Golden CO.

While the large installation outside of Buffalo Bill's Wild West did not introduce the American bar or the American cocktail to Britain, it did help popularize them. One observer remarked that in London, "straight drinks are the rule . . . and they know nothing more about mixed drinks than what little knowledge they have imported from the United States." Newspapers reported that American cocktails became a rage during the exhibition, and a wave of bars serving these drinks opened in London and elsewhere. Two years later it was noted that no London restaurant could be considered whole without an American bar, complete with shakers, lemon squeezers, and lots of crushed ice, since "no American bar would be of any account without its ice . . . a necessity of life to the vast majority of Americans." One of the best-known hotels in London, the Savoy, opened an American bar in 1893. It is still in operation, serving American cocktails with plenty of ice.[10]

Also available on the grounds around the amphitheater were another uniquely American treat—popcorn balls. These balls of sugared popcorn were exceedingly popular, and the demand was so great that eleven stands were erected. To meet this demand, Nate Salsbury ordered one hundred bushels of popcorn from New York. By the end of the season, the number of popcorn stands had increased to thirty. It was reported that "at every exhibition given by the Wild West company the audience feasted their eyes on performances while devouring the balls of sugared popcorn."[11]

While American newspapers initially claimed that Buffalo Bill had introduced popcorn balls to England, some of their readers stated that popcorn had been there years earlier and produced evidence to that effect. But as one "sturdy Briton" stated, although he did not introduce popcorn to England, "Buffalo Bill may have made eating popcorn more fashionable." Buffalo Bill's Wild West certainly helped turn it into a commercially viable product. Confectionery stores were soon advertising popcorn balls in London newspapers. For the Wild West, it became a regular product sold in its concession stands elsewhere in Europe and later back in America.[12]

The business of feeding the large company continued in dining tents behind the Wild West encampment. The show kept local purveyors at Covent Garden, Smithfield Market, and Billingsgate busy supplying fruits and vegetables, fish, flour, coffee, and six thousand pounds of fresh meat daily. The meals served to the show's personnel reflected American diets, and like the rib roasts and American-themed luncheons hosted by Cody and Burke, they were often shared with special visitors. These were frequently served in Buffalo Bill's guest tent and catered by the same cooks who provided food for the company. A correspondent for a San Francisco newspaper noted that "such personages as General and Lord Beresford, Hartington, Churchill, and hundreds of their kind, have dangled their lower limbs under Cody's improvised mahogany." Seating eight people, the table was illuminated by a combination of incandescent and gas lights, as well as candles, and presented "a really oriental and brilliant appearance." These meals not only helped promote the show but also were much easier for Cody to attend because he did not need to leave the exhibition grounds.

They were often staged before or after a performance. Cody later wrote that even the princess of Wales came by after a show for a cup of tea.[13]

The princess of Wales was not the only royalty entertained by Buffalo Bill in his dining tent during the stay in London. Later, the prince of Wales ate an American meal with Cody, Crown Prince Wilhelm of Germany, and the duke of York. William Langan, the camp's head cook, provided the prince with a personal tour of the show's kitchen as well as recipes for chicken salad and Maryland-style chicken. The prince of Wales visited the Wild West again two years later while it was in Paris, and as King Edward VII, he visited it yet again when it returned to London in 1902. During the meal, Crown Prince Wilhelm extended an invitation for Buffalo Bill to bring the Wild West to Berlin, which he did three years later.[14]

William F. "Buffalo Bill" Cody was now one of the most popular celebrities in London. The show's arrival, he wrote, "commenced a long series of invitations to breakfasts, dinners, luncheons, and midnight lay-outs, garden parties and all the other attentions which London society delights to honor what it is pleased to call the distinguished foreigner." Between mid-April, when the show arrived, and its opening on May 9, Cody had already attended so many dinners and parties that his nephew, who had accompanied his uncle to England, wrote that Buffalo Bill was starting to look fat. Cody finally had to regulate when and where he would go. Even so, both British and American newspapers were filled with stories of his appearances around town. British newspapers trumpeted his popularity, one even referring to him as the "great lion of the season in London."[15]

Americans often saw humor in the situation, with one New York newspaper referring to him as "The Biggest Man in London" but remarking that he had so many invitations to 5:00 teas that he might "kill himself with tea." After he dined with some members of Parliament, one American paper mused that when he returned to the States, he would "call everything 'bloody,' and parade other evidences of his familiarity with the customs of England's most exclusive social circles." One could argue, however, that he had more of an influence on England's social circles than vice versa.

Another newspaper observed of his many dinner invitations that "scalps and Buffalo Bill reign in the very same rooms that a year or two ago were the temples of the sunflower and Oscar Wilde."[16]

William Cody did indeed frequent England's most exclusive circles. A painted Indian basket on the camp table in his tent at the show was filled with "perfumed notes of invitation, begging the honor of the presence of this American exhibitor in marble halls, whose vassals wait in plush and satin to receive him." He was able to accept relatively few of the invitations because of the show's rigorous schedule of afternoon and evening performances. But he made time for special invitations, like those from royalty or members of Parliament. While visiting the House of Commons, he spent several hours in the dining room regaling Colonel Francis Hughes-Hallett, Lord Charles Beresford, and other members with tales of the American West. And the "great lion of the season" even found time to have tea with one of Britain's literary greats, visiting the home of Mr. and Mrs. Oscar Wilde on July 13. It was held from 4:00 to 7:00 p.m., conveniently between afternoon and evening performances.[17]

Cody also spent a great deal of time with Henry Irving, the best-known actor in Great Britain during the second half of the nineteenth century and the first actor to receive a knighthood. Irving met Cody during a visit to Buffalo Bill's Wild West while it was appearing at Erastina in 1886. He loved the show and gave it his personal endorsement before it arrived in London the following year. Irving attended the Wild West on opening day of the American Exposition in Earl's Court and maintained a private box for the duration of the show's appearance. Cody met writer Bram Stoker through Henry Irving, and the three of them dined together. Stoker worked as Irving's manager, and wherever Irving went, Stoker was sure to be found. Stoker later included a character resembling Buffalo Bill in his most famous story, the novel *Dracula*. Cody's blooming friendship with Henry Irving helped smooth his introduction to London society. Irving was a man about town and accompanied Cody to many social events and dinners. He also hosted frequent dinner parties for Cody at the Lyceum Theatre's Beefsteak Club. Irving was a fixture at London's Lyceum Theater, appearing there over the course of several decades. The first Beefsteak Club originated in London in the early eighteenth century, with the purpose of eating lots of beef and drinking lots of wine. The tradition had begun to die out when Irving revived it in 1878 at the Lyceum. The presence of Buffalo Bill, a representative of the American West and lover of beef, made the parties immensely successful.[18]

Even with all the attention and the alcohol flowing liberally, Buffalo Bill managed to keep his promise to Nate Salsbury to forgo drinking during the show season. Salsbury later remembered that after a performance for Queen Victoria at Windsor Castle, they were invited to the private apartment of the nobleman in charge of her horses. "As Cody did not drink anything that summer, I did duty for both of us in a glass of wine." On another occasion, a group of guests in Cody's dining tent drank freely of all kinds of wine, provided by their host. Yet, they noted, Buffalo Bill consumed only milk. His forbearance from alcohol was so dedicated that some even thought he would become an advocate for the temperance movement.[19]

Buffalo Bill became so popular that a bakery began advertising "Buffalo Bill Cakes." Reid's College Street Biscuit Factory claimed to be the largest cake factory in the world, baking thirty thousand cakes per day. Baked in a "Yankee oven," these cakes were "warranted to soothe the Wild West savages." The nature of the Yankee oven is not clear, but it may have been a tin reflecting oven. The Buffalo Bill Cakes, as well as Albert, Fatma, Chicago Plum, and Queen's Own cakes, were available by parcel delivery "to all parts of the United Kingdom."[20]

After the conclusion of the American Exhibition in late 1887, Buffalo Bill's Wild West stopped in Birmingham and Manchester. It eventually departed from Hull to the United States on the steamship *Persian Monarch* in the spring of 1888. For the rest of the year, the show appeared in states in the Northeast, revisiting Erastina on Staten Island for two of the months. Then in April 1889 Buffalo Bill's Wild West returned to Europe, this time to France. Over the next two years it traveled around the continent, then in 1891 it crossed the English Channel to Great Britain.[21]

Among the members of the cast that year were leaders and participants in the Ghost Dance, a movement that had been popular among the Lakotas in 1890. After the Ghost Dance was put down by the U.S. Army, some of its leaders were allowed to travel with the Wild West to Europe as an alternative to jail. They were well satisfied with the treatment they received while with the show. Short Bull, a key leader of the Ghost Dance, praised the food they received while traveling in Britain but said he did not care for the weather.[22]

Leeds was the show's first stop in Britain after leaving the European continent in 1891, followed by several weeks each in Liverpool and Manchester, and then it was on to other destinations in Great Britain. Everywhere the show traveled, visitors observed the cooking operations with great interest, fascinated by the large amounts of food consumed. Some noted that members of the cast especially liked cooked tomatoes, with several hundred prepared at a time in a large stew pan. John Burke told a reporter, "We have no such things as rations here, if anybody wants ten eggs for breakfast and a whole sirloin for dinner, they can be had." Excessive drinking was cause for dismissal from the show, however, and Burke explained, "We don't mind how much they eat, and though there is plenty of beer, whiskey, and brandy in the store, we discourage excessive drinking, because if the men drink too much you cannot rely upon them to do their work." The British particularly enjoyed hearing cook John Keanan quote Shakespeare while he was cooking.[23]

After visits to Brighton and Croydon, where the Wild West had a final show on October 24, it headed north to Glasgow, Scotland. There it spent the winter, performing indoors in the East End Exhibition Building, a structure that had been modified to accommodate the show. The new amphitheater within it could hold seven thousand people. Next door, a former Boys' House of Refuge provided accommodations for the cast, including personal quarters for Buffalo Bill and a dining room for the show's personnel. Since the show was only appearing in Glasgow, people traveled by rail from all over Scotland to see it, coming from as far away as Inverness and Dumfries.[24]

Cody was the toast of town, just as he had been everywhere else he traveled in Europe. On November 6, ten days before the show opened, he was a guest at a dinner thrown by the Dramatic Club of the Glasgow Athenaeum in honor of his friend Henry Irving.

The dinner, served in the Athenaeum's great hall, began with a fish course of cod à la béchamel and fillets of whiting au gratin. Croquettes of chicken à la française and fricasseed tripe followed. The main courses were roast turkey and tongue, roast beef with horseradish, and York ham. For dessert, Bakewell pudding (a flaky pastry spread with jam and topped with a custard of egg and almond), compote of green figs, wine jelly and vanilla creams were served with coffee. Port, claret, champagne, brandy, Erbach beer, maraschino liqueur, lemonade, and Very Old Highland Whisky were the beverages enjoyed during the meal.[25]

Eighty people were in attendance at the event, which went past midnight. During the program, Irving introduced Cody to the group as a person whom he respected and loved. Cody in turn thanked the members of the club for honoring Irving, whom he credited with inspiring him to bring his show to Britain and being one of the first to greet him on his arrival. The evening stretched into the morning and concluded with the singing of Robert Burns's "Auld Lang Syne."[26]

Buffalo Bill rendezvoused again with Irving and Stoker at the Glasgow Institute of the Fine Arts on November 27. It was a dinner event sponsored by the Pen and Ink Club, an organization that promoted and supported the liberal arts. Held in one of the institute's galleries, the event included 137 guests and honored Irving. The evening's entertainment consisted of a variety of toasts to Irving and even some to Buffalo Bill, as well as a rendition of the Robert Burns song "Willie Brewed a Peck o' Maut," by a local glee club.[27]

Buffalo Bill was not the only member of the company feted during the show's stay in Glasgow. On December 4 restaurant proprietor John Campbell Galloway hosted a 1:00 p.m. dinner in his establishment for chiefs Short Bull, Kicking Bear, No Neck, and other male members of the Lakota contingent. Attendees also included John Shangrau and George Crager, both translators with the show. The meal was uniquely British and quite different from anything the Lakotas had eaten before. It began with kidney soup and continued with steak pie, mutton cutlets, stewed rabbits, corned beef, ox tongue, and boiled ham. Desserts were apple pie, tapioca pudding, cabinet pudding (a steamed pudding made from sponge cake with dried fruits such as raisins or cherries and covered with a sweet sauce), and stewed prunes. When the meal concluded, No Neck addressed Galloway, thanking him for his hospitality and noting that while they "could not repay him for his kindness, God, who gave the good things, would."[28]

Cody was recognized by Glasgow's 1390 Club on December 22 with a special 2:00 p.m. luncheon where he was given an honorary membership. The event was held in the Grand Hotel, one of the finest in Glasgow. The repast began with Argonaut Soup, a concoction of water added to water, with its tongue-in-cheek recipe attached to each menu. Fortunately for the diners, the remainder of the distinctively Scottish menu consisted of real foods, with civet de lièvre (a stew prepared with rabbit, onions, garlic, and red wine) and kari de poulet (curried chicken) opening the meal. These were followed by haggis and "auld Scottie" (a Scotch whiskey sauce), sheep's head and trotters, black pudding (blood sausage), and white pudding (a meat sausage). The main course was sirloin of beef, roast turkey and tongue, roll of hunter's beef, rabbit pie, spatchcock (butterflied) chickens, York ham, deviled kidneys, grilled pig's feet, and salade à l'américaine (a large garden salad). The meal finished with plum pudding with cream, popcorn soufflé, and Californian jelly. The last two desserts seem designed to emulate American food, but no recipes or descriptions remain.[29]

Following the meal, club members joined Cody and Burke in the large hall of the hotel. There a big crowd had already gathered, listening to music provided by the Wild West's cowboy band. Once Cody and the club members had entered the hall, the show's American Indian performers entered, did a dance, then sang "Nearer, My God, to Thee" in Lakota. The newspaper account of the event noted that other ceremonies followed, and all in attendance were "very favourably impressed with the character of the wild Indians of the Far West."[30]

The season ended in Glasgow with the final show on February 27, 1892. A few performers stayed in Scotland, entertaining in other venues, but most of the troupe returned to the United States. When the International Horticultural Exhibition opened in London on May 7 at Earl's Court, not coincidentally, Buffalo Bill's Wild West also opened in Earl's Court on that same date, the troupe having gathered again in London for a final five-month stand. The exhibition was on the same grounds that had been occupied by the American Exhibition five years earlier, and the Wild West was back in the amphitheater that had been constructed for it. A ticket purchased for the horticultural exhibition also granted access to the show. Newspapers reported that the Wild West's entertainment was generally the same show that was so successful in 1887, but several new features had been added, and they "are even more startling and the individual performers more clever than they were then."[31]

The exhibition opened with a variety of special events and banquets; once again Cody found himself rubbing elbows with lords, ladies, and other celebrities. One banquet thrown by the International Society was set up in a tent right next to the Wild West. Buffalo Bill and his friend General Sheridan were among the honored guests. These opening events were followed by numerous invitations to breakfasts, luncheons, dinners, teas, and garden parties. On July 4, 1892, Cody was invited to dine at the Hotel Albemarle on Piccadilly Circus. The Albemarle was among London's newest and most fashionable buildings. While the meal was a celebration of American independence, the menu was presented in French, and the foods were given international names (fig. 17). The offerings included haricots verts à la anglaise (English-style green beans), salade moscovite (Moscow salad), and a bombe brésilienne (Brazilian bombe, an ice cream dessert). Cody saved the invitation and menu to this event, as well as many others, in a scrapbook documenting the places he visited and the people he met during his London stay.[32]

As before, Cody kept busy hosting special guests at the show and trying to keep up with invitations to dining and tea. The press complimented his special meals for them as "cozy banquets" superior to other soirees. On this trip to London, the Wild West no longer held rib roasts; the show had dropped them when it returned to Europe in 1889. Now the meals, overseen by William Langan, were served on plates at nicely laid tables. One "breakfast," served at 1:00 p.m., consisted of clam chowder, spring chickens fried in cream, corned beef, hashed beef, salt pork, cornbread, sweet corn, lemon

Fig 17. The menu from the 1892 Fourth of July banquet attended by Buffalo Bill at the Hotel Albemarle. He kept it in a scrapbook with dinner invitations and other memorabilia from his London visits. Object ID#72.014.7–23a, Buffalo Bill Museum and Grave, Golden CO.

custard pie, and pumpkin pie. It was all washed down with wine and coffee. The guests "came away with respect and a dash of envy for American cookery."[33]

By the time the International Horticultural Exhibition, including Buffalo Bill's Wild West, closed in mid-October, it was estimated that nearly two million people had attended. On October 13 and 14 the show sold 150 horses, plus some wagons and other rolling stock, at auction. Buffalo Bill and his American personnel then departed on the steamship *Mohawk* for New York City.[34]

After the departure of Buffalo Bill and his Wild West, one London poet wrote about his culinary legacy in Britain:

There was beef, and ham,
And lots of beer, and imported cham,
So with forks and knives
We worked away, as for our lives,
At Colonel Cody's party.[35]

The Wild West did not return to Great Britain until 1902, when it spent two years traveling about the island. The tour started in London, as it had in 1887, and then the show visited cities and even small towns throughout England, Wales, Cornwall, and Scotland. The Atlantic crossing from the United States to Britain was rough, with angry seas. Luther Standing Bear, making the crossing for the first time, was seasick and later recalled, "I even hated to hear the dishes rattle, and for nine days I suffered the tortures of the damned." He managed to keep up his strength by eating some dried meat and Indian corn, which he was able to keep down. On landing, they proceeded to London, where he said, "after nine days of total abstinence," the aroma of mutton cooking "was mighty comforting to me." The Lakotas were served the meat they had smelled, along with potatoes, vegetables, and greens. They sent everything but the meat back to the kitchen. Standing Bear told the head waiter afterward that from then on, they wanted lots of meat and no vegetables. They had their appetite back, but within limits.[36]

The show's performances in London began the day after Christmas, observed by the British as Boxing Day, and ended four months later. Buffalo Bill's Wild West, now much expanded with the Rough

Riders of the World, did not return to Earl's Court, where it had performed previously. Instead, it set up at Olympia, an indoor facility that enabled the show to perform through the winter. Once again Cody made his rounds of teas, meals, and parties in London. Some of them, like a dinner at the London Press Club, were necessary for him to attend in promotion of the show. He also hosted special meals and banquets at Olympia for a variety of guests, including General Nelson Miles and other old friends from the States as well as Londoners.[37]

The show in London closed on April 4 and headed to Manchester for a return visit, opening there on April 13 and closing on May 2. This was the longest, after London, that it stayed in any British city on this return visit. From Manchester, the show meandered around England and Wales, following the best train connections. Citizens in the towns it visited were fascinated by both the show and the activities behind the scenes. The massive range wagon was an impressive sight as Buffalo Bill's Wild West arrived in Cheltenham, as described by one newspaper: "The first wagon, drawn by eight magnificent horses, splendidly handled by the driver, contained the commissariat department, kitchen ranges, cookers, large mess tents, etc., and it was on the work of a quarter of an hour ere fires were lighted, tents erected, and the whole colony of helpers busy preparing breakfast."[38]

British visitors often marveled that everyone ate together, with Cody eating the same food as the troupe. "It is a fact worthy of notice that the men fare exactly like the 'bosses.'" On its journey through Wales, the show set up in Priory Meadows in the ancient town of Abergavenny. There members of the local press were again amazed at the egalitarian manner in which the show fed its personnel. One mused on what the long-deceased monks of the old Benedictine priory would think if they knew "the Red Indian, the Cossack, the Arab, and the men from Uruguay would meet there in friendly conclave with the Briton, and sit down peaceably to dine with him." The show closed for the season at Burton-on-Trent on October 23, 1903, having spent ten months in England and Wales. Cody and most of the cast returned to the United States on Cunard line's ss *Etruria*.[39]

The following April the season began at Stoke-on-Trent, in the heart of Staffordshire. Buffalo Bill's Wild West and Congress of Rough Riders of the World was now associated with the Barnum and Bailey Circus, which had its winter quarters in Europe there. During the winter, the railroad cars, show wagons, and other supplies had been repaired and painted by a contingent of around two hundred people employed for that purpose.[40]

Staffordshire was the center of England's pottery-producing industry, particularly in the manufacture of transferware products. Transferware was created by a process whereby inked scenes on tissue paper were transferred to the pottery in a heated kiln. In 1904 Charles Eldridge Griffin, a performer with the show, took time to explore the potteries, where he "found the process of making an ordinary dinner plate both complex and interesting." About a decade earlier, a set of Buffalo Bill transferware dishes had been made in Staffordshire, inspired by the popularity of Buffalo Bill's Wild West on its first visit to Great Britain. They imaginatively depicted a horseman lassoing wild horses in a mountainous setting.[41]

During the 1904 season, the show traveled to Cornwall and Scotland in addition to England and Wales. These travels included a return to Glasgow as well as a first visit to Edinburgh. At Dumfries, members of the show made a special visit to the mausoleum of Scottish poet Robert Burns, where they laid a wreath. The troupe made other sightseeing trips along the way to Land's End near Penzance on the southernmost point in Britain and John o' Groat's on the northernmost coast of Scotland.

The season ended as it began, in Staffordshire, on October 24. The livestock, wagons, trains, and other supplies went into winter storage once again in the Barnum and Bailey barns at nearby Stoke-on-Trent. Griffin later remarked that Britain was "the fairest and squarest country in the world to a stranger." It was his opinion that the season was the best in the history of the show. It was also the last that Cody and his crew would see of Great Britain and vice versa. In the spring, the animals and rolling stock were sent across the channel to join the rest of Buffalo Bill's Wild West and Congress of Rough Riders of the World in France. There the show would begin its tour of the continent in Paris, just as it had in 1889.[42]

11

Introducing American Cuisine to Europe

Buffalo Bill is teaching Paris to eat popcorn and peanuts.
Sacramento Daily Union, 1889

Over the course of Buffalo Bill Cody's trips to and from Europe, he booked passage on some of the most prestigious ships of the day: the *Persian Monarch* (1889), *Normandie* (1890), *Switzerland* (1892), *Umbria* (1892), *Etruria* (1892, 1903), *Servia* (1892), *Compania* (1904), *St. Paul* (1905), *Kaiser Wilhelm der Grosse* (1905), and *Zeeland* (1906). While aboard, Cody enjoyed gourmet fare similar to that served in the finest restaurants and hotels. The seasickness that had caused Cody to lose his appetite on his first voyage to Great Britain in 1887 did not appear to bother him as much, if at all, on subsequent trips. A dinner served to Cody and his cast during their return to the United States on the ss *Persian Monarch*, on May 17, 1888, only three days before the ship arrived in New York City, served as a celebration of the season in Great Britain. The meal began with mulligatawny soup, followed by salmi of duck (roasted duck in sauce) and braised sheep's head. Next came roast beef and corned beef with carrots. The meal ended with plum pudding, blancmange, rock cakes (small cookielike tea cakes), and cheese. The food was included in the cost of passage, but the cast paid an extra fee for wine and spirits. The extensive liquor list included sherry, port, claret, champagne, white and red wines, and beer. The ships also served a variety of liqueurs, brandies, and whiskeys, including some brands familiar today, such as Hennessy, Martell, and Glenlivet.[1]

Cody's successes in Great Britain in 1887 paved the way for his return to Europe in 1889. Buffalo Bill's Wild West arrived in France to great fanfare and with great expectations. Cody and company visited Barcelona, Rome, Berlin, and Brussels, then returned to Great Britain, all in the course of three years. The grand tour began in Paris on the occasion of the Exposition Universelle. The show was not part of the exposition, as it had been during the Queen's Jubilee in London. Instead, it was located several kilometers away, near the popular Bois de Boulogne park in Neuilly, a Paris suburb.

Its distance from the exposition did not discourage the Parisians, who visited the Wild West in record numbers. Their enthusiasm was undoubtedly encouraged by "the immense painted posters over the city to advertise Buffalo Bill—his portraits pasted all in a row, many times larger than natural; the cowboys on their wild horses; the Indians, looking very savage." One observer thought that "never before was such a financial venture in the show business inaugurated under such auspicious circumstances, and never were more clever advertising tricks played on unsuspecting people." The posters caught the imagination of the Parisians, and they flocked to the show. The city seemed consumed by Wild West fever.[2]

That fever was intensified as the show's performers were seen on the Champs Elysees, at various sites around the city, and in the Exposition Universelle. Shortly after the show opened, John Burke escorted the Lakotas, in their full performing regalia, to the exposition and along the main city boulevards. This visit was met with "delighted enthusiasm" by the locals. It also included a trip to the Eiffel Tower, erected specifically for the exposition and its main attraction. Members of the Wild West troupe visited the tower frequently during their months in Paris. Perhaps reminiscent of the American Exhibition in London two years earlier, an American bar was on the first floor of the tower and offered "the best view" of the Seine River. From the top of the tower, the show's encampment near the Bois du Bologne could be spied as a long row of white tents in front of the dark background of trees in the park.[3]

The grounds for the Wild West were spacious and wooded. The horseshoe-shaped arena had seating for twelve thousand, with an elaborate set on the open end. Ravines, rocks, and waterfalls were painted on the backdrop, in front of which was a small log cabin.

It was a vision of the American wilderness in the City of Lights. As visitors paid admission and then promenaded to the arena at the far end of the grounds, they could follow four routes. Two passed between the tent of Buffalo Bill and those of the cowboys. Cody's tent was distinguished from the rest by a mounted buffalo head over the entrance, flanked by American and French flags. Another route went by a restaurant and several groups of tepees, and the fourth took visitors past a large tent that housed the show's main bar, once again dispensing American cocktails. A slightly smaller bar awaited guests just as they came upon the arena, presumably providing liquid refreshments for enjoyment during the show. Following the afternoon show, guests were able to walk among the tents and tepees to meet their inhabitants.[4]

The Exposition Universelle opened on May 6; Buffalo Bill's Wild West opened soon after, on May 18. The Wild West's opening was a huge event, with crowd estimates ranging from thirteen thousand to twenty thousand. The numbers included "nearly all the Americans in Paris," journalists, and members of the French government. President Sadi Carnot of France and his entourage were met at a private entrance, given a personal tour of the grounds, and escorted to a private box decorated with tricolored bunting representing the French flag. After the matinee was over, John Burke escorted the journalists on a tour of the camp that ended with an evening meal among members of the company in the food tent.[5]

People who had seen the show in Great Britain, including the prince and princess of Wales, crossed the English Channel to get more of Buffalo Bill and his Wild West. The show also had an impact on the Paris art scene. Artist Paul Gauguin went to see the show twice, then purchased a Stetson hat. Later, in Tahiti, he painted a self-portrait of himself in the hat. Norwegian Edvard Munch, studying art in Paris, also attended the show and wrote enthusiastically about it in letters to his father and aunt. Even Rosa Bonheur, known for her animal paintings, deviated from her preferred genre to depict Buffalo Bill on horseback. Bonheur was a constant visitor to the Wild West camp, doing studies of the Indians and animals, making friends with everyone, and often joining the crew for lunch.[6]

Buffalo Bill, dubbed Guillaume de Buffalo by the newspapers, found himself at the center of Parisian culture, attending and throwing breakfasts, luncheons, and dinners. One American visitor observed that after every performance, Cody changed from his buckskins into a dress suit and attended a dinner or reception. One of his first big society functions was a breakfast/luncheon thrown for him on May 29 by the Vicomtesse Chandon de Briailles and "attended by many members of the leading families of France."[7]

A French newspaper later composed a satirical, though not particularly good, poem about the event:

> Yesterday Mme. Chandon de Briailles
> Gave a great tralala.
> Buffalo Bill regaled himself
> With a fine dish of chicken.
> Madam X call him her Phoenix,
> As she ate her orange salad.
> Buffalo Cody felt his oats,
> "My little angel," he murmured.
> Madam Z whispered over her finger bowl.
> "Come to see me tomorrow morning.
> I shall be at home."
> The Countess Y said:
> "I should have wed
> A man who would be my master.
> Now my husband is on his last legs.
> He is only an old count."[8]

The poem, while scoffing at both Cody and society women, highlights his attractiveness to the ladies of Paris. A dashing presence at any table, he was forty-five years old, had long graying hair, and was tall and lean. His excellent horsemanship and his tales of the West were said to "lend romantic interest to his smiles." It was noted that "many beautiful women squabble for the honor of lunching *le charmant Guillaume*, and for these fair admirers the name of Buffalists has been invented." One American paper speculated that the Parisians had not yet decided "whether to class him as art or dressed beef," perhaps a late nineteenth-century equivalent of the twentieth-century "hunk." Cody was so popular that he received at least twenty-seven proposals of marriage, and American newspapers declared him "the hero of the hour." One newspaper worried that his role as social lion, including adopting stylish continental dress, might change him so much that "his Nebraska friends would not recognize him" and would find it "impossible to believe he was once a scout on the Western plains." It was similar to earlier journalistic speculations that he would become too British while in London.[9]

A week after his lunch with the vicomtesse, Buffalo Bill held another breakfast/luncheon with her husband, Count Frederic Chandon de Briailles, the duke de Vallombrosa, Nate Salsbury, and several American friends. Served in Cody's private tent at the Wild West, the American-themed repast consisted of trout, ribs of beef à l'américaine, quail on toast, sweetbreads, chicken mayonnaise, asparagus, American corn, and new potatoes in cream. Tea, coffee, and corn bread were served as dessert. Perhaps that meal allayed any concerns the count might have had about Cody's designs on his wife, or vice versa.[10]

American foods were at the center of a breakfast/luncheon at the Wild West on August 27, served "In Honour of Our American Friends" for Thomas Edison. Edison was one of the celebrities of the exposition and was allocated eight thousand square feet in the main pavilion to show his various inventions. The center of his exhibit was a forty-foot-high model of an incandescent light bulb, composed of twenty thousand bulbs. On either side of the model were French and American flags, also made of incandescent light bulbs. The American breakfast staged by Cody was described by Edison as consisting of "pork and beans, fried beef, mince pie and peanuts." He neglected to mention that sole, quail on toast, steak with mushrooms, clam chowder, and Maryland-style chicken were also on the menu, along with sides of popcorn, hominy, corn bread, and biscuits. In addition to the mince pie, pumpkin and apple pies were also served. Edison later said that of the many dining experiences he had in Paris, the breakfast given in his honor by Buffalo Bill was the most enjoyable. This breakfast was the beginning of a business relationship between the two men. Cody later hired Edison's firm to supply electric lighting for his shows, and Edison documented Buffalo Bill's Wild West on film. He also preserved Cody's voice on a wire recording.[11]

The peanuts that figured in the American meal for Edison were among the foods served to the French at concession stands when they visited the Wild West. Roasted peanuts, popcorn, doughnuts, and pulled candy were consumed by visitors as they watched the reenactments and other acts. For those who did not stop at the bar for an American cocktail, the show also offered cold lemonade. Americans were incredulous that two of their entertainment staples, popcorn and peanuts, were not familiar to the Parisians. The wire services spread the word that "Buffalo Bill is teaching Paris to eat popcorn and peanuts," and this appeared throughout the United States in small-town papers eager for news from Europe. One American newspaper observed that the peanuts would help keep peace in France, which was still recovering from the Paris Commune conflict of 1871 and other unrest, reasoning, "It is utterly impossible for a man to have his pockets filled with roasted peanuts and heart filled with dissatisfaction and fight at the same time."[12]

The Parisians initially approached the Wild West's popcorn somewhat warily but soon were consuming it with delight, and it had an impact beyond the show grounds and even beyond 1889. By October it was said that the people of Paris "seem to go to the theatre to eat, for they munch and absorb during the entire performance." This habit at theatrical venues was "a new fashion set by Buffalo Bill with his popcorn." Nearly ten years later, an American newspaper observed that popcorn was introduced to Paris by Buffalo Bill and had caught on so well over the years that five tons had just been shipped to Paris.[13]

The Exposition Universelle closed in Paris on October 31, 1889. Likewise, Buffalo Bill's Wild West folded its tents and departed for the rest of Europe, but not before the Lakotas celebrated their successful experience in Paris with a dog feast and ox rib roast. On the show's departure, one wire service article mourned, "A great gap yawns in the social life of Paris." Rather than close for winter, the show continued on to Lyon and Marseille before crossing the Mediterranean to Barcelona. The Wild West arrived in Barcelona at Christmastime and stayed until mid-January. A special reenactment of Columbus discovering America added to the show's popularity there. But it was the first and only time Buffalo Bill visited Spain; the Spanish-American War of 1898 later made all things American unwelcome in that country.[14]

Leaving Barcelona, the Wild West headed to Italy. The crew again crossed the Mediterranean, landing safely in Naples after passing through a major storm at sea. A New York newspaper observed, "A troop of American Indians within the shadow of Mount Vesuvius is an indication of how distances in this great world are now annihilated." During the show's three weeks in the shadow of Vesuvius, Buffalo Bill stayed at least some of the time in the Grand Hotel Alfred Hauser. He wrote from the hotel, "My outfit consists of 243 persons, 200 horses and mules and 29 buffaloes: quite a large family, you will say, to take around." He continued, "I go from here to Rome and will make a desperate effort to perform in the old Roman colloseum [sic], where gladiators of old fought and died."[15]

As Cody suspected, the effort to perform in the Colosseum was a vain attempt, rejected by the Roman authorities. Instead, the show set up at the Piazza D'Armi, an army parade ground (no longer standing) between the Vatican and the Castel Sant'Angelo. This did not, however, dissuade the newspapers from drawing parallels between the gladiatorial feats of old and those of the Wild West. The location made it easy for Buffalo Bill and members of the cast, most notably the Lakotas, to be present for the commemoration of Leo XIII's twelfth anniversary as pope. Cody was invited to join the Italian nobility in the Sistine Chapel for the occasion, while the rest of the show's members were outside in the Ducal Hall. As the pope passed by the Lakotas, dressed in their native garb for the occasion, he leaned forward and blessed them. When the papal party passed through the Sistine Chapel, he also blessed the nobility gathered there, including Buffalo Bill.[16]

Following several successful weeks in Rome, the Wild West traveled to Florence. There a local newspaper editor noted that the show had two large eating tents, one occupied by the Indians and the other by the cowboys, vaqueros, and other employees. He observed, "The Indians eat meat and bread like we do, only three times as much. . . . Yesterday between the Indians and the Americans they ate an entire cow." Members of the show also consumed one thousand eggs a day, purchased from the San Donato dairy farm outside of Florence. Before the show opened, a banquet was thrown in Cody's honor at the Florence Club. This gathering of Americans and their friends living in the city consumed a dinner of salmon, turtle soup, and York ham. Pauillac, an expensive wine from a small region north of Bordeaux and near the French coast, and magnums of champagne lubricated the evening. After a toast from the entire assembly, Cody made some remarks, noting that the wheels of the show's wagons still bore traces of Roman mud, which he intended "to take to America as a bit of the Eternal City that led the civilisation of the world." Within a week, Florentine mud added to the Roman mud as torrential rains made the arena a quagmire. Despite the weather, the show was quite successful, with special trains coming from many towns in the area, including Siena and Pisa. The popcorn and caramel candy concession did very well after each performance, when "a crowd three deep besieged the booth."[17]

The Wild West's remaining destinations in Italy were Bologna, Milan, and Verona. In Verona, Cody finally got his wish to perform where the gladiators had fought, with a single show in the amphitheater, even older than the Roman Colosseum. Thousands attended from nearby Venice, where Cody and the Lakotas had been photographed a day before at the Doge's Palace and riding in a gondola. While the show was pronounced very successful, the camp, in a deserted garden not far from the amphitheater, was also of great interest. There visitors saw the tents and tepees of the cast, as well as long tables spread with western fare: chunks of beef, fried pork, potatoes, and boiled beans. A *New York Times* reporter observed that "sad experience had taught the managers that it was better to make no innovation in the accustomed menu," referring to such European foods as spaghetti, frogs' legs, polenta, or sauerkraut. The cooks with the show served only American foods, and that was how it was going to stay. Having concluded its time in Italy, the show's next destination would be the land of sauerkraut: Germany.[18]

The first stop on the show's northward trek from Italy that spring was Munich. After a relatively short visit, the show moved on to

Vienna and three weeks of performances at the Prater amusement park. During that time, the Lakotas with the show were invited to a special reception with the American minister to Austria, the German ambassador, and other European diplomats, where they enjoyed Viennese "ices" (ice cream).[19]

The Wild West's trek across Germany took it all the way north to Hamburg. By then the show's peanuts had been renamed "Algerian almonds." They were joined by "American bonbons" wrapped in silk paper. Show visitors who tasted them were heard to exclaim, "Why, it's maize and honey." These were the sugared popcorn balls that had proven so popular in London three years earlier. While Buffalo Bill may not have introduced popcorn balls to Great Britain, they certainly were new to the Germans.[20]

One of the most important and highly publicized visits in Germany was to its capital, Berlin, where the show was set up on Kurfürstendamm near the Charlottenburg Palace. Wilhelm, the crown prince who had seen the show in London and invited Cody to Berlin, was now Emperor Wilhelm II. He not only made a return visit to the show but also sent his military advisors to observe the efficiency with which it transported men, equipment, and animals. The advisors looked at all aspects of the show's operation, including the manner in which Cody's "mimic army" was fed.[21]

The German newspapers were meticulous in their descriptions of the show and its operations. Upon arriving at the Wild West, visitors approached twelve pay booths, with entrances based on seating categories. Inside were a police station, telephone room, medical room, post office, press room, and various sales booths with souvenir items. Some booths offered champagne and Russian liquors. Food was provided in concessions operated by local restaurants Löser und Wolff, Unter den Linden, and Café Bauer. The popular "American bonbons" were hawked by young locals on behalf of the show.[22]

After spending a month in Berlin and making additional stops in Bremen and Hamburg, the Wild West headed south along the Rhine. The show concluded the 1890 season in the city of Strassburg, which was the capital of the Alsace-Lorraine region, an area of dispute between France and Germany for several hundred years.

In 1890 it was part of Germany, having been captured twenty years earlier during the Franco-Prussian War.

John Burke later wrote that the decision to stop at that point, rather than head farther south for a winter season, was motivated by attacks on the show by reformers back in the States. One of the biggest charges was that the Lakotas were being poorly fed. Nate Salsbury remained with the troupe in winter quarters at an abandoned castle and abbey in Benfield, near Strassburg, while Burke and Cody returned to America with the Lakotas to address the charges. After being cleared by the secretary of the interior, Cody traveled to Nebraska to assist his friends General Nelson Miles and Governor John M. Thayer during the Ghost Dance. When he returned to Europe the following spring, he was joined by Short Bull and other Ghost Dance leaders who chose to perform with the Wild West as an alternative to jail. The secretary of the interior had not only cleared Cody of the accusations but even allowed members of the movement to join the show.[23]

The 1891 season opened with shows in Strasbourg in mid-April. Then the Wild West traveled back up the Rhine, visiting cities it had missed on its southward trip the previous fall. The last city the show visited in Germany was Aachen, onetime capital of the Emperor Charlemagne. Nate Salsbury escorted an American correspondent around the show grounds, where he saw the separate dining tents of the Indians and the rest of the show, with a "kitchen-on-wheels" between them. Near the kitchen stood John Keanan, stirring a cauldron full of asparagus and quoting from Shakespeare's *Macbeth*.[24]

Departing Aachen, the show proceeded to Brussels for two weeks. While the show was performing, Buffalo Bill stayed at the Hôtel Bellevue, with neighboring rooms occupied by Cornelius Vanderbilt and John Jacob Astor IV, grandson of the western fur trader. Cody attended several banquets, including one with other Americans at Wiltcher's Hotel and a gala dinner party celebrating the birthday of Belgium's queen Marie Henriette. Among the choices offered on a menu printed with gold on "vegetable parchment" were inventive entrées created for the occasion, including Salade Nelson, Chaufroix, De Mauviettes á l'Indienne, and Chamounix en Fromage.[25]

Buffalo Bill, Burke, Salsbury, the Lakota Indians, and other members of the cast all visited the Waterloo memorial on June 2, where they had a photograph taken on the steps while the cowboy band played "The Star Spangled Banner." They then retreated like Napoleon, but only so far as the Hôtel du Musée, where Cody treated everyone to glasses of milk. Two days later the women of the Wild West, including riders Georgia Duffy and Della Ferrell, visited the monument in the early morning and stopped at the same hotel for breakfast.[26]

The grand tour of the European mainland ended at Antwerp on June 17, 1891. From there the company set sail to Great Britain and, as John Burke put it, their "cousins of the isle." After several years of hearing languages that were foreign to them, the members of the Wild West were pleased to arrive in a place where they spoke a common language with the inhabitants.[27]

Buffalo Bill's Wild West returned to the European mainland again in 1905 after spending two years in Great Britain. By that time the show, as well as Buffalo Bill himself, had gone through significant changes. The Congress of Rough Riders of the World was added in 1893 for the World's Columbian Exposition in Chicago and remained a primary focus of the program. After years of quarreling with his wife, Louisa, Cody had attempted to divorce her during the winter of 1904–5, with disastrous personal and public relations consequences. Buffalo Bill's marriage problems were splashed across newspaper headlines throughout the United States. For him, a return to Europe was an opportunity to get away. As one newspaper observed, "Buffalo Bill sailed for gay Paree Saturday. He goes away to forget his family troubles."[28]

Buffalo Bill's Wild West and Congress of Rough Riders of the World opened in Paris in 1905, on the Champs de Mars near the base of the Eiffel Tower (fig. 18). Paris was the first stop on an itinerary taking the Wild West throughout France and much of the European mainland, including Italy, Austria, Germany, and Belgium, as well as Hungary, Slovakia, Ukraine, Serbia, Romania, Poland, Croatia, and the Czech Republic in eastern Europe.[29]

The Wild West left Paris on June 4. Cody's employees were happy to get on the road, since, as performer Charles Eldridge Griffin wrote, "Nine weeks is too long to stay in any one place for those accustomed to one-day stand circus life in America." They surely got their wish as the show traveled throughout France over the next five months, visiting 113 cities and finishing the season in Marseille.[30]

The tour began again in spring of 1906, continuing along the French and Italian Rivieras to Rome. As was his practice, John Burke took the Lakotas to see the sights when they were not performing. Following a visit to the Spanish Steps, they stopped at Caffè Greco. Nearly 150 years old at the time, it was a Bohemian hangout known for the many famous writers, composers, and artists who haunted it throughout the nineteenth century, discussing their craft over cups of coffee. Particularly attractive to the often near-starving artists was the inexpensive food; when the Wild West group visited, a beefsteak cost sixteen cents and a bottle of wine five cents. As a writer, Burke undoubtedly felt a kinship with many of those who had frequented the café. He wrote, "Few distinguished strangers visited Rome without a paying a call there," and he would have considered himself one of that number. A photograph of Burke, misidentified as Cody, and two Indians perusing their menus still hangs on the café's walls.[31]

Buffalo Bill's renowned hospitality continued throughout the tour, particularly to Americans visiting his show. When journalist George Ade and novelist Booth Tarkington brought twelve other American writers to the show's encampment on Rome's Piazza D'Armi, the same location the Wild West occupied back in 1890, he made sure they were served plenty of eggs, ham, and buckwheat cakes. Ade apologized for bringing so large a group, to which Cody replied, "I wish you had brought three hundred instead of thirteen; I'd guarantee to fill all the Americans in Italy with ham and eggs and be glad of the opportunity." He followed that up with tickets to the show and a ride in the stagecoach, a privilege he frequently extended to dignitaries. It was reported that "they proved a happy lot of pilgrims and seemed to enjoy themselves immensely." After the bad publicity regarding his failed divorce action, Cody knew it was in his best interest to show his journalistic visitors a good time.[32]

Despite some successes, the Wild West experienced troubles in Europe that it had not previously encountered. Horses in the show

Fig 18. Buffalo Bill's Wild West and Congress of Rough Riders of the World on the Champs de Mars in the shadow of Paris's Eiffel Tower in 1905. Object ID#2016.012, Buffalo Bill Museum and Grave, Golden CO.

were infected with glanders, a highly contagious and fatal illness, after leaving Paris. By the time the show closed in Marseille, many of the horses had died, and local authorities forced Cody to kill the rest of them to keep the illness from spreading beyond the show. When the show resumed traveling in the spring of 1906, with new horses from the States, it met with suspicion that they were still carrying the disease as it traveled into Italy and beyond. The show had planned on playing Pisa on April 4 but was barred from that city because of fears about glanders, disappointing members of the cast who had looked forward to seeing the famous Leaning Tower.[33]

While in Vienna, the show appeared once again at the Prater amusement park, characterized by show personnel as Vienna's Coney Island. The park's vendors capitalized on the show's presence by selling "American sowerkraut" and "American beer," probably neither in reality. But trouble continued to follow the Wild West. Buffalo Bill was accused of mistreating the horses by putting "thorny chains" under the saddles to make them buck. Cody, who loved horses and had been brokenhearted over their loss in Marseille, turned away scornfully from his accusers. Members of local humane societies tracked the handling of the show's horses as it moved across Hungary, but they found no evidence of ill treatment, and nothing more was said.[34]

Throughout the season, rumor had it that Buffalo Bill was thinking of retiring because of disappointments with the show, ongoing family difficulties, and ill health. He wrote back to the States, "Strongly deny reports of failing health, bad business and retirement. Never in life felt better and business immense." Despite such assertions, the show simply did not have the successes of its earlier travels between 1889 and 1892. As the troupe traveled through the countries of the Austro-Hungarian Empire, they encountered more poverty than anticipated, and show revenues were disappointing. After three months, a return to the richer towns of Germany helped make up for the loss of income in eastern Europe.[35]

After a successful week and a half in Belgium, the show left for the United States on September 22, 1906. Charles Eldridge Griffin, who had traveled with the show through Great Britain and Europe for the entire four years, wrote that despite the obstacles and troubles, "the tour was a most successful one, both financially and artistically." John Burke summarized the trip by saying, "We have shown Europeans how we do things in the United States, and, in much modesty, I believe that our methods left a very favorable impression upon the people."[36]

Buffalo Bill wrote in 1888 that the accolades that the Wild West had received in the United States had excited his and Salsbury's "ambition to conquer other nations than our own." Encouragement from Mark Twain and the offer from John Whitley to join the American Exhibition in London had given that ambition substance. After its first year in Great Britain, the show briefly returned to the United States, then made a triumphant entry into the European continent for Paris's Exposition Universelle. By the end of its last trip to Europe in 1906, Buffalo Bill's Wild West had indeed conquered many other nations.[37]

The first visits to Britain and Europe between 1887 and 1892 made Cody an international celebrity, setting him up for greater fame and fortune once he returned to the United States. Annie Oakley wrote many years later, "Tepee and palace were all the same to him. And so were their inhabitants." Cody's egalitarian attitude reflected American ideals, which in turn were reflected throughout Buffalo Bill's Wild West. The return of Buffalo Bill's Wild West and Congress of Rough Riders of the World from 1902 to 1906 broadened the story, showing peoples from the entire world interacting, competing, and cooperating. In some ways the show was a microcosm of America, a country of immigrants, made up of the peoples of the world.[38]

Cody and his Wild West were cultural ambassadors. Just as Mark Twain had suggested, they brought something uniquely American to the mother countries. Buffalo Bill's Wild West made a lasting impression on Europeans' vision of America. His version of the American West, with its peoples and its history, brought to life the stories, images, and news articles that had been making their way across the Atlantic for decades. One Englishman observed that the show rendered "reading books, or viewing the works of the sculptors and artist on these subjects more easily comprehended and enjoyed in years to come." This paved the way for movies in Europe just as it did in America, with westerns being the first and most popular genre on the silver screen. After their encounters with Buffalo Bill's Wild West, reinforced by western movies, it is no surprise that well into the twentieth century, Europeans thought the American West was entirely populated by cowboys and Indians.[39]

Celebrities of the day, such as Oscar Wilde and Paul Gauguin, were drawn to Buffalo Bill's Wild West. Americans, including notables like Thomas Edison, enjoyed the show as a patriotic expression of their homeland. On the diplomatic front, kings, queens, princesses, prime ministers, and other political leaders visited the show. There is good reason to believe that the Wild West's trip to the American Exhibition in London, honoring the jubilee of Queen Victoria's reign, did indeed help American and British relations, as Buffalo Bill and John Burke later asserted. And why not? As Burke often insisted, Buffalo Bill's Wild West was not just entertainment; it was an educational exhibition.

In 1897, five years after the show's first tour of Europe concluded, a writer remarked that it was Buffalo Bill's Wild West that had introduced the trendsetters of Europe to corn bread, corn cakes, and all that could be made of corn. Cody "thus indirectly created a market for American corn which has resulted in the sale of millions of bushels." The writer suggested that all the other contributions Cody had made in terms of introducing American life paled in comparison to this, and that few others had done more for America than "Buffalo Bill did when his hospitality introduced American corn to the cities of Europe." Whether one agrees with that conclusion, it was the food shared with the show's European hosts that served as the social cement connecting Europe to America. Burke later observed, "Living in their own camp, eating American food, the people of the Wild West did much to educate foreigners into a taste for American hams, corn-meal, and other luxuries." Thus, in many ways—the meals shared between the cast and their visitors, snacks of popcorn and peanuts, and the promotion of American cocktails and western cuisine—foods helped introduce the New World to the Old World.[40]

12

Fourth of July Feasts

No matter in what part of the globe he may be with this Wild West show, no anniversary of the natal day passes by without "extra doings" on the occasion.

Columbus (NE) Journal, 1903

Buffalo Bill's Wild West was intended to be a showcase and celebration of things American, particularly its western history and culture. The prolonged tours outside the United States made the Fourth of July a poignant day for Cody and his employees. It was the one holiday of the year that they were on the road, often far from home and feeling more than a little nostalgic. It was also Buffalo Bill's favorite holiday. Even though the regular performances went on as scheduled, the entire company made merry and let their patriotic colors fly. The dining tent was gaily decorated in red, white, and blue; all wore their nicest clothes; and the troupe enjoyed a meal that celebrated the occasion.

One of the myths regarding Buffalo Bill's Wild West revolves around Independence Day. As the story goes, Cody had been traveling and returned to his home in North Platte just before July 4, 1882. He was appalled to discover that no plans were in place for a celebration, so he put together an event that recruited cowboys from all over Nebraska to compete in a rodeo-like event that was the forerunner to the Wild West. Yet in telling stories of his life, Cody never referred to this supposedly pivotal moment. When he described the founding of his show in *Story of the Wild West and Campfire Chats*, published in 1888, he did not mention it at all. John M. Burke's 1893 biography, *Buffalo Bill from Prairie to Palace*, which did its best to promote Cody and his patriotism, said nothing of it. The legendary status and name of North Platte's "Old Glory Blowout" appear to have been the invention of Louis E. Cooke, a circus promoter who worked for Cody twenty years later.[1]

North Platte did have an Independence Day celebration in 1882, and not being one to miss such a celebration, Buffalo Bill was on the planning committee. By then the Buffalo Bill Combination had reached the height of its popularity, and as a show business celebrity, Cody was asked to be marshal of the town's parade. The festivities also included speeches, singing, horse races, and some demonstrations of cowboy skills, including riding a saddled buffalo. But outside of the parade and cowboy feats, it bore little resemblance to what visitors experienced a year later at Buffalo Bill's Wild West. It had no battle re-creations, displays of pioneer life, vaquero exploits, or opportunities to see American Indian culture. The Wild West, which was organized the following spring and rehearsed in Columbus, Nebraska, had many sources, not just the Old Glory Blowout. Over the years, the story of the celebration grew . . . even in the memories of the North Platte folks, who claimed to recall such things as Cody stating he was going to start a show called Buffalo Bill's Wild West and Congress of Rough Riders of the World. However, that name did not evolve until ten years later. Although Cooke and many people in North Platte asserted that the Old Glory Blowout was the beginning of Buffalo Bill's Wild West, it was not.[2]

Even if the Wild West did not begin as the Old Glory Blowout, Independence Day and the patriotism associated with it were important to Cody. In 1887 the cowboy band played "The Star-Spangled Banner" at every performance in London. By that time it was a regular part of the show. Buffalo Bill was among the first to use the song in such a way, before the U.S. Navy adopted it in 1889, before President Wilson declared it the national anthem in 1916, and long before it was officially recognized by Congress in 1931. One could argue that the consistent playing of the song before every Wild West show, heard by millions of Americans, helped establish it as a favorite patriotic song.[3]

The practice of observing the Fourth with "extra doings"—specifically, a banquet for the Wild West troupe—appears to have begun while the show was in London in 1887. In this early effort to provide a special meal for the occasion, the menu selections may have been distinguished more by their interesting titles than by any uniqueness in their preparation. Like the food tent, made less ordinary with patriotic bunting, the foods were likely the show's regular fare, dressed up with names reminiscent of home.

The meal format loosely followed French banqueting tradition, giving it an appearance of sophistication. The 1887 banquet menu, saved by Nate Salsbury, was carefully separated into courses, each of which was described. The dinner opened with a "Soup" course of Wild West style bean soup, followed by boiled halibut in parsley sauce as the "Fish" course. The "Roast" course consisted of saddle of veal in Omaha Sauce, Texas beef and brown potatoes, and chicken à la North Platte. That was followed by two "Entrées" of chicken salad à la Wyoming and baked pork and beans, Boston style. At French banquets, the entrées were usually the third course, but in this case, they followed the roast course. The French would have served a hot dish in sauce or a cold dish, or both, for the entrée course. This banquet followed that approach with a distinctly western flair by offering hot pork and beans and cold chicken salad. New green peas, American corn, and new potatoes and cream constituted the "Vegetable" course. For dessert, the "Pastry" course, offerings were Wild West Pudding, lemon pie, apple pie, and assorted cakes. "Fruits" were the final course, with strawberries and cream, oranges, and mixed nuts. As was the case with all meals served to show personnel, each person could choose any or all of the offerings. This first banquet on the Fourth established a tradition of using printed menus for each year's celebration; many of those menus remain.[4]

In 1889 the show observed the Fourth of July while at the Exposition Universelle in Paris (fig. 19). Here, as one would expect, the menu followed the French banqueting tradition fairly closely, with soup, fish, entrée, roast, vegetable, and dessert courses. For this occasion, the foods on the menu were named after individuals associated with the troupe, such as Rabbit à la Cody, Roast Beef à la Mode d'Arizona John (John Burke's nom de plume), Assorted Sweets à la Little Nate Salsbury Jr., and even Calves Head à la the

Staff. The front of the menu was decorated with the crossed flags of the United States and France and noted that the meal was presented "Compliments of Cody and Salsbury for the Boys in Camp Paris." Following the meal, the show held its matinee performance, and Cody departed for a huge reception and banquet given for Americans in Paris by the new minister to France, Whitelaw Reid. A thousand people enjoyed champagne and food in abundance. Cody wrote to his sister Julia the next day that after the two meals, "today I am off my feed." Even a man with Buffalo Bill's zest for food and drink had to take a break.[5]

Buffalo Bill's Wild West and the newly added Congress of Rough Riders of the World spent the 1893 season in Chicago during the World's Columbian Exposition. One reporter noted that the Independence Day meal at the show was a "splendid spread." It included a dozen different vegetables, venison and wild game, roast beef and mutton, and a wide variety of "dainties" for dessert. The most popular dessert was ice cream, a rare treat. The mutton, served with a caper sauce, was well liked by one of the cowboys, although he said he had no interest at all in the "sour peas" in the sauce. Such delicacies as capers and frog legs were just too exotic for many of the performers, as was discovered the next year while the show was in Brooklyn at Ambrose Park. That Fourth was celebrated with a breakfast featuring frog legs imported from Canada. While members of the French cavalry and some of the cowboys enjoyed them, the Cossacks ate them sparingly, and the Arabs rejected them altogether. It was observed that "the Rough Riders are all good eaters, but frog legs are rather delicate for them."[6]

July 4, 1897, in Toronto, was described as a festive occasion at the show. In the patriotically decorated food tent, "large boiling kettles were steaming away merrily, and great joints were roasting in the portable range." That was the range wagon, in regular use by that time. Twenty-five gallons of ice cream were in one corner of the tent "to enable the diners to cool off." In 1899 the show was in Lawrence, Massachusetts. William Langan, who had been in charge of the meal in 1887, continued to oversee the process, with William Thall as the head chef. The banquet menu was considerably more ambitious than the first one in 1887. It also abandoned the

Fig 19. Food tent decorated for the Fourth of July, probably while the show was in Paris in 1889. Cody, already balding in his forties, is seated in the left foreground. Object ID#90.0396, Buffalo Bill Museum and Grave, Golden CO.

French manner of dividing the meal into courses and simply listed the food as it would be served. It included consommé, tenderloin of trout, fillet of sole in anchovy sauce, chicken breasts in cream, turkey wing fricassee, roast prime rib of beef au jus, beef fillets with mushrooms, roasted sugar-cured ham, and turkey with cranberry sauce. The vegetables were new potatoes, mashed potatoes, string beans, sweet corn, and pickled beets. Other offerings were lobster salad, chicken salad, lettuce, radishes, and a cheese course. New England cheeses and Roquefort were served with Bent's Water Crackers, produced by a Massachusetts company begun in 1801 and in operation until the twenty-first century. Water crackers were similar to hardtack, something Buffalo Bill had consumed many times in his youth on the frontier. This may have accounted for the popularity of these crackers among Wild West performers. Assorted cakes and ice cream finished the meal, which they washed down with plenty of tea and coffee.[7]

When the show unloaded in Syracuse, New York, for its performances on July 4, 1900, one of the first things off the train was the large range wagon, so heavy that it took eight workhorses to pull it from the train to the show grounds. From there William Langan and the Buffalo Bill's Wild West Company Dining Department oversaw the festive feeding of a show whose numbers had swelled to over six hundred. Even though the official title of the show was Buffalo Bill's Wild West and Congress of Rough Riders of the World, for brevity it was frequently referred to as Buffalo Bill's Wild West, and this short title appeared on the Fourth of July menus. The menu in Syracuse consisted of nearly the same foods provided to the troupe the year before, including the cheeses with Bent's Water Crackers. New additions were roast lamb with green peas and a curry of giblets and rice. Langan later remarked that it took nearly fifteen hundred pounds of meats to supply such a meal, plus breakfast and lunch.[8]

Whether the show was in New England or old England, it always observed the Fourth of July. When in foreign lands, it was a time for the American cast members, always in the majority, to reminisce about and reconnect with the country of their origin. The show returned to Great Britain in late December 1902 and celebrated the next Fourth of July in Aberdare, Wales. By that time William Langan had moved on, and it was now the job of DeWitt Ballard to coordinate the occasion. Ballard decided to return to the previous practice of listing courses, perhaps for an air of sophistication while in Britain. The front of the menu wished employees "Many Happy Returns of the Day" on behalf of Colonel William F. Cody and James A. Bailey. Bailey, of Barnum and Bailey fame, had become a partner in the late 1890s as Nate Salsbury became more sickly and less involved. Bailey brought an infusion of capital as well as new ideas, such as the addition of a Varieties Tent with a moss-haired lady, a blue-skinned man, and other sideshow acts. Ballard also added some new ideas to the Independence Day meal: boiled Columbia River salmon in hollandaise sauce, ox tongue and spinach, banana fritters, and Stilton cheese, considered by the British to be the king of cheeses.[9]

The following Fourth of July the Wild West was still in Great Britain, this time in York. Charles Eldridge Griffin, who managed the sideshows in the Varieties Tent, later wrote that the whole show was decorated with red, white, and blue bunting and the cowboy band played patriotic songs. "The entire company sat down to a regular Yankee dinner, which almost made us forget, for the time being, that we were 'strangers in a strange land.'" The Yankee dinner, again overseen by Ballard, included boiled York ham with cabbage, boiled turbot in hollandaise sauce, fried chicken Maryland style, apple fritters in a wine sauce, roast sirloin of beef with Yorkshire pudding, spring lamb with mint sauce and green peas, and stuffed turkey. New potatoes, stewed corn, and string beans were the vegetables. The dessert course included pumpkin pie, cakes, and ice cream. The meal finished with Stilton and Cheshire cheeses.[10]

The Wild West returned to Paris in 1905, then toured throughout France. On July 4 the show concluded a four-day stand in Lille, near the Belgian border. Once again the show grounds were bedecked with red, white, and blue bunting; the band played patriotic songs; and the members of the company were treated to a grand banquet. James Bailey visited from the States to help Cody host the event. It was his last time with the show; he died in early 1906. The food was similar to that served at past Independence Day banquets, with only minor variations. In Lille, asparagus cream soup started the meal, followed by boiled salmon in an egg sauce. The previous year's Maryland fried chicken, lamb, and ham were replaced by chicken fricassee, ox tongue and spinach, banana fritters in wine sauce, and veal with dressing. The meal concluded with coffee and tea, on which the performers thrived. Each meal required around ninety gallons of coffee and forty-five gallons of tea. While in Lille, Ballard arranged for all the tea and coffee consumed at the show to be provided by the Meert confectionery and tearoom, which dated back to 1677 and is still in operation today.[11]

It was perhaps in Szeged, Hungary, where the Wild West company celebrated Independence Day in 1906, that the members felt the most like "strangers in a strange land," according to Charles

Eldridge Griffin. He said it seemed they were on "the frontier of Europe and Asia." There and in the countries of Serbia, Romania, Ukraine, Poland, and the Czech Republic, they were confronted by languages and cultures with which they were completely unfamiliar. The show had been on the road for nearly four years, and even though some of the staff returned to the States between seasons, many stayed in Europe through the winters. So when they celebrated the Fourth of July in Szeged, the holiday decorations became even more poignant reminders of home, a place to which they would return in a few months.[12]

Griffin noted that Hungary's agriculture at the time of their visit was comparatively primitive, which may have been reflected in a Fourth of July menu with fewer offerings, since most of the ingredients for the entrées were locally sourced. The menu still included ham and short ribs of beef, but the main entrées were poultry: chicken pie, stuffed duckling, and young goose in a giblet sauce. Lima beans also made their first appearance at this Independence Day banquet.[13]

Thinking about his show's return to America in 1906, Buffalo Bill mused, "I was glad to get back to America. No matter where I am, outside of the United States I am a foreigner. . . . In the future I shall live where I was born and brought up, in my own country." And that was exactly what he did.[14]

DeWitt Ballard continued to serve as the show's food manager or caterer through 1913, planning and executing Fourth of July meals along with his other tasks. In 1907, in Fitchburg, Massachusetts, the menu opened with a brief dialogue referring to the merriment of the occasion: "Ah! What noise is that?" "Your pardon, Madam; only a harmless entertainment after my own country fashion." The list of food items that followed, however, was anything but "country fashion." Offerings included green turtle soup with a relish of radish and olives alongside, boiled salmon in hollandaise sauce, boiled leg of mutton with caper sauce, prime rib in gravy, spring chicken with new peas, stuffed Rhode Island turkey, and saddle of veal with braised mushrooms, as well as vegetable side dishes and an assortment of desserts.[15]

The Wild West returned to Massachusetts in 1908 with a one-day show in Springfield on the Fourth. The menu was decorated with an image of George Washington on the cover, and inside was a poem commemorating the immortal patriots of the nation, including Washington. The poem ended with the words "Hail Columbia," referring to the female figure standing alongside Washington on the cover. This time the soup was cream of green corn, the fish was boiled sea bass in anchovy sauce, and the entrées were sirloin of beef with mushrooms, young goose with apple sauce, chicken sauté à la Newburgh, and duckling with currant gravy. Crab and lobster salad was also on the menu, as were vegetable side dishes and desserts.[16]

In 1909 Buffalo Bill's Wild West and Congress of Rough Riders of the World combined with Pawnee Bill's rival show to create Buffalo Bill's Wild West and Pawnee Bill's Far East. This combination was reflected on the front of the 1911 Fourth of July menu. Inside was a flippant reference to George Washington, who had appeared on the 1908 menu, saying, "O, you George!" The offerings were similar to those from that year, with the addition of Philadelphia capon, a popular item in restaurants and at banquets at the time. Capons were young male chickens that were sterilized and fattened to develop a delicate, full-flavored flesh, and those from Philadelphia were considered the best.[17]

The last Independence Day celebrated by Buffalo Bill's Wild West was in 1913 in Chicago. The menu was simple, with only an American flag, the date, and the show's location on the cover. The simplicity of the menu cover may have reflected the show's current financial situation. At the beginning of each season, loans were often secured based on expected income. The 1913 season had not gone well, and Buffalo Bill's Wild West and Pawnee Bill's Far East owed money to Denver businessman Harry Tammen when the show arrived in that city on July 21. The show was seized by the Denver sheriff on Tammen's behalf and put up for auction. By August Buffalo Bill's Wild West was no more.[18]

The following year Cody was forced to appear with a show organized by Tammen. Billed as the Sells Floto Circus and Buffalo Bill Himself, the show still held its annual Independence Day dinner. That year it was in Sioux Falls, South Dakota, offering a menu not greatly different from those at the banquets Buffalo Bill had thrown for over twenty-five years. It started with green turtle soup, included a variety of relishes, and offered a variety of meats. Newly added were sweetbreads in Bordelaise sauce, Waldorf salad, and asparagus. This holiday must have been bittersweet for Cody because it celebrated independence, something he no longer had under Tammen.[19]

After traveling with the Sells Floto Circus for two years, Cody was able to leave it and join the 101 Ranch show. This was a Wild West show, not a circus, and he enjoyed it much more. It also gave him top billing, so the Fourth of July menu for 1916 read "Buffalo Bill Himself and the 101 Ranch Shows Combined." The banquet, held after the show in Fall River, Massachusetts, opened with consommé followed by Roman punch, a frozen drink prepared with or without alcohol and typically consumed between courses on festive occasions. Baked bluefish, boiled Smithfield ham with spinach, prime rib of beef with mushroom sauce, and Vermont turkey with oyster dressing were served next. Strawberry shortcake, vanilla ice cream, nuts, and cheese and crackers finished the meal.[20]

Many of the special foods acquired for the Fourth of July banquets were locally sourced, which explains some of the differences in the menus over the years. Seasonal produce varied depending on location and availability. Some fruits, like strawberries, were nearly always on Fourth of July menus because the holiday occurred during the height of their season. Sales of fresh foods by local purveyors to Buffalo Bill's Wild West for the Fourth of July banquets proved to be of tremendous economic benefit to any community. The extra doings also made every Fourth of July something for everyone to celebrate.

While the Old Glory Blowout is largely a myth, invented by one of the Wild West's promoters, the importance of Independence Day to the Buffalo Bill's Wild West cannot be overemphasized. No matter where the Wild West traveled, the Fourth of July became a reminder of home and all that it meant. Everything from the printed menus with patriotic themes to the food tent decorated with flags to the banquets of favorite foods helped the staff recall just what they celebrated in the arena every day. It might even be safe to assume that on that day, the cowboy band played "The Star-Spangled Banner" with a little more feeling than usual.

13

Caterers, Cracker Jack, and Red Lemonade

> It is a mistaken notion that a show of this sort takes an immense
> amount of money out of every town it visits. . . . We take in a
> mint of money, to be sure, but we also disburse a great deal
> and the net sum we take away from each large town is com-
> paratively small.
>
> Wild West employee, *Buffalo (NY) Courier*, 1895

Buffalo Bill's Wild West was an economic powerhouse, whether in
Europe or in the United States, and food had a lot to do with it.
Communities large and small were eager to host the show, not only
because it was an entertaining spectacle but also because it proved
to be an economic boon to any place where it appeared. Everyone
benefited, from the merchants who supplied meats, produce, breads,
and other goods to the show's caterers to the concessionaires who
worked under contract to sell food and souvenirs. These local and
sometimes national companies often advertised in the show's programs. Local hotels and restaurants also benefited from the influx
of visitors to the communities hosting the show. Even independent
vendors who set up for the parades and outside the show grounds
experienced an economic windfall. Over the years, Buffalo Bill's
Wild West journeyed across two continents, eating, entertaining,
and spreading money in its wake.

The first community to benefit from the presence of Buffalo
Bill's Wild West was Columbus, Nebraska, where in early May 1883
Cody and his business partner Doc Carver gathered and rehearsed
a troupe of cowboys, vaqueros, American Indians, and support
personnel, following Cody's vision of a show about the American
West. That first group, numbering around 120 people, spent a week
in Columbus, rehearsing the new show. Their presence made a

difference for a small town like Columbus, as hungry cast members sought out food and libations. Many gathered at Bucher's Saloon, which had opened seven years earlier. The saloon is known today as Glur's Tavern and is still in operation.[1]

Following the rehearsals, the show premiered in Omaha, Nebraska, on May 17. It received acclaim, and one newspaper observed that "the resources of the state and adjoining territories were taxed to their utmost to furnish materials." Those materials included wagons, a stagecoach, bucking horses, buffalo, and even several elk from Colorado. Provisions were also needed to feed the company and the livestock. It was an auspicious beginning to a wildly popular, yet financially unsatisfying, season. Neither Cody nor Carver was a good manager, and they parted company in the fall. Cody dropped Carver's name from the title, changing it to Buffalo Bill's Wild West and joined up with Nate Salsbury, who guided it to financial success.[2]

Providing food for the Wild West company was a big task, particularly as the show grew. Over time, in addition to purchasing food for the troupe, Buffalo Bill's Wild West added concession booths to feed the thousands in attendance. During the British tour of 1887, food and souvenir concessions were handled by the Wild West, with popcorn stands making as much as $500 per show. It was estimated that popcorn alone grossed $20,000 during the show's operation in Britain that year.[3]

As Buffalo Bill's Wild West traveled across Europe in the late 1880s and early 1890s, procurers for the show purchased local meats and produce, while businesses took advantage of the show's popularity. Reid's College Street Biscuit Factory in Glasgow sold "Buffalo Bill Cakes" throughout Great Britain. Restaurants in communities the Wild West visited encouraged attendees to stop for food before or after the show. While the Wild West was in Paris in 1889, it had a locally operated restaurant on site where visitors could dine. In Berlin, dining at the show was provided by three local restaurants. Since the show had no intermission, vendors from the Wild West also walked through the bleachers selling popcorn, peanuts, doughnuts, and cold lemonade.[4]

When the show returned to the United States in 1893, it set up at the Columbian Exposition in Chicago. During the six months there, it purchased supplies from vendors throughout the city. These included the Troy Bakery, Bremner Bakery, W. E. Aldrich and Company (another bakery), New York Biscuit Company, and Bryce Baking Company. Popcorn for the concessions was purchased from Columbia Pop Corn Works in quantities from four hundred to eight hundred bags per day. In addition to the popcorn and other concession items, the Wild West also offered visitors meals for fifty cents.[5]

Chicago was the center of America's meatpacking industry, which meant ample beef, pork, and mutton to feed the hungry performers. Chicken was the "crowning dish" each Sunday, with over four hundred fowl sacrificed for the occasion. The abundance of food at the Wild West was in marked contrast to the fare provided to many of the performers in the exposition's Midway Plaisance, including a group of American Indians who went on strike demanding a good square meal.[6]

The 1893 World's Columbian Exposition did bring significant food innovations to the American palate. For nearly a decade, the cooks at Buffalo Bill's Wild West had been making griddle cakes from scratch for breakfast, as had cooks all across the country. The first griddle cake mix, called Aunt Jemima's Pancake Flour, was introduced at the exposition and immediately became popular. Juicy Fruit gum premiered at the fair, as did Vienna Beef hot dogs. Pabst Beer received a blue ribbon, which became a trademark for the company, and Milton Hershey was inspired to move from the production of caramels to chocolate. Hershey sold his caramel division to the American Caramel Company, which promoted its products by including trading cards. In 1910 its Wild West trading card series included Buffalo Bill, Sitting Bull, and John Burke. Popcorn, which originated in the New World and had been served in its candied version all over Europe by Buffalo Bill's Wild West, was combined with peanuts and molasses and sold in a stand at the fair. Eventually the recipe was perfected, boxed, and sold as Cracker Jack. "Cracker Jack" was a slang term that referred to someone who had special athletic ability and was somewhat mischievous, symbolized by the boy on the box. Eventually the confectionery tents at Buffalo Bill's Wild West sold Cracker Jack rather than making their own candied popcorn (fig. 20).[7]

When the show was moving from town to town, spending only a day or two in each place, no effort was made to provide a restaurant on the grounds. But when it was in a single location for several weeks or months, as had been the case in Paris and Berlin, the show often included a restaurant. In 1893 the close proximity of the grounds to myriad restaurant options in Chicago, including the White and Coleman's Wigwam Restaurant across from the show entrance, did not discourage the Wild West from having its own restaurant. Cody contracted with restaurateur Charles E. Vankeuren to set up a restaurant on the grounds, with the Wild West receiving a quarter of the proceeds. A joint ticket was offered for $1, which included admission to the show and a full dinner.[8]

After 1893 Buffalo Bill's Wild West and Congress of Rough Riders of the World rarely stayed in any one place for more than a week, which led to the use of local restaurateurs. Once James Bailey became involved with the show, touring assumed a near breakneck pace, with the show arriving in a town and pitching its tents in the morning, doing an afternoon matinee and an evening performance, then taking everything down and traveling by railroad to the next place where the whole process was repeated. During the 1896 season the show traveled ten thousand miles and made 132 stops. Given this, the staff had barely enough time to erect the food tent for the employees, let alone a restaurant tent. On occasion, a local vendor might have erected a lunch tent, not unlike food booths at festivals today. Most often the only foods available on the premises were snacks from the show's confectionery tent or vendors in the stands. More substantial foods had to be obtained from local restaurants and cafés. A one-day visit in the small of town of Ottawa, Kansas, nearly overwhelmed local eating houses with "the throngs of people in to attend Buffalo Bill's Wild West show."[9]

Independent street vendors sometimes set up booths outside the grounds in an effort to capture business from people on their way to the show. During the show's 1895 appearance in Buffalo, vendors offered a variety of refreshments, from "red circus lemonade" and popcorn to "temperance" drinks and beer. Three years later a newspaper noted that New Yorkers at the show in Albany overindulged in "the intoxicating peanut and popcorn, and the contemplation of the lemonade when it was pink." Lemonade could be had in every color of the rainbow on these occasions, but red was the most popular with the crowds thronging to the Wild West. In 1899 a Bridgeport, Connecticut, newspaper observed that "all along State street the small boy had his peanut stand or red lemonade dispensary, and many colossal thirsts were quenched by the wayside."[10]

The Wild West had a large confectionery department; in 1896 it consisted of twelve employees plus a superintendent. That year the show purchased a variety of goods from the New York Confection Company, which catered specially to circuses, railroads, and other businesses, providing candies in sealed packages for easy transport and sale. Candy sales netted $491.95 between July 6 and 13. That income helped offset the $1,424.30 cost of feeding the company during the same period.[11]

When the show visited Madison Square Garden in 1897, one newspaper remarked that the evening shows were patronized by the city's "stellar lights in the world of fashion." Afterward, the fashionable New Yorkers moved on to "late suppers at Delmonico's and the Waldorf."[12]

In 1899 the show's route took it back to New York, New Jersey, then into New England. From there it headed to the midwestern states. William Langan said, "We buy all our provisions in the town where we show, and spend a pile of money in that way." In Long Branch, New Jersey, those provisions included a ton of ice, 210 dozen eggs at breakfast, and twenty bushels of potatoes. The Wild West purchased fifty pies, twenty-five dozen doughnuts, and 750 loaves of bread from Beihl's, a local bakery. Baked goods were critical to dining at Buffalo Bill's Wild West. Chace's Bakery, the largest in Fall River, Massachusetts, supplied 250 pies, forty dozen doughnuts, and seven hundred loaves of bread. In Fond du Lac, Wisconsin, Langan purchased pies, rolls, doughnuts, and three hundred pounds of bread from Jake Gerherdt's bakery. Sometimes a town did not have a bakery large enough to supply the show's

Fig 20. Confectionery vendors at Buffalo Bill's Wild West in front of the Cracker Jack tent in 1910. Object ID#2011.0029.26, Buffalo Bill Museum and Grave, Golden CO.

needs. Back in 1895, when the Wild West was in Wilmington, North Carolina, Mrs. E. Warren and Son, owners of the local Vienna bakery, provided the show with thirty-five hundred loaves of bread and then shipped another seven barrels of bread ahead to its next stop in Goldsboro.[13]

The Wild West tour of the northern tier of the country was unquestionably of great benefit for community after community, as each performance attracted thousands. At Winsted, Connecticut, "the population of the back country towns came in a body." Over two hundred people dined at the Winchester Hotel, the finest in town, while the other local hotels and restaurants were full. As one local remarked, "It was a great day for Winsted." Austin, Minnesota, another moderate-sized community, also experienced large crowds. Fifteen thousand people came to see Buffalo Bill's Wild West and Congress of Rough Riders of the World, filling the town's hotels, lunch counters, and restaurants. At least one dining establishment ran out of food, while downtown stores of all kinds were filled with shoppers. Some reported it was their largest business day in years, making it a "day of exceeding joy for all."[14]

"Buffalo Bill Makes Triumphal Entry" trumpeted a headline marking the beginning of the 1901 season in New York City. The mayor and Mark Twain, who was an enough of an enthusiast to name one of his cats Buffalo Bill, had box seats for the big opening at Madison Square Garden. New York businesses also rejoiced because the show's five hundred employees were expected to stay for nearly three weeks and spend weekly sums of $2,500 at local boardinghouses and hotels, $1,000 on feed for the show's horses, and $1,000 for "delicacies," presumably snacks and other foods. And those numbers did not include the daily outlay for feeding the entire company.[15]

By 1902 Buffalo Bill's Wild West souvenir programs, sold at the show for ten cents apiece, had grown to over eighty pages in length. Nearly twenty of those pages were occupied by advertisements, printed at the beginning and end of the informational content. Food products were prominent among them, including full-page ads for Curtice Brothers' Blue Label Tomato Catsup inside the front cover and Sen-Sen Gum on the outside back cover. The Sen-Sen ad pointed out that it was "pure and wholesome" and "positively the only gum sold with this exhibition." Smith Brothers Cough Drops and Sa-Yo Mint Jujubes "for coughs and throat irritations" were sold at the show for five cents per box, so no one would miss a moment of action due to a fit of coughing. After the show, anyone tired out by all the excitement could purchase Stored Energy bonbons at one of the stands for the slightly higher price of ten cents per box. And so that all the sweets eaten at the show did not lead to cavities, Dentacura toothpaste, "recommended by three thousand dentists," was also advertised in the program.[16]

Show attendees each received a free show program of several pages that listed the performances they would be seeing. The ten-cent souvenir programs, more substantial and usually printed in bulk before the season began, contained advertisements for products available nationally. The free programs, sometimes referred to as "tip-in" programs since they were also glued into the souvenir programs, were dominated by advertising because they were free with admission. These were produced for specific stops, with local ads. While the show was in Boston in 1902, the eight page tip-in program contained three full-page ads, including front and back covers, with over half of the rest of the pages touting a variety of products and services. One of the full-page ads was from the chain of Jayne's and Company Drug Stores in Boston, which offered everything from insect powders to Moxie cola. Albert J. Hogdon of Boston advertised Garrick Club Whiskey. That advertisement plus the ad for Old Crow and Scotch whiskeys in the larger souvenir program made it clear to the people of Boston that Cody was no temperance advocate, particularly not if it interfered with making a profit.[17]

At the end of 1902 the Wild West took off for Great Britain and Europe. Buffalo Bill's account book for the next year shows income from the candy stands ranging anywhere from seven to fourteen English pounds per day (taking inflation into account, fourteen English pounds in 1903 would be equivalent to $2,130 in 2020). A reporter in Bedford who visited on September 16 recorded that in the show stands, "vendors of programs, books of views, photographs, and American confections moved briskly to and fro, and shouted their wares." He reported that the show received 1,400 pounds of meat daily under a contract from Liverpool but that produce and other groceries came from local sources, having been arranged by an advance man from the show. Those included 700 pounds of potatoes and 300 pounds of other vegetables. He noted appreciatively that while he was visiting, a cart arrived at the show from a local bakery that was contracted to deliver 150 pounds of bread. The following year during a one-day stand in Gainesborough, England, the Granby Hotel received a contract from the show to provide refreshments on site. The hotel provided ales, spirits, sparkling water, and sandwiches to showgoers.[18]

Both free and souvenir programs for Buffalo Bill's Wild West continued to be dominated by advertising for the next decade. The 1907 free program for Chicago had two one-third-page ads for Berghoff's Brewing Company, offering "the real German beer which has no peer," as well as a one-third-page ad for Pabst Blue Ribbon beer. The Quaker Oats Company of Chicago covered most of another page. Aimed at specific populations, official programs could also cater to localized tastes. After Buffalo Bill's Wild West joined with Pawnee Bill's Far East, the official program for its 1909 appearances in Georgia held an ad for Red Snapper hot sauce from Memphis, something that probably would not have appealed to Chicago tastes at the time.[19]

The souvenir program produced for 1911 had full-color full-page ads for Baker's Chocolate and Pabst Blue Ribbon beer inside its front and back covers. Together with ads for automobiles, firearms, and Stetson hats were promotions for Heublein's Club Cocktails, Scotch Mints, A1 Sauce, and Cracker Jack. The ad for Cracker Jack noted that it was for sale at the show. In fact, it was placed prominently in the confectionery tent and pushed by vendors in the stands, as it was critical to the show's refreshment income. The canny combination of advertisements in programs with confectionery tents and vendors hawking their wares netted a good income for Buffalo Bill and Pawnee Bill. The sales of concessions, primarily confections, accounted for $19,855 in 1910 (the equivalent of $539,460 in 2020).[20]

The advertising in the 1912 souvenir program, titled *The Pioneer Scouts: A Book of Border Life*, did not just dominate the informational content but nearly overwhelmed it. The back cover was devoted to an ad for "the world's leading chewing gums," Sen-Sen, Adams, White's, Beeman's, and Chiclets, making clear that all were sold at the show's confectionery tent. Inside were advertisements for Sunshine Biscuits, Dubonnet liquors, chocolate popcorn Fluffs, Luden's Cough Drops, and two full pages devoted to Pabst Blue Ribbon beer. Ads also touted sparkling Vin Fiz grape drink, which was sold at the show. A Vin Fiz wagon was even part of show parades and parked on the grounds.[21]

The primary meat purveyor in Bisbee, Arizona, a vendor to the show in 1908, advertised in the local newspaper, "Buffalo Bill Cody is eating E. A. Tovrea & Co's. meats today. He took away all he could carry." It went on to say that he chose them because he had cultivated a taste for choice meats "from the Sioux lodges of the Little Bighorn to the incomparable cafes of Vienna and Paris." The year before, a silhouette of a well-dressed couple having cocktails, along with the Bismarck Restaurant and Hotel's address, was all the establishment felt it needed by way of advertisement in the free program. One of Chicago's best restaurants, the Bismarck offered fine dining, with such entrées as porterhouse steak and desserts including French pastries.

Cody ensured that his troupe received the finest meats and other foods for their meals and ate with them most of the time, but he also appreciated dining at restaurants. The Bismarck advertised with the show, so Cody undoubtedly ate there at least once during the two weeks in Chicago. He had cultivated a taste for fine dining on his first visit to New York City in 1872 and never lost that taste. Dining out was also his opportunity to pursue his many business interests and friendships.[22]

WEEKLY SUPPLY OF FOOD FOR BUFFALO BILL'S WILD WEST IN 1894

Beef, 5694 pounds; veal, 1250 pounds; mutton, 750 pounds; pork, 966 pounds; bacon 350 pounds; ham, 410 pounds; chicken, 820 pounds; bread, 2100 loaves; milk, 3260 quarts; ice, 10 tons; potatoes, 31 barrels; cabbage, 7 barrels; spinach, 9 barrels; onions, 8 barrels; eggs, 570 dozen; butter, 298 pounds; fish, 720 pounds; green peas, 2 barrels; succotash, 14 cases; sweet corns, 12 cases; string beans, 12 cases; buckwheat, 150 pounds; rice, 250 pounds; vinegar, 6 gallons; catsup, 15 gallons; Worcestershire sauce, 15 gallons; mustard, 15 gallons; pepper sauce, 3 dozen; jelly and jams, 220 pounds; condensed milk, 5 cases; pepper, 20 pounds; sugar, 3.5 barrels; salad oil, 5 gallons; crackers, 10 boxes; oatmeal, 60 pounds; lettuce, 250 heads; radishes, 250 bunches; young onions, 250 bunches; watercress, 2 barrels; sago, 20 pounds; farina, 15 pounds; tapioca, 25 pounds; lard, 200 pounds; olives, 4 gallons; horse radish, 4 dozen bottles; asparagus, 200 bunches; tea, 25 pounds; coffee, 225 pounds; salt, 100 pounds; pickles, 1.5 barrels; pickalilli, .5 barrel; mackerel, 1 barrel; pig's feet, 1 barrel; flour, 4 barrels; cornmeal, 200 pounds; syrup, 10 gallons; pies, 500; cheese, 3 American dairy, 10 Edam, and 1 Gruyere.

"Buffalo Bill's Steward: His Taste of Fare Is Suited to the Tastes of All Nations," *New York Times*, August 26, 1894

14

Dining Out with William F. Cody and Friends

> Buffalo Bill was at lunch the other day, together with John
> Willis, my old hunter. Buffalo Bill has always been a great friend
> of mine. I remember when I was running for Vice-President I
> struck a Kansas town just when the Wild West show was there.
> He got upon the rear platform of my car and made a brief
> speech on my behalf.
>
> President Theodore Roosevelt, 1904

Buffalo Bill was also William F. Cody. While his nickname and his
given name were often used interchangeably, they reflected two
different personas. A writer in 1898 observed, "Talk about Dr. Jekyll
and Mr. Hyde! You ought to know Buffalo Bill and Col. William F.
Cody. They are one and the same person, but their personalities are
as different as March and May." Buffalo Bill was a frontiersman and
entertainer, while William F. Cody was an influencer and captain
of industry. The dual roles allowed him to interact freely with the
movers and shakers of his day. Buffalo Bill wore buckskins, made
and colorfully decorated by American Indians, whereas William
F. Cody wore fine suits, made by the most skilled tailors of the day.
Twice while he was in London, he purchased bespoke suits from
Henry Poole and Company on Savile Row. With such a wardrobe
to draw on, he dressed in either buckskins or a suit, depending
on the circumstances.[1]

Buffalo Bill Cody moved from tents to hotels as easily as he
changed outfits. He often said that he stayed in his tent because
he enjoyed being on the show grounds with his men. But as he
aged, that sentiment changed. Already forty-one years old when
the show was in London in 1887, Cody preferred to spend nights
in his room at the Hotel Metropole rather than in the tent erected

for him. A year later, while awaiting the show's opening at Erastina on Staten Island, he stayed at the Hoffman House, one of the finest lodging establishments in New York City. A decade later William F. Cody was back at the Hoffman House, while Buffalo Bill was found at Madison Square Garden when performing. From that point on, Cody stayed exclusively at the Hoffman House whenever the show was in town. After the press interviews and the evening show were over, he left the grounds and spent the night on a nice bed rather than a cot.[2]

When the show was on the road, his private train car, which had a sleeper, became his more frequent place of lodging, although he still spent nights in hotels or his tent during extended stays in larger cities. Since the show frequently moved from one engagement to another during the night, sleepers were a necessity for the entire staff. Even while on the road, when he spent one day in a town and then moved on, he was able to switch personas, emerging from his private car as Buffalo Bill or as William F. Cody, depending on what was needed. Fortunately, both personas allowed him to indulge in fine dining, whether it was supplied by the show's cooks while he was in camp or by chefs at restaurants.

Throughout each year, execution of his business activities required attendance at myriad social events, parties, and dinners. And for William Cody, sans the show business mantle of Buffalo Bill, that meant fine dining. Whenever he left the Wild West to dine, it was noted in the social pages of the newspapers. Those occasions were most frequently banquets thrown in his honor. On July 10, 1885, the Philadelphia Herd of the Beneficial Order of Buffaloes hosted the members of the company at a dinner in Cody's honor at the Belmont Mansion, where the evening began with "bumpers of beer." Later, wines were the featured beverages at an 1887 banquet honoring Cody at London's United Arts Club, with Moët brut champagne, white Rhine wine from Rüdesheim, claret, and sherry. John Burke, Nate Salsbury, Lakota Chief Red Shirt, Broncho Bill, and the show's announcer, Frank Richmond, accompanied Cody to that event. He sat between actor Henry Irving and his host, Captain C. A. Thimm, a British military man and fencing enthusiast.[3]

William F. Cody and Nate Salsbury were honored guests at many banquets and dinner parties during the 1893 World's Columbian Exposition in Chicago. The American Newspaper Publishers Association visited Buffalo Bill's Wild West Camp for the afternoon and evening performances, then Cody and Salsbury attended the organization's farewell dinner at Kinsley's restaurant. Herbert M. Kinsley was considered Chicago's leading restaurateur and had assisted exposition organizer Daniel Burnham with restaurant logistics for the fair. Since the dinner was sponsored by a publisher's association, each item on the menu was accompanied by a newspaper quotation. The offerings included consommé, planked whitefish, fillet of beef, broiled snipe, and a salad of lettuce and tomatoes. For drinks the menu had a variety of wines and Roman punch. Dessert was rainbow-colored ice cream in the shape of a newsboy clasping a bundle of newspapers under his arm. Three years later Cody returned to Kinsley's restaurant for a meal with the Fellowship Club, an organization of sixty leading citizens of Chicago. He was invited by Melville Stone, newspaper publisher and general manager of the Associated Press, who assured him that the club's dinners "have unquestionably been the finest ever given in the West." Having dined at Kinsley's during the exposition, Cody doubtless agreed.[4]

Over the years after his first tongue-tied words onstage in 1872, Buffalo Bill Cody evolved as a public speaker, going from actor to orator. After his early colorful interviews for newspapers, it was only a matter of time before he was asked to provide his thoughts as a guest at banquets. When he spoke at a banquet in his honor in North Platte in 1886, the local newspaper noted, "Mr. Cody has somehow acquired the art of talking, and his eloquent description of his Wild West was a drama of itself." He was particularly adept at toasts, which often turned into testimonials. At a banquet for his friend Major General Nelson A. Miles, he spoke emphatically that as long as Miles remained commander of the U.S. Army, "no foreign invader would ever set foot on American soil." He concluded by saying to Miles, "If they do, just write to me." The comment elicited laughter from the other banquet guests, which included

Vice President Adlai Stevenson. One newspaper covering the event observed, "Col. Cody is no mean orator."[5]

Consequently, as America entered a new century, Cody was sought out not only as a banquet guest but also as a speaker. He was asked to talk about a wide range of topics, from his early experiences in the West to current events. When Buffalo Bill's Wild West was in New York City during May 1902, Cody hosted a dinner at the Hoffman House. The guest of honor was Broadway actress Lulu Glaser. During the dinner, Cody gave a brief speech, informing his guests that he was "the largest farmer in Uncle Sam's domains" and describing the agricultural developments he was overseeing in Wyoming's Bighorn Basin. Six years earlier he had been instrumental in founding the Bighorn Basin town of Cody, named after him. Another banquet that month included Bighorn Basin celery and beefsteak from Buffalo Bill's TE Ranch near Cody.[6]

In 1913 William F. Cody helped organize the Showmen's League of America and became its first president at a meeting of two hundred people in Chicago's Saratoga Hotel. Today the Showmen's League is still in operation. It maintains a cemetery in Chicago, provides scholarships for students interested in the amusement business, and is involved in a variety of other charitable activities. A month after it was organized, the league held its first annual convention, at Hotel La Salle in Chicago, with a concluding banquet. The La Salle's main hall was transformed into a "big top" with a brightly decorated marquee at the room's entrance and sawdust scattered on the floor. Waiters scurried about in circus outfits, while a circus band played and vaudeville entertainers kept the guests amused. Each attendee received a souvenir menu decorated with western scenes and an image of the evening's guest of honor, Buffalo Bill. The dinner began with Manhattan cocktails, Blue Point oysters in cocktail sauce, and relishes. The soup course was lobster bisque, and the fish course was baked halibut in an Italian sauce with pommes Parisienne, which were typically sprinkled with parsley. These were followed by sweetbreads wrapped in bacon and new peas. Chicken cooked in sauterne with watercress and a romaine salad with oranges completed the main courses. Dessert was ice cream with petit fours and mignardises (miniature tarts), truffles, macarons, and other small sweets. The meal finished, guests received white rock candy demitasse sticks to enjoy while Buffalo Bill regaled them with tales of his life in the Old West.[7]

When William Cody met Thomas Edison in Paris in 1889, they cemented a relationship over a bountiful breakfast/luncheon that proved mutually beneficial. Throughout his career, similar dining experiences played a huge role in connecting him with the movers and shakers of his day. When Buffalo Bill's Wild West played in New Haven, Connecticut, on March 31, 1895, one of the spectators in the audience was an old friend he had first met on the western plains of Nebraska. Professor O. C. Marsh was a paleontologist who aided in founding the Peabody Museum and competed with Professor Edward Cope in the infamous "Bone Wars" of the late nineteenth century. Marsh met Cody on his first foray onto the fossil-laden fields of the Great Plains in 1871. Buffalo Bill was supposed to guide him but was called away for several skirmishes with the Lakotas. They did have several hours together before Buffalo Bill had to depart, during which time Marsh entertained him with "yarns" about the dinosaurs. Cody later wrote that those stories "seemed too complicated and mysterious to be believed by an ordinary man like myself." But he was clearly impressed with Marsh's knowledge.[8]

That first meeting was significant to Cody, who met Marsh again while visiting New York City for the first time in 1872. He traveled from the city to New Haven, where the professor threw a reception and dinner at the Tontine Hotel, one of the finest establishments in the city. Buffalo Bill had recently turned down an offer to play himself at the Bowery Theatre, but the two still discussed the idea of touring a show about the American frontier. One year later Cody invited Marsh to see him perform in *Scouts of the Prairie* at New Haven's Music Hall. Marsh gave Cody and his fellow actors, including Texas Jack and Ned Buntline, a tour of Yale. In January 1874 Buffalo Bill and Wild Bill Hickok joined Marsh for another meal at the Tontine Hotel while performing in town. Since all three were accomplished storytellers, the meal must have been as entertaining as Cody and Marsh's first meeting in 1871.[9]

Cody and Marsh missed each other when the Combination returned to New Haven again in December. Cody sent Marsh a letter in which he stated that he had left an $80 check with the night clerk at his hotel in repayment of a loan the professor had made to him. That amount would be over $1,800 in today's dollars, suggesting it was no small loan and had certainly been helpful to Buffalo Bill's Combination in its first year. Cody also wrote that he hoped to repay Marsh's kindness someday. It was twenty years before he returned to New Haven, this time with Buffalo Bill's Wild West and Congress of Rough Riders of the World on March 31, 1894. Cody hosted Marsh and some of his Yale colleagues at the show, giving the professor a chance to see that his loan at a critical time in Cody's career had been the foundation for a great project. Marsh died in 1899. When the show returned to New Haven in 1902, a local newspaper noted that Marsh had encouraged Cody's efforts to reproduce the Old West and that when Buffalo Bill came to visit, it had always been a special day for the professor.[10]

William Cody's interests included art, and he considered himself a patron. Over the years, he purchased a variety of paintings of the West, which he exhibited in his homes and business properties. Artists Paul Gauguin and Edvard Munch attended Buffalo Bill's Wild West, and Cody had friendships with other well-known artists as well. Most notable among these were Frederic Remington, Albert Bierstadt, Rosa Bonheur, and James McNeill Whistler. Before Buffalo Bill's Wild West opened in London in 1887, Whistler joined Cody and Nate Salsbury in the Drury Lane Theatre's royal box. Best known for his portraiture, most notably what is commonly known as *Whistler's Mother*, the American artist also painted scenes. He later did a sketch of Buffalo Bill's Wild West. Whistler and writer Oscar Wilde, once friends, had a falling out so severe that Wilde included a murdered artist based on Whistler in his novel *The Picture of Dorian Gray*. Cody, who later had dinner with Whistler and tea with Wilde, managed to maintain a friendship with both. That year Whistler even asked Cody if he could paint his portrait.[11]

Whistler never got around to painting Cody, but when the show returned to London in 1892, the two were present at a gala banquet given in honor of American deputy consul general E. J. Moffat.

Moffat was returning to the States after ten years in the position to work with his father, David Moffat, a Denver businessman and railroad magnate. The guest list reads like a *Who's Who* of Americans in London, including Whistler. Held at London's Hotel Metropole, where Cody had resided five years earlier, the event had a menu featuring a similarly notable list of French foods and fine wines. Each course was carefully paired with an appropriate wine. After assorted hors d'oeuvres, the soup course of consommé with lettuce was accompanied by a dry sherry. A white Rhine wine from Rüdesheim followed with the fish course of salmon in hollandaise sauce. Cutlets of wild pigeon and sweetbreads with cucumbers were next. The diners cleansed their palates with a Neapolitan sorbet and an 1884 dry champagne from Max Sutaine and Company, then tucked into mutton and ham in Madeira sauce, this time with Bollinger and Company champagne. Quail on fried slices of bread, petite peas in butter, and potatoes in a Roman-style sweet-and-sour gravy were then served with salad. Desserts included molded gelatin with Montmorency cherries and various fruits in gelatin, Scottish shortbread, an ice cream bombe with hazelnuts, and fondant cake, along with various liqueurs. The evening's toasts to Moffat by those in attendance were made with Château Leoville wine and Cockburn's Old Bottled Port.[12]

Albert Bierstadt and William Cody discovered they had a lot in common while dining together. Each was trying to capture the essence of the American West and give it substance. For Cody, it was through performance, and for Bierstadt, it was on canvas. They were both fascinated by the Yellowstone area and supported efforts to preserve it. And they shared a concern for the buffalo. Cody transported and exhibited the large mammals and called for their preservation. He wrote in 1883 that their decimation on the plains had "been criminally large and useless." Bierstadt depicted the buffalo in his paintings and also spoke out for their preservation. Given their mutual interests, their friendship was inevitable.[13]

Bierstadt said that he met Cody and became a friend while attending Buffalo Bill's Wild West during its appearances at Erastina on Staten Island in 1888. He was working on a new painting of a buffalo hunt and took a sketch box to the show. The show's buffalo and its Lakota members became his models for the painting. That summer Buffalo Bill hosted Bierstadt for a "towatapee," a Lakota term for "good eat," at the Wild West camp, where he ate rib roast, roast corn, pickles, and pumpkin pie.[14]

That fall Bierstadt completed his buffalo hunt painting, *The Last of the Buffalo.* The next spring it was sent to Paris, where, even though it was rejected for exhibit in the American art pavilion at the Exposition Universelle, it appeared in several galleries during the fair. Bierstadt shipped the painting to Paris and then stood at the dock in New York to wave goodbye to Cody and members of the show as they departed for France on the *Persian Monarch.* In Paris the Lakotas with Cody's show made a point of visiting the painting, which reminded them of their homeland. Rocky Bear, who had attended the towatapee, went to see the painting several times and later stated that Bierstadt had "given breath and life to the glorious past of the redskin and to the buffalo." Buffalo Bill also took famous French artist Rosa Bonheur to see Bierstadt's painting. Before that, she had corresponded with Bierstadt and received several sketches of buffalo from him.[15]

Buffalo Bill's Wild West figured prominently in Rosa Bonheur's work during 1889. Well known for her depictions of animals, Bonheur was a popular artist throughout France. The same fascination with the animals of the American West that led her to write Albert Bierstadt also drew her to the Wild West. She visited the show repeatedly, as often as four times a week, to sketch and paint what she saw. Bonheur found herself captivated by both the animals and humans who were part of the show and later remarked, "It's unbelievable how I get the old fire back when my pencil brings to life those thrilling scenes." She created more than fifty sketches and paintings, including depictions of Buffalo Bill and Rocky Bear on horseback. Bonheur later invited Lakota performers Rocky Bear and Red Shirt to breakfast at a restaurant in the Bois de Boulogne. She frequently lunched with Buffalo Bill and his staff while at the show, and she hosted Cody at her château outside of Paris, taking him out to the Hôtel de France in Fontainebleau for lunch. They then visited the famed Château de Fontainebleau, former residence of French kings, where they strolled through the gardens. She gave Buffalo Bill her painting of him, which ended up in his home, and he used it to promote the Wild West. It remains one of her most famous works. After the Wild West left Paris, one newspaper observed that "Buffalo Bill and Rosa Bonheur have become great friends."[16]

Another great friend of Buffalo Bill's was Frederic Remington. In 1889 Calhoun Printing Company borrowed several illustrations by Remington for posters it created to promote the Wild West in Paris. Cody and Remington finally met in London in 1892, when the artist was on assignment to write an illustrated article about Buffalo Bill's Wild West. Both were as enthusiastic about food as they were about the West, and they dined together that summer. The article was published in *Harper's Weekly* and helped propel Remington's career upward as well as promote Cody's show. Recognizing Remington's growing reputation in the States, Cody reprinted the article in his 1894 program. For several years the Wild West's publicity department also ensured that a portion of the article was distributed to local newspapers before the show's arrival. Remington again visited Buffalo Bill's Wild West that year, creating a set of illustrations for *Harper's Weekly*. While working on the illustrations, which provided a behind-the-scenes look at the show, he received a thorough tour of the grounds at Ambrose Park and posed with Cody, Salsbury, and other members of the show for a group photo. In August he wrote to invite Salsbury and Cody to join him for dinner at New Rochelle. The collaborations continued, with Cody providing the preface and Remington doing the illustrations for a history of the Santa Fe Trail by their friend Colonel Henry Inman. After the book was published in 1897, Inman went with Cody on a monthlong trip into Yellowstone and environs, later remarking that they ate "grub fit for a king."[17]

Following the trip with Inman, Cody asked Remington to create illustrations for a biography written about him by his sister Helen. Later, an image of Buffalo Bill from one of the illustrations was used for the cover of the 1900 Wild West program (fig. 21). In 1899 Buffalo Bill also arranged a trip for Mr. and Mrs. Remington to the town of Cody, where they dined and danced with the Cody family, though Buffalo Bill was on tour and unable to participate in the visit. Remington thanked him with a painting, *Portrait of a Rancher*, done during the visit. That year the artist was also commissioned to paint a battle scene backdrop for the show. Later, while performing in New York City in 1902, Nate Salsbury threw a special dinner for a small group of friends in the Wild West's dining room at Madison Square Garden. The menu, called the Grub Pile, was signed by everyone present, including Cody and Remington. The feast was sumptuous, with "tender prime rib," "toothsome roasts," lamb, fish, and fowl. Bent's Water Crackers, ever popular with the Wild West cast, accompanied Roquefort cheese just before a jelly roll dessert. Everything was washed down with coffee and "wet goods galore." In 1907, while his show was appearing in Brooklyn, Cody and his daughter Irma had lunch with Remington. The following year Remington visited the town of Cody in late summer but once again missed Buffalo Bill. Cody wrote to his friend George Beck, requesting that he make sure there was plenty of whiskey on hand because Remington and the men accompanying him were "good steady drinkers."[18]

One of Buffalo Bill's other artistic associations, while imaginative, proved less fruitful, In 1908 Buffalo Bill and the Wild West cast visited Philadelphia's famous Wanamaker's department store, where they posed for a group photograph. They were there at the request of Rodman Wanamaker, the owner and son of the store's founder. Wanamaker later financed several photographic expeditions to the West to document American Indian life. A motion picture from the 1909 expedition included footage of Buffalo Bill's Wild West. Following a viewing of the motion picture at Wanamaker's New York City store, Cody, in evening dress, and Lakota chief Iron Shell, dressed in his own Native finery, were hosted at a banquet in Sherry's restaurant. There Rodman Wanamaker introduced a large gathering of politicians, military men, and other influential people, including Frederic Remington, to his new plan. He proposed to erect a statue of an Indian in New York Harbor, near the Statue of Liberty and equally large. Following dinner, Cody was invited to be the first speaker on behalf of the project. He said that he could think of no more fitting tribute to "the first Americans— the Indians—than a statue in the harbor with arms outstretched," welcoming the world. The other speaker at the event was General Nelson Miles, who also paid tribute to the Indians, then concluded with a brief accolade to Cody. Miles said that Cody not only knew the Indians better than any other man but also "knew where the best grass, water and whisky could be had."[19]

Nearly a year later, a bill enabling the creation of the statue was introduced to Congress. It was to be sculpted by Daniel Chester French, who later created the statue of Lincoln in the Lincoln Memorial. The Indian statue would be placed atop a museum situated on a bluff on Staten Island, overlooking the harbor. Not enough funds were gathered, however, and the project was abandoned.[20]

Having served with the military and made his reputation as a scout, Buffalo Bill frequently dined with old friends from those days. Like Cody, they had moved up in the world. Charles King was a lieutenant when he and Cody first met at Fort McPherson in 1871. They often went on hunts together, where they formed a fast friendship. An injury forced King to retire from the army in 1879, and he took up writing, becoming well known. He devoted some of his writing to reminiscences of his service during the Indian Wars and continued his interest in the military. That interest led to his becoming a general in the Wisconsin National Guard. On August 22, 1899, Buffalo Bill stepped away from the show to have dinner with King at the Chicago Press Club. Over sandwiches and beer, the two reminisced about their experiences on the plains almost thirty years earlier, while members of the club listened in. Not coincidentally, a reporter for the *Milwaukee Journal* witnessed their dinner together. The story of their meeting ended up in that paper the next day. It wound up being an effective promotion for a visit by Buffalo Bill's Wild West to Milwaukee six days later. Human interest stories about Buffalo Bill swapping tales of the Old West with old and new friends were always fodder for publicity.[21]

General Nelson Miles was another friend with whom Buffalo Bill had served during the Indian Wars. Cody and Miles shared not just friendship but also confidence in each other, so it was natural that Cody was asked to be one of the speakers at a banquet in Miles's honor. The event was held on January 31, 1896, at the Chamberlin Hotel in Washington DC, considered the best hotel

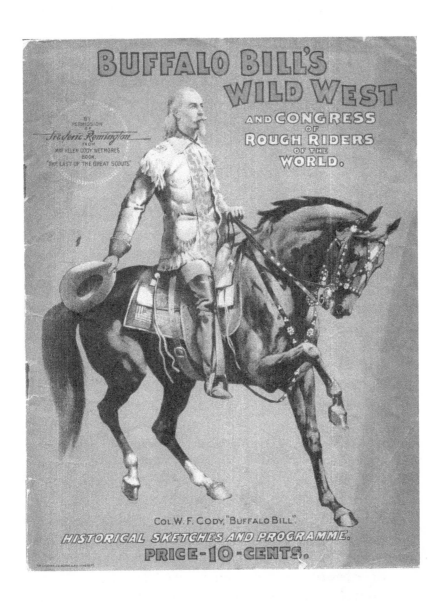

Fig 21. Painting by artist Frederic Remington on the cover of the show's 1900 program. Buffalo Bill, the subject of several Remington paintings, cemented his fifteen-year friendship with the artist over lunches, dinners, and drinks. Author's collection.

in the city and an oasis of fine dining. Among the attendees were Washington politicians, including Vice President Adlai Stevenson, and a number of retired military men, most of whom were known to Cody. The hotel belonged to John Chamberlin, a noted hotelier, restaurateur, and gourmet who was referred to as "the Napoleon of epicures" and set a sumptuous table.[22]

The dining table was decorated with red and white roses, while Indian headdresses, tomahawks, and a shield made of buffalo hide hung on the walls. The meal started at 8:00 p.m. with Blue Point oysters and crab bisque, accompanied by Spanish oloroso sherry and Johannisberg riesling kabinett, a white wine from the Rhine. Chicken croquettes with a cream and truffle sauce, relishes, potato croquettes, and saddle of mutton followed. The wine for that course was Mumm's extra dry champagne. Dishes prepared with terrapin, or turtles, were quite popular at the time, and the next course included Terrapin à la Chamberlin and cold asparagus points. "Marschino," or maraschino, punch, a cold fruit drink, was offered as a palate cleanser. Served in hollowed-out oranges, maraschino punches were all the rage at luncheons and dinner parties in the 1890s. With cleansed palates and unsated appetites, the guests then turned to the main course, roast capon stuffed with truffles, along with roasted potatoes. The wine for the main course was from the Château du Clos de Vougeot, a vineyard in Burgundy with origins in the twelfth century and still in operation. The dessert course followed, with sliced Smithfield ham, lettuce salad, rum omelets, Camembert and Stilton cheeses, assorted liquors, and coffee. A newspaper observed that the meal was "prepared under the personal direction of Chamberlin himself." It was one of his last magnificent dinners; he passed away eight months later. Chamberlin's obituary included William F. Cody among the friends who would miss him and his hospitality.[23]

Cody's first dinner with a president was in 1873, when he was invited to the White House for a meal with President Ulysses Grant. Over the years he got to know Presidents Grover Cleveland, Benjamin Harrison, William McKinley, Theodore Roosevelt, and William Taft. In 1889 he hosted Harrison's son Russell for a breakfast in Paris, where "baked beans, with the flavor of savory pork, corn bread, custard pie and ice cream" were served, as well as other American and French dishes. The meal concluded with many toasts. Cody counted Theodore Roosevelt among his friends, and Roosevelt wrote after a lunch together in 1904, "Buffalo Bill has always been a great friend of mine." Cody reinforced that friendship by supporting Roosevelt's candidacy for vice president and speaking out on behalf of his efforts to create national forests, parks, and other preserves.[24]

From that fateful day in 1872 when he received a standing ovation at the play about himself at the Bowery Theatre, Cody's star was ascendant. Each new venture added to his celebrity. As his Buffalo Bill persona became one of the best-known figures of his time, William F. Cody found himself an influencer. His opinions on current issues were sought out and could be read in the newspapers. He was able to speak out about things that mattered to him, like women's and Indians' rights and conservation. The dinner table also became a forum where he could trade ideas with the influential people of his day, including artists, military figures, captains of industry, and even presidents.

15

Meanwhile, Back at the Ranch

> When Colonel Cody is playing in big luck, his ranch is a cen-
> ter of lavish and even reckless hospitality. Away out there on
> the frontier, senators and members of congress tell us they
> have seen banquets and wine suppers which even the Chinese
> legation in Washington would never attempt to outdo.
>
> *Wilkes-Barre Times Leader*, 1893

In 1905, after a particularly grueling season traveling across France
ended in Marseille, an exhausted Cody returned to the United States
just in time for Christmas. He stopped in Chattanooga, Tennessee,
for Christmas dinner at Fort Oglethorpe with his daughter Irma;
her husband, Second Lieutenant Clarence Stott; and members of
the Twelfth Cavalry. The mess hall was decorated with evergreens
and a "gaily decorated Christmas tree, illuminated by small wax
candles." The meal featured roast turkey with oyster dressing, pork
loin, baked fish, and a most unusual entrée, roast possum. Fifty
people enjoyed the Christmas repast, and a good time was had by
all. Cody then resumed his journey back to the West to spend time
with the rest of his family and friends.[1]

When each show season ended, everyone went home to their
families or worked at other jobs until the next season began. Buffalo Bill packed away his buckskins and became Will Cody. As a
leading businessman and celebrity, he continued dining with the
people who were influential in his day. But much of his time was
spent on and around his properties in the West, where he could
also unwind and hunt.

During his first years with the Wild West, Buffalo Bill's off-season
destination was North Platte, Nebraska. There he would relax at
his ranch, which he named Scout's Rest, or at his house in town,

called the Welcome Wigwam. He had roots in North Platte, having worked as a scout at nearby Fort McPherson when the town got its start, and had made many trips to the growing community. Even though he was on the road most of the time, it was the only place he could truly call home, and after briefly settling his family in West Chester, Pennsylvania, and then Rochester, New York, he returned to North Platte for good.

The Cody family's first house in North Platte was the Welcome Wigwam, built in 1878. Around the same time, Buffalo Bill invested in a ranching operation near the Dismal River. During roundups to the property, he always made sure to have a wagon filled with liquid refreshments "as antidotes against snake bites and other accidents." When the liquor ran out, he promptly sent the wagon into town for replenishments. He kept that ranch until 1882, by which time he had invested in land nearer to North Platte. That became his Scout's Rest Ranch, and he built a house on it in 1886. There he had a herd of 125 Herefords, Angus, and other breeds of cattle. He also raised Thoroughbred horses. The ranch house was later remodeled, adding a larger kitchen plus a main dining room and a dining room for the hired hands. The large dining room was accessed from the kitchen through a twenty-two-foot hallway that served as a butler's pantry, with all sorts of china, silver, and glassware. After the first Welcome Wigwam burned, Cody used some of the income from the 1893 World's Columbian Exposition to acquire a much larger house in town, which the family also called the Welcome Wigwam. It was reported that the house had "a well-filled larder, choice cigars for the male guests and a wine cellar stocked from the vineyards of the old and the new worlds." Sharing space in the wine cellar were fine French champagnes and "dew drop" (whiskey) from Kentucky.[2]

By 1886 William F. "Buffalo Bill" Cody had become both North Platte's and Nebraska's most famous son. After the show closed at Erastina that September and before it opened at Madison Square Garden in November, he visited Nate Salsbury in Chicago, and the two went to the theater. Then he traveled on to North Platte for a hero's welcome. Upon arrival at the train depot on the morning of October 6, he was met by "about every man and boy and many of the ladies" plus a brass band. He was then taken by friends to the Pacific Hotel and treated to breakfast. The town's grandest welcome, however, was reserved for that evening, when eighty of the town's leading citizens gathered again at the Pacific Hotel for a banquet in Cody's honor.[3]

The banquet began shortly after 9:00 p.m., when local lawyer and former Nebraska state senator Beach Hinman kicked off the evening with a speech of welcome and a toast, for which everyone stood and downed glasses of Mumm's extra dry champagne. Cody's response included the statement that the men of the West "who made this wilderness blossom like the rose, deserve a place in the memory of this mighty nation." Since he was not performing with the show and not bound by his promise of temperance to Nate Salsbury, Cody felt free to imbibe to his heart's content at the banquet. He often did this on his visits to North Platte. But this fondness for alcohol, acquired during his scouting days, eventually came to haunt him.[4]

North Platte was a major center of operations for the Union Pacific during the laying of the transcontinental railroad and remains so today. Any goods that moved on the Union Pacific, from east to west and vice versa, were available to the town. The banquet therefore had food and drink equal to that served in any major city in the United States. After enjoying a generous feast, guests were served more Mumm's champagne, California angelica, port, Catawba, sherry, brandy, and Otard cognac. The evening festivities, including more toasts and speechmaking, did not conclude until 1:30 a.m.[5]

That morning was the opening of the Lincoln County Fair, one of the reasons Cody had chosen to return home at that particular time. Perhaps still a bit bleary-eyed from the festivities, yet happy to be home, Cody walked around the fairgrounds, shaking hands and greeting old friends. His new house at Scout's Rest Ranch was completed, and before leaving North Platte for Denver the next day, he had a reception there for many of those friends. When he returned from his business in Denver, he attended an "elegant reception" given by some friends and then cohosted forty guests at a gala birthday party for his niece at the new house on the ranch, now managed by his sister Julia and her husband. The party featured a "superb supper," dancing to waltzes and other music provided by an orchestra, and the presentation of birthday gifts. When he left for New York City several days later, it was the last that North Platte saw of him for quite a while. After the show closed at Madison Square Garden, it was loaded onto the *State of Nebraska* and everyone went to London, where the Wild West took part in the American Exhibition of 1887.[6]

The show was immensely successful in London, but Cody did not make a triumphant return to North Platte in 1888. Instead, he went to New York, where he remained while the Wild West made a return appearance at Erastina, then traveled to other locations on the East Coast. While in Washington DC, he also took seventy-five of the show's Lakotas to meet with President Cleveland. Following that, the Lakotas returned to Pine Ridge, and Bill finally went home to Nebraska, where he stayed for the next two months. It was November and fully two years after his previous visit. He made a tongue-in-cheek statement to the *Lincoln Evening Call*, saying, "I am going to my home in North Platte to be introduced to and cultivate the acquaintance of my family, not having seen them in nearly two years." He also announced that he would be going to France for the next season. He was not greeted by welcome home celebrations on his return, but Cody hosted a group of friends at Scout's Rest for a rib roast similar to those he had thrown in England. Not long after that, he attended a dinner in his honor in Wallace, Nebraska. Other guests included several English lords who were visiting and had probably first met Cody while he was in London. The meal featured a whole roasted pig and baked beans.[7]

For next several decades, North Platte was Buffalo Bill's main base of operation between show seasons. From there, it was easy for him to travel on the Union Pacific to all parts of the continent. North Platte was also a good jumping-off point for hunting expeditions on the Great Plains and in the Rockies. Invariably, when he returned home, he was greeted with much the same enthusiasm as he had experienced in 1886. His generosity may also have been a factor in that enthusiasm, as he made donations to everything from local churches to civic organizations like the town band. At the town's saloons, he frequently provided free drinks for everyone present, and he threw generous parties at the Welcome Wigwam and Scout's Rest Ranch.

In 1893 one newspaper observed that when Cody was feeling flush and happy, his North Platte ranch became "a center of lavish and even reckless hospitality." He would also ride into town, "asking everybody to accompany him to the best bar in town and setting up the wine for all hands." Members of the community later recounted how Cody "used to have a public reception upon his return from a season on the road. Everyone was invited to the reception and the supper, preachers, gamblers, society folk—everyone went, for it was a community affair." Buffalo Bill's generosity became almost legendary in Nebraska, and he rarely visited without spreading his money around. At least once he did this quite literally, scattering coins in the street for local children from two half-bushel containers as he walked through town. On another occasion, during a trip to Omaha, he ran into some old friends and treated them to a meal at Maure's, one the city's more expensive restaurants, then took them on a shopping trip where he bought them silk handkerchiefs. He even bought a fine coat for one of the friends. Back in North Platte, he frequently took his daughter Irma to the Keliher Ice Cream Parlor, where he would buy her a box of their finest candy. If any other girls or women happened to be in the shop, he would treat them to candy as well.[8]

Buffalo Bill's Wild West visited North Platte several times. The first visit was on October 12, 1896, for a state Irrigation Fair, sponsored by North Platte and celebrating the progress in irrigation throughout the state. Even though he expected to lose income, Cody's affection for the town, as well as a growing interest in irrigation projects, led him to offer the Wild West as an attraction at the fair. Out of gratitude, and probably capitalizing on Cody's fame, the town had a life-size marble statue created of Cody to stand at the fair's entrance to welcome visitors. When he arrived in town, 2,500 people were waiting at the depot to greet him. The fair was a rousing success, with 19,200 in attendance at the afternoon and evening Wild West performances. When a group of cowboys, in town for the fair and the show, rode up to Guy Laing's saloon, Buffalo Bill joined them, laying $200 on the bar and ordering drinks for everyone. The visit turned out better than he could ever have imagined, with no loss in income at all. He returned with the Wild West two years later.[9]

Three days before that return, another big Nebraska tribute was given to Bill Cody at the Trans-Mississippi Exposition in Omaha, when August 31, 1898, was declared Cody Day and united him with many of his old friends. Nebraska senator John Thurston opened the day with a brief speech. Thurston was followed by Alexander Majors, co-founder of the Pony Express and Cody's first boss back during the early days in Kansas. Cody responded, noting, "In all of my wanderings I have kept the flag of our beloved State unfurled to every breeze from the Platte to the Danube, from the Tiber to the Clyde." Dexter Fellows, a press agent for the Wild West, later remarked that it was one of the happiest days of Cody's life. Fellows wrote, "It was a big day, fat with oratory, but the night was bigger with food and drink." Cody hosted Majors, Thurston, five governors of Nebraska, and other Nebraska celebrities at Markel's Café in Omaha for dinner, followed by wine, champagne, whiskey, cigars, and tale telling.[10]

Despite his affection and longtime attachment to North Platte, Buffalo Bill never opened any businesses there and invested little money in the community other than his donations. It was no longer the wilderness of open spaces he had first known. He said, "Down in Nebraska, there is nothing now but farms and damned barb-wire fences." He wanted to be nearer to the wild places he had loved his whole life. During conversations with his friend O. C. Marsh, who had led paleontological expeditions into Wyoming's Bighorn Basin between Sheridan and Yellowstone, Cody learned of the basin's geology. The area had fertile soil and mineral riches, and it offered excellent hunting in the Bighorn Mountains to the east and Absaroka Mountains to the west. Increasingly, his interest and his money were drawn to that region. It was an area that was ripe for development, and Bill Cody decided to stake his claim there.[11]

Initially, he decided to follow his mother's family tradition of opening and managing hotels, undaunted by his earlier failed attempted to run the Golden Rule House back in Kansas. In the years after that failed enterprise, he had spent time at his uncle Henry Guss's Green Tree Hotel in West Chester, Pennsylvania, and since then had stayed in more hotels than most people of his era. So in 1892 he formed the W. F. Cody Hotel Company. Then the show's successful 1893 season in Chicago left him flush. When the opportunity presented itself to invest in a hotel, he had the knowledge and the funds. That hotel was the Sheridan Inn in Sheridan, Wyoming, near the Bighorn Mountains. It had been built by the Burlington and Missouri Railroad, which needed an investor to operate the hotel. Cody stepped in, bringing along hotelier George Canfield, of Omaha's Canfield House, as manager.[12]

Cody was not a silent investor. After the inn opened, he frequented it and often threw large parties there. The inn's restaurant was known for its fine food, and whenever he made a stop at its luxurious saloon, he treated everyone present. He also invited special guests on "fox hunts" using hounds but seeking coyotes instead, then concluded the day with mint juleps at his friend George Beck's ranch just west of Sheridan.[13]

Cody also decided to follow in his father's footsteps and become a town founder. He had made an abortive attempt to start the town of Rome in western Kansas back in 1867. In 1895 he made a much more successful effort in the Bighorn Basin as co-founder of Cody, Wyoming. The town of Cody began to replace North Platte in his attention, investments, and affection, eventually eclipsing it. Unlike North Platte, Cody was his town, a realization of his dream. He persuaded the Burlington and Missouri Railroad to extend its tracks to the new town and rode into town on the first train on November 12, 1901. By that time the new town had nearly one thousand residents, most of whom turned out for the occasion, which featured a big parade, followed by a barbecue and speeches in the evening.[14]

Yellowstone National Park opened as the world's first national park in 1872 but was nearly inaccessible. With the completion of the railroad line, the town of Cody became the gateway to Yellowstone. Buffalo Bill's next hotel project was the Irma Hotel, named after his youngest daughter, which opened in 1902. He asked his sister Julia to manage the place for him once it opened. He suggested she spend some time at a friend's hotel in Rawlins to study how to run a hotel, including "the buying of provisions, cooking them, serving them," and other tasks. Bill was actively involved with the operation, discussing with Julia whether dining should be offered on the European or the American plan. He also arranged for a chef from his favorite New York hotel, the Hoffman House, to act as head cook. He purchased a farm, which he called "the hotel farm," outside of Cody to supply chickens, butter, and vegetables for the cook's use. He later wrote to Julia inquiring how that arrangement was working out, noting, "I like to hear of these little things." In 1904 the Irma offered a fine Christmas dinner with a fixed-price menu that included lobster Newburg, leg of mutton in caper sauce, pork loin with apple sauce, and the obligatory turkey with cranberry sauce. The meal concluded with an assortment of cheeses, lemon and apple pies, and a steamed fruit pudding with rum sauce.[15]

Pahaska Tepee, Buffalo Bill's hunting lodge and resort just outside Yellowstone, opened to the public the next year (fig. 22). It was a jumping-off point for sightseers to the national park and hunters in the mountains outside the park. The lodge, built of logs and much more rustic than the Irma Hotel, had a dining room with long tables and a kitchen with a large wood-burning stove. One account remarked that the dining hall, "with roaring fireplace at one end, the long table in the center, loaded with juicy elk steak, venison roast and bighorn stew, reminded the guests of scenes presented by Sir Walter Scott."[16]

A somewhat less ambitious project, the Wapiti Inn, midway between Pahaska Tepee and the town of Cody, was also completed in 1905. With the Irma Hotel, Pahaska Tepee, and Wapiti Inn all operating, several different brochures advertised "Buffalo Bill's Hotels in the Rockies." By 1913 increased automobile traffic made the trip from Cody to Pahaska relatively short. Consequently, the Wapiti was torn down, and the salvaged lumber was used for remodeling Pahaska Tepee. From 1895 to 1913, Bill pumped a great deal of money into projects in the Cody area, including founding the *Cody Enterprise* newspaper. He also bought ranchland around the town, moving cattle there from his ranch in North Platte. Before long he had created the Rock Creek Ranch, Sweeney Ranch, and

Irma Lake Ranch. Buffalo Bill was bullish on Cody and the Bighorn Basin, promoting it heavily during newspaper interviews and in Wild West programs. The graphic accompanying one advertisement even showed wagonloads of settlers streaming into the area.[17]

The flagship of Buffalo Bill's operations in the Bighorn Basin was the TE Ranch, which he acquired in 1895. It was the main place to which he returned on his visits to Cody. It had a big kitchen and two dining rooms, one for the family and one for the help. As his fortunes declined later in life, he finally opened it to guests as a dude ranch. In 1916 he wrote, "The dudes live on young sage chickens and fish, mostly which they kill and catch themselves." Buffalo Bill knew sage hens well, having frequently dined on them during his forays into the high plains and mountains of Wyoming. A couple of years earlier, he had written to the TE ranch manager a nostalgic memory of cooking sage hens for breakfast while hunting in the Beartooth Mountains, saying, "I never spent three happier days than I did when we rode the range." The ranch offered much more to live on if the dudes wanted it, with the brochure touting "fresh meat, home-killed; vegetables from the garden, fresh eggs, fresh milk and butter, all produced on the ranch." On one visit to the ranch with his wife, Louisa, Bill even had a chance to relive a bit of his boyhood when the couple gathered two bushels of wild gooseberries.[18]

With seven months spent on the road each year, it was difficult for Bill Cody to manage all his operations in his town, many of which required an attentive eye. In 1915 he wrote to his lawyer W. L. Walls several times asking him to look into operations at the Irma Hotel, which was losing money. He was particularly concerned that someone might be skimming money from the bar receipts. It was not the only problem that came with being an absentee owner. The following year Horace Albright, an attorney for the Department of the Interior who later became the first superintendent of Yellowstone National Park, visited the Irma with Stephen Mather, who became the first director of the National Park Service the next year. Albright later wrote that they spent an uncomfortable night after receiving "bad food and terrible service" in the dining room. They went on to have lunch at Pahaska Tepee the next day, which

Fig 22. Pahaska Tepee, Buffalo Bill's hunting lodge and resort just outside of Yellowstone. Opening in 1903, it offered a rustic atmosphere and served wild game. Author's collection.

he pronounced "as bad as the Irma, if not worse." That fall Albright and Mather met Buffalo Bill at a party in Washington DC. When Cody thanked them for visiting his establishments, Mather replied that he would not visit again if conditions were not improved. Cody took the criticism in good humor and said, "Send me a list of sad conditions. We'll see they're corrected."[19]

"Back to the New West, the Wild West I leave with you," declared Cody in a brochure promoting his town-founding efforts. That New West, as far as Buffalo Bill was concerned, was the Bighorn Basin. As the new century rolled on, he returned to Cody more frequently than North Platte. In November 1909 he was given a banquet there in celebration of the successful season he had just completed. He announced his intention to remain in Cody and his ranches there throughout the rest of the winter. He still made a brief return visit to North Platte that winter, where he was once again greeted by a crowd of several hundred and a brass band. With his travels around Europe, as well as business in Cody and elsewhere, it was his first time back in ten years. His daughter Irma and her husband, Fred, were now managing Scout's Rest Ranch and threw a large barbecue there for him, which was attended by over a hundred of his Nebraska friends.[20]

Something that was not a family tradition was Buffalo Bill's interest in natural resources. He recognized the need for irrigation in the Bighorn Basin and became a partner in the Shoshone Irrigation Company. He even promoted these efforts in Buffalo Bill's Wild West programs, with images showing produce grown with water from the company's Cody Canal. Based on O. C. Marsh's early assessment of the mineral-rich areas of Wyoming, Buffalo Bill also invested in mining and oil exploration. As his friends grew excited about discoveries of gold in Arizona, Buffalo Bill caught gold fever from them and invested heavily in mines in the Tucson area. In 1910, after spending much of November in Arizona, he enjoyed a farewell dinner thrown for him at the best hotel in town, the Santa Rita. It was where he typically stayed and where he wined and dined local businessmen and investors in his mining projects. By this time he was in his sixties and attracted to Arizona by the warmer winter weather as well as the mines. Over the next several years he spent enough time in the state that some locals urged him to run for U.S. senator from Arizona, something he did not choose to do. Despite his high hopes for the mines, he did not find the wealth he was seeking. Like so many of his investments, they broke even at best. He fancied himself an entrepreneur, but his bread and butter came from the Wild West.[21]

Another area where Buffalo Bill made no money, but was proud to be involved, was in the preservation of natural resources. He frequently spoke out for the protection of wild lands, lands that he loved but that were rapidly disappearing. He was a supporter of Yellowstone National Park and was an early advocate for saving the Grand Canyon. He often praised the efforts of Gifford Pinchot and Theodore Roosevelt to preserve America's forests and wild lands. A big part of his motivation for preserving these lands was his love of hunting. It gave him a chance to get out in nature and brought back memories of his earlier years. He was an early advocate for wildlife and game management. Despite earning his name as a buffalo hunter, he decried the decimation of the buffalo and overhunting of any species. He said in 1904, "We've got more game left in the Wyoming mountains than any other part of the country. By strict game laws we're keeping it too."[22]

While he enjoyed being a celebrity and all the trappings associated with that, including fine dining, his hunting trips during the winter months afforded him the opportunity to set aside both his show business persona of Buffalo Bill and his business persona of William F. Cody and just be Will Cody. It was a time he could truly relax and enjoy the frontier life he had loved ever since he was a young man. The town of Cody was in an ideal area for a hunter, surrounded by mountain ranges and forest on nearly all sides. He made frequent hunting trips in the Bighorn Mountains to the east of Cody and commissioned artists C. S. Stobie and Irving Bacon to create paintings of those hunting experiences, titling each painting *The Life I Love*.

After months of eating food prepared by the Wild West cooks and by chefs at fancy gourmet feasts at banquets and in restaurants, the hunting trips gave Buffalo Bill a chance to return to his frontier comfort foods. Smoky bacon and beans cooked over a wood fire, sage hen, and antelope were among the foods he had grown up with and had often cooked himself. He also discovered that his guests on hunts enjoyed those foods as much as he did. Not long after Buffalo Bill's Wild West became well known, Cody invited a group of military officers on a hunting expedition in the Rockies. Wishing to impress them, he engaged a French chef from the Brown Palace Hotel in Denver at great expense to prepare all the meals in camp. The chef served a haute cuisine meal the first evening, complete with fine china and linen. He continued to do so for two more days, until the members of the hunting party rebelled. They wanted western food. Cody reportedly "beamed with delight," saying that haute cuisine and Rocky Mountain trails did not go together well. Two of the scouts hired for the expedition were enlisted as cooks, and the chef was told to relax for the duration. Cody even took a turn at cooking, the results of which the group declared to be "first class."[23]

While Bill Cody occasionally cooked on hunting trips, there is no record that he ever cooked at any other time. Buffalo Bill enjoyed food, so much so that one could call him a foodie, but he was neither a gourmet chef nor an everyday cook. He left that to professional cooks at the Wild West or at fine dining establishments when he was away from home. His wife, Louisa, was a good cook and enjoyed cooking; even though the Codys had a cook on their household staff, she did much of the cooking herself. She particularly loved to make pickles, jams, and jellies. In 1909 Louisa moved to Scout's Rest Ranch, where her daughter Irma and family were living. They frequently had picnics with friends on the grounds, preparing lemonade and homemade ice cream, while the cook baked cakes and made sandwiches for everyone. Buffalo Bill never partook in those picnics, as he was on the road with the Wild West at the time.[24]

Over the years, particularly after Buffalo Bill's death, people have claimed to have been his personal chef. It was not unusual for people to add to their résumés by either elevating their roles in Buffalo Bill's Wild West or inventing stories of having worked for Cody. Otto Fleissner, a chef in a Seattle hotel in 1905, said he had worked as Buffalo Bill's personal cook to support his endorsement of a patent medicine for kidney and bladder problems. In 1923 W. F. Ford, a cook at a lumber camp, asserted he had been Buffalo Bill's personal cook. William Royce, before his death in a hospital for the criminally insane, also said he cooked for Cody.[25]

There have been other impostors as well. In 1932 ninety-two-year-old James Lyman Brown, who dressed like Buffalo Bill in later life, said he had been Cody's first cook in 1870. However, in 1870 Bill and Louisa were living in a cabin near Fort McPherson, where he worked as a scout under contract. The family barely scraped by on his income, and Louisa did all the cooking. Brown also claimed to have later served as Cody's Portuguese cook. While some of the different ethnic groups who performed with Buffalo Bill's Wild West occasionally prepared their own food, there is no evidence that Cody had a personal chef who prepared Portuguese food. Brown, like the other pretenders, got away with his claims because those who might have challenged him had passed away.[26]

Not everyone who said they had been Buffalo Bill's personal cook was an impostor. In December 1912, M. Alfred Heimer and his wife, Elsie, were among a gathering of Wild West personnel, both retired and active, in New York City. The group included Wild West band leader William Sweeney and John Burke. Heimer, proprietor of Billings, Montana's Rex Bar, served as a private steward to Cody for eight years, and his wife had often cooked for Buffalo Bill. Twenty-two years later Heimer reminisced to the Billings newspaper about his experiences with Buffalo Bill. As a young man working at the Opera Hotel in New York City, he had met John Burke. Over the next several years he begged Burke to get him a job at the Wild West. Finally, in 1897 he was hired to work as a steward in Buffalo Bill's private train car. That essentially meant he had to get snacks for Cody while the show was on the road, deliver breakfast to him from the camp in the mornings, run messages, and keep things organized. During the winter of 1901, with the show closed, Heimer met and married his wife. That spring, when he told Cody he could no longer work with the show since he was married, he was asked to "bring her around." When Buffalo Bill met Elsie, he asked if she could cook. When she replied that she could, Cody invited her to cook for him, and Alfred resumed work as his steward.[27]

Since, with the exception of breakfast, Cody usually ate with the show's cast in the food tent, neither Alfred nor Elise was his personal chef, as some of the impostors claimed they had been. Instead, she probably only occasionally cooked for him. The couple stayed with the show until 1904, when Buffalo Bill asked Heimer to take charge of the Irma Hotel bar. After three years there, he established his own bar in Cody, then moved to Billings, where he opened the Rex Bar.[28]

Harry Leonard Wiard took charge of the Irma kitchen when Heimer left. Wiard later remembered that meals were cooked on a twelve-foot-long Majestic kitchen range, with a meat broiler, hot ovens, and steam tables. He also recalled that Buffalo Bill's favorite meals at the Irma were grilled beef tenderloin, chicken fricassee with homemade noodles, and rump roast with vegetables.[29]

Among Alfred Heimer's comments about Buffalo Bill to the Billings newspaper was that accusations of drunkenness during the show, causing Cody to turn in a poor performance, were patently untrue. He said he saw Cody drink only twice while working at the Wild West, both times when he got together with old friends from his scouting days. Buffalo Bill was so true to his promise to Salsbury that many temperance advocates saw him as a man for their cause. Yet for many years he drank alcohol, even going on binges, during the off-season. His longtime relationship with alcoholic beverages was much more complicated than most people imagine. By 1905, when Heimer was working at the Irma, it also played a role in Cody's divorce trial from Louisa.[30]

Part 3

The Last Stands

16

Tanglefoot, Ginger Ale, and a
Tempestuous Marriage

Col. Cody doesn't drink anything stronger than ginger ale
sometimes.

Joplin (MO) Herald, 1898

Drunkard, teetotaler, philanderer, family man . . . all were names
used to describe William F. Cody. When his personal life was scru-
tinized during his 1905 divorce trial, all stories were correct and
all were incorrect, depending upon the witness. His personal life
was complicated, and alcohol had a lot to do with it.

Buffalo Bill's relationship with alcohol was complex. Newspaper
accounts of the period suggested he was a paragon of sobriety, and
some of his friends remarked on his restraint when it came to alcohol. Yet others commented on his drunkenness. Cody was capable
of being drunk on some occasions but critical of drunkenness on
others. His relationship to alcohol was like his relationship to his
wife: it ran hot and cold.

Will Cody's first encounter with alcohol was as a young boy, when
he and a friend got into a barrel of hard cider, and the aftermath
left him with a strong dislike for the drink. Twenty-five years later
newspapers reported that he was resorting to soft, or fresh, cider
as an alternative to stronger drinks. He also drank ginger ale, lemonade, and buttermilk. This led some people to conclude that
he had taken up the temperance cause. But he had not, and his
early negative experience with hard cider certainly did not turn
him against alcohol.

He was probably introduced to whiskey during his forays across
the Great Plains in the company of teamsters who drank heavily

despite the best efforts of Russell, Majors, and Waddell to enforce abstinence among its workers. In 1860 Missouri had twenty-two distilleries and Kansas had one. It is likely that some of the whiskey that Will Cody consumed in his younger days came from Holladay's distillery in Weston, which would have been accessible to him and his fellow teamsters. Whiskey and other spirits also came by boat from back East and even from Europe.[1]

Cheaper and less reputable whiskeys were available as well. Many stories mention the abundance of cheap whiskey on the western frontier. When Cody was traveling across the plains with the wagon trains, any alcohol was acceptable, just as any coffee was preferable to none at all. He frequently referred to cheap whiskey as "tanglefoot." In the West, tanglefoot was often rectified whiskey, which meant it was redistilled whiskey, often originally of poor quality. Rectified whiskey was nearly flavorless and colorless but high in alcohol content. All sorts of flavorings were added to make it resemble a higher-quality whiskey. Some of those additives, like kerosene, could be dangerous, so rectified whiskey was often called "rotgut." But rectified whiskey was certainly cheap, which made it attractive to hard-drinking westerners on a budget. Even U.S. Army commissaries sold it. And, like many young men, Will Cody was often indiscriminate in his consumption of alcohol.[2]

Cody wrote in his autobiography that in late 1863, grief-stricken over his mother's death, "I entered upon a dissolute and reckless life—to my shame, be it said." He continued this "dissipation" for two months, until one day, "after having been under the influence of bad whiskey," he awoke to discover he had enlisted in the Seventh Kansas and went to war for the northern cause.[3]

During his scouting days, while conducting hunts for celebrities and army brass, just as he discovered finer foods, he also discovered a better class of alcohol than the tanglefoot he had consumed in his youth. By the time Cody was involved in show business, he no longer drank tanglefoot. He even criticized those he saw as under its control, willing to drink anything to become drunk. Cody was usually in control. He didn't refrain from the occasional overindulgence, however; he just drank a better quality of beverage.[4]

While Buffalo Bill was stationed as a scout at Fort McPherson, he frequented Dave Perry's saloon in North Platte, a practice he continued on subsequent visits to the town during his show business career. His sister May, who lived with the family part of that time, remembered that while her brother drank, so did all the other men at the fort, including officers. "He didn't drink any more than any other western man at that time," she observed. It was a time when one of the many measures of a man was his ability to drink liberally and still hold his alcohol.[5]

A few men refrained from drinking, but they were very few. Buffalo Bill and his friends remarked how unique fellow scout Jack Crawford was because he never drank. Cody had a favorite story about Crawford back in their scouting days. Crawford safely transported a gift bottle of fine whiskey three hundred miles to Cody without drinking a drop, then politely refused to join him in a drink. Cody noted, "I was never a lone drinker, I invited General Carr over to sample the bottle."[6]

Surrounded by hard-drinking men, Cody drank liberally but didn't allow it to interfere with his work when buffalo hunting or scouting; no complaints were ever lodged against him for drinking on duty. Show business was an entirely different situation, and learning the ropes involved knowing where and when not to drink. When he launched his Buffalo Bill Combination with Texas Jack Omohundro and Wild Bill Hickok in his second season onstage, he received a small cask of whiskey from a fan. He invited Texas Jack and some other friends to polish it off over the course of a weekend. On another occasion, Cody, Texas Jack, Wild Bill, and their scouting friend Frank North were drinking, but reportedly not drunk, and settled the issue of who would pay the bill by having a horse race. These events passed largely unnoticed by the press, but Cody eventually discovered that maintaining good public relations was a lot more important in show business than it was in scouting. On his way to New York City for the opening of his 1880–81 season, Buffalo Bill stopped in Chicago to sell livestock from his ranch and stayed over for several days. He lodged at the Briggs House hotel and spent the evenings drinking at Splan and Marshall's saloon. One evening he consumed around two quarts of gin and lost $900 throwing dice. "Buffalo Bill Badly Beaten" was the title of an article about the occurrence in the *Chicago Tribune*. It went out on the wire and was published in the *Brooklyn Daily Eagle*, where it was read by potential audience members for his show in New York City the following week.[7]

By 1882 Cody was more discreet. Newspapers reported that Buffalo Bill was now drinking only soft cider. In private, however, he was still getting together with old friends for a tipple or two. That year he wrote to his friend A. H. Patterson of Fort Collins that he'd like to get together and reminisce about old times, suggesting a fishing trip. He concluded the letter, "I ain't much on the fish catch, but I could do the drinking."[8]

Cody's discretion lapsed when he and Doc Carver created Buffalo Bill's Wild West a year later. Reportedly, one car of the train that transported the show was filled with liquor. Pawnee Bill, who later became a partner, joined the show during its first season. He later wrote of his disappointment at seeing Cody frequently drunk during the show's first five weeks. Buffalo Bill's Wild West had record attendance but was financially unsuccessful because both Cody and Carver spent their off hours drinking rather than paying attention to business.[9]

When Nate Salsbury became Cody's business partner the next season, he quickly brought Buffalo Bill's drinking to an end after discovering Cody and some old friends drunk after a show. It was something that he never forgot and never let Will Cody forget. Conscious of the poor public relations that could result, he demanded that Buffalo Bill pledge to abstain from getting drunk during the show season if he wanted Salsbury to remain as his business associate. Cody agreed, responding, "You will no longer see me under the influence of liquor." And he kept that promise. Even during the show's disastrous stand in New Orleans the following year, Cody refrained from drinking, although he wrote to Salsbury, "When the show is laid up for the winter I am going to get on a drunk that is a drunk," but "till then I am staunch and true." And he continued to be "staunch and true" a year after the New Orleans season. When Cody's nephew Ed worked with the show, he wrote to his mother Julia that he never saw his uncle touch a drop of alcohol. In 1892 Buffalo Bill told a reporter in Manchester, England, "I never drink—or, at least, never when on tour." And for the most part, he observed that practice for the next twenty years.[10]

Even before Salsbury's reprimand, Cody had been able to confine his drinking to those times when he wasn't working. Cody often registered his disapproval of men who drank so much that they were unable to do their work. In 1879 he wrote to Buckskin Sam, who wanted to work in his stage show, "Tanglefoot gets away with you. And I will have no one with me that's liable to let whisky get away with him, in this business a man must be perfectly reliable and sober." Even when Buffalo Bill did drink, the whiskey rarely got away with him. His friend and employee Robert "Pony Bob" Haslam observed that it was difficult to tell when Cody was drunk because "he kin stand a powerful lot." When he was sent by General Nelson Miles to bring in Sitting Bull during the Ghost Dance, several army officers who were allies of Indian agent James McLaughlin tried to delay Cody by getting him drunk, as McLaughlin wanted to handle Sitting Bull himself. The agent's friends invited Cody to the officers' club when he stopped at Fort Yates for the night, hoping to drink him under the table and delay him by a day. They were unsuccessful, and after sleeping until 11:00 a.m. the next day, Cody continued his mission. One of the officers later remarked on his "capacity."[11]

Buffalo Bill never put his name on a distilled beverage, but he came close to doing so when he joined his old friend Frank "White Beaver" Powell in the production and sale of a patent medicine. White Beaver's Cough Cream was promoted as a cure for "coughs, colds and all diseases of the lungs," made from "an extract of roots and herbs such as has been used by the Indians of the Northwest." But like many other patent medicines, it consisted of mostly alcohol, in this case 86 percent. It also contained 12 percent chloroform and 2 percent opium. With these ingredients totaling 100 percent, that didn't leave much room for the extract. Cody and Powell were listed as equal partners in the enterprise, which was centered in La Crosse, Wisconsin. They also sold White Beaver's Wonder Worker and Yosemite Marrow, both patent medicines. The business lasted from 1884 to 1894, failing at the same time as the Cody-Powell Coffee Company, another of their businesses.[12]

While Cody was in Chicago at the World's Columbian Exposition, Powell came up with a coffee substitute that, for a while, provided Buffalo Bill with a new nonalcoholic beverage. It was promoted as much healthier than coffee and equally good for everyone in the family, from "the nursing babe to the worn-out old man." This "wholesome and delicious" beverage was called Panmalt, presumably since it consisted primarily of barley malt. Like the cough cream, it was produced in La Crosse. Cody wrote to his sister Julia on August 29 that the partners had many orders and were ready to manufacture thousands of pounds a day. The new product was advertised throughout the Midwest and promoted to Wild West visitors. A reporter from the *Chicago Times* followed his nose to Buffalo Bill's "private kitchen" at the Wild West, where Cody and John Burke provided him with a cup, telling him that it was the only kind of coffee being provided at the show. Despite their enthusiasm, the public was not nearly as excited about the product, even though it cost less than regular coffee. The partners' venture into the production of a coffee substitute ended a year after it began, when Cody told Julia he "had to close coffee factory down." The show's chefs resumed serving regular coffee, and nothing more was said about Panmalt.[13]

The need for sobriety in show business was a theme throughout Cody's Wild West years, and he remained true to his pledge to Salsbury. On the way to London in 1887, he and Salsbury asked Jule Keen, who had been with Cody as part of the Buffalo Bill Combination and continued as a treasurer for the Wild West, to take a pledge of sobriety. Keen presented them both with a letter stating that he would refrain from intoxicating liquors for the next two years. Cody expected his employees to maintain sobriety and tried to be a good example during the show seasons.[14]

Some weren't entirely sure that Buffalo Bill would be able to maintain his sobriety during the show's European travels between 1887 and 1892. One American newspaper observed, "If he keeps sober he will not disgrace his country, for he is shrewd enough to know his own defects and he conceals them splendidly by a retiring and courteous manner." Indeed, some of that splendid concealment occurred before he departed, when other newspapers assured their readers that Cody "never drinks anything stronger than lemonade, because fire-waters do not agree with him." This news item even appeared in Columbus, Nebraska, where four years earlier he had enjoyed the local saloons after the first rehearsals for the show. By all accounts, Buffalo Bill successfully abstained from alcohol during the European tours. Glasgow and Edinburgh newspapers reported that Cody was a teetotaler and that performers in the show were generally abstainers, because the hazardous nature of the work required "self-possession at all times." When the Wild West returned to Great Britain in 1891, Cody continued to be a paragon of restraint as far as the press was concerned. Entertained in Cardiff, he drank ginger ale while everyone else in the group drank champagne.[15]

Cody was particularly careful to maintain sobriety during his extended tours of England, in particular, where the temperance movement was strong. He was so careful that some people considered him an advocate of temperance and asked for his support of that cause. General William Booth, the founder of the Salvation Army, even put Cody's image on a banner. But in their desire to have such a prominent person as a supporter, the temperance people were fooled by appearances. Although Cody did abstain, it was only for the portion of the year when he was performing. One Missouri newspaper observed, "Col. Cody doesn't drink anything stronger than ginger ale," then added "sometimes." When the shows were over, Buffalo Bill returned to his Great Plains nurtured love of liquor. A Denver newspaper commented, "If Bill ever got on one of those whooping prairie tears of his he would break up any foreign temperance community in about one hour." He consistently demurred when asked to become a temperance advocate, knowing he would not give up alcohol entirely.[16]

Buffalo Bill's state of mind toward prohibition was quite obvious at the end of the 1900 season, when he said, "We close at Memphis Saturday. Monday I'll be in Omaha, Tuesday I'll be in North Platte, the next day I start for the ranch. A week from today I'll be drunk." After months of abstaining during the show, Buffalo Bill was ready to let loose. As he passed through Omaha and North Platte, he was joined by friends who rode the rails with him as far as they could, since the railroad did not reach Cody, Wyoming, until the next year. When laying out the plans for the town of Cody with his friend George Beck, Buffalo Bill had observed that it could not get along without a "gin mill" or saloon. By 1900 the town had four saloons, and the group immediately headed to one of them on arrival. There, more friends awaited to celebrate the homecoming. After several days in town, Cody headed out to the TE Ranch with some of his guests.[17]

Buffalo Bill loved being surrounded by friends while drinking. That was the way he lived during his scouting days and before he made his pledge to Salsbury. He was, above all else, a social drinker. When Scout's Rest Ranch was furnished in 1886, Cody wrote to his sister that he wanted a sideboard with "some nice decanters and glasses." He continued, "I don't propose to make a bar-room," and suggested instead, "Put it up in my bedroom—then if anyone gets full I can put them to bed." His old friend Pony Bob Haslam often joined him and other friends at the ranch, acting as barkeeper. Haslam said he tried to keep the alcohol "light" when he mixed the drinks, "so they wouldn't get loaded too quick." Entertaining friends at the ranch, in saloons, and on hunting trips by offering them drinks was an important part of Buffalo Bill's idea of hospitality, whether he was drinking or not. For him it was all about the camaraderie and conviviality.[18]

Buffalo Bill's financial success during the 1893 World's Columbian Exposition in Chicago gave him ample opportunity to treat his friends in local bars upon his return to North Platte that fall. He also freely indulged in the alcohol he had denied himself all season, getting "lit up" at a banquet thrown in his honor. The following year another banquet was thrown for him on his return to town, at which time, according to a Lincoln, Nebraska, paper, he demonstrated his continued love for "all kinds of drinkables, from beer to vermouth." Cody could abstain when needed but, once released, could overindulge with the best of them. Nevertheless, even then he did not drink to the point of being incapacitated.[19]

Cody continued his seasonal romance with alcohol through most of his thirty years at the helm of Buffalo Bill's Wild West. He remarked that when the season was over, he drank for recreation, and it enabled him to throw off the "thoughts of work and labor for the time being." Dexter Fellows handled much of the publicity for the show for seven of those years. He later observed that except for a visit to several Nebraska cities in 1898 when Cody was honored at the Trans-Mississippi Exposition in Omaha, he never saw Buffalo Bill under the influence of alcohol during the show season. Back in his old stomping grounds and caught up in the celebration, Buffalo Bill drank with his friends, but the rest of the time he was "sober as a judge."[20]

Cody typically provided drinks for his guests when they visited Buffalo Bill's Wild West, even as he refrained from imbibing. Fellows remembered that Buffalo Bill kept a stock of liquor in his private train car for entertaining. When General Fitzhugh Lee visited the Wild West, he remarked that he had been told Cody made "the best old-fashioned cocktail ever put together." According to Fellows, Cody mixed a full-size drink for the general and poured a very small glass of it for himself to keep his guest company. On another occasion, three of Buffalo Bill's friends from his scouting days dropped by when the show was in Oklahoma City in 1900. He invited them to his private car, where they reminisced while his guests enjoyed his private collection of whiskey. He then suggested they ride with the show to Texas. They did, in what Fellows described as "an alcoholic tour de force, in which Cody took no part except as a fatherly host." He had his ginger ale, cider, lemonade, and other alternatives.[21]

Cody claimed that he missed only ten performances during his years with Buffalo Bill's Wild West, and he could not have done that had he been a drinking man. In 1901 he wrote to his friend Mike Russell that he was feeling particularly well because he had stopped drinking. In 1904 he said he had drunk wine, beer, or liquor only three times since 1901, and two of the times it had been prescribed for him by a doctor. The third time, he said, he accidentally drank a ginger ale highball instead of a ginger ale horse's neck. The horse's neck was a nonalcoholic combination of lemon juice, ginger ale, and cracked ice, with the spiral peel of an entire lemon placed around the inside of a tall glass. The highball he was served was a horse's neck with brandy added, something made popular by the Hoffman House, his favorite New York hotel. Buffalo Bill apparently felt his forbearance was enough to call himself an abstainer on his next trip to Europe, from 1902 to 1906. In England he was quoted as saying, "I am an abstainer and have been for some years past. I was led to abandon alcoholic liquors because I found it best for health, purse, reputation, and, more especially, as an example to those under me." It was a story he repeated as the show traveled across England, where the temperance movement had a great deal of influence. But he was not yet a teetotaler.[22]

Alcohol played a major role in pushing his hot-and-cold marriage to Louisa to its breaking point. Bill Cody's family life was anything but ideal. The arrival of each of his children was a cause for celebration, and he doted on them. Two of his children, his only son, Kit, and daughter Orra, died while young. His other daughters, Arta and Irma, grew to adulthood, and he spent as much time as he could with them. When they were of age, he occasionally took them along while traveling with the Wild West. He was rarely at home, however, and left the raising of his children up to Louisa. While such behavior by a husband as breadwinner was not unusual at that time, Cody was absent more than most because of the nature of his work. And when he was at home, he and Louisa frequently argued.

Their arguments were mostly about his drinking and relationships with other women, which he claimed were friendships but she said were infidelities. Louisa was very jealous and suspicious of him—and for good reason. As it would have been put during his day, Cody had an eye for the ladies. And they certainly had an eye for him. He was handsome, dashing, and famous, and he always seemed to have plenty of money to throw around. At their divorce trial, when Louisa accused him of frequent intimacies with other women, the judge ruled out her testimony, saying it was "manifestly unjust, false and brutal." If Cody had been unfaithful, it would not have been unexpected, given his many opportunities, months away from his family, and frequent clashes with his wife when they were together. He and Louisa fought over everything, not the least of which was his drinking with friends at local saloons. The arguments made his visits unpleasant, and he frequently escaped the house to meet with friends to drink. Not only did Louisa make him feel unwelcome, but she also was frequently rude to his friends and sisters. Even her own friends said she could be a difficult woman and had quite a temper.[23]

Cody thought of divorcing Louisa several times, most notably in 1883, when he wrote to his sister Julia, "I have got out my petition for a divorce with that woman." But each time he was ready to file, a momentous event in his life occurred that caused him to put those plans on hold. In 1883 it was the formation of Buffalo Bill's Wild West, and at other times it was the arrival of a child. His on-again, off-again relationship with his wife came to a head in April 1904, after his two remaining children were married. As he explained it, "I simply stood it as long as I could. I thought I'd wait till the children were married and then get free." He filed for divorce, thinking that Louisa would be happy with a settlement and ready to part company. But she was not and contested the divorce.[24]

During the next year, much of the family's dirty laundry was aired in both national and international papers. Louisa accused Cody of affairs with other women, while Will spoke of her mistreatment of him, his friends, and his sisters, with whom she did not get along. He also accused her of trying to poison him. Her reply to his accusation was that he had been "administering poison to himself for years" in the form of alcohol. This was all great fodder for the newspapers. When the trial began in Cheyenne in early 1905, a parade of witnesses sided with one or the other. Each party accused the other of wanton drunkenness, and one witness testified that Louisa drank to the point where it affected her temper, making her "boisterous and quarrelsome," while others said she never drank. Will contended that when forced to spend an evening with his wife, he would grab a bottle of "red eye" and drain it because "this is the only way to tolerate a quarrelsome and jealous woman." One headline noted, "Buffalo Bill and His Wife Both Appear to Poor Advantage." The testimony continued until March 23, when the judge denied Buffalo Bill's request for a divorce. His admonishment of Will was stinging, characterizing Louisa as a devoted mother and wife and stating that her husband had heaped indignities on her and been cruel. The embarrassment of having the whole drama play out on the world stage was compounded by newspaper statements such as "There seems to be a certain dimness about Buffalo Bill's halo" and "His name seemed to lose its luster." Little had been accomplished by either, other than undermining each other's reputation.[25]

Fortunately for Cody, Buffalo Bill's Wild West opened in Paris on April 2, and he did not have to stay in the United States to face the embarrassment. He threw himself into his work, while Louisa returned to their house in North Platte. Over the next two months he doubtless did a good deal of soul-searching. He wrote to his sister Julia on June 14, "It's in my old age that I have found God—And realize how easy it is to abandon sin and serve him." He also wrote that as a result, he had decided to stop drinking entirely. It was a kind of spiritual awakening. Will had previously given little thought to faith and religion, but from this point on, he became much more forthright about believing in God. In one of his speeches, he admonished listeners, "Look to God and put your trust in Him." He even asked his sister to invite her minister in Cody to the TE Ranch to give a sermon and have dinner when Will returned at the end of the 1906 season. It was a marked change from his boyhood practice of chasing away the yellow-legged chickens on their farm so the minister would not stop for dinner. And, it appears that Buffalo Bill was embarking on a serious effort to stop drinking.[26]

After the trial, the Codys split from each other, still married but with every intention of living apart. During the trial, however, they had not just made grievous accusations about each other but expressed some affection as well. As the wounds healed from the trial, that affection grew. Efforts of their family to reunite the two were successful, and in late March 1910 news was carried throughout the nation that they had "adjusted their domestic difficulties" and discovered that "love still held a place in the hearts of the old couple." To celebrate, Will and Louisa held a reception for everyone in North Platte at the Elks lodge. It wasn't just an effort to polish their images after being tarnished in the trial. A year later they were still happily together and feted by daughter Irma and her husband, Fred Garlow, for their forty-fifth anniversary. Two dinners were held at the Garlows' home, one hosting fourteen people and the other twelve. Each dinner consisted of seven courses. Two years later, Louisa could be seen wearing Buffalo Bill's favorite watch fob on a chain around her neck in a photograph with Will, his hand resting affectionately on her shoulder (fig. 23).[27]

With the return of Buffalo Bill's Wild West from Europe in 1906, Cody also returned to some of his old habits. On a trip to Deadwood with George Beck, they were joined by other friends at a saloon, where he became quite "hilarious." That appears to have been an aberration in his efforts to abstain, however. On a later visit to Deadwood in 1909, some of the same friends were surprised to learn that he would not be drinking any whiskey with them. Instead, he indulged in buttermilk and reportedly drank every drop of it in town. The newspapers reported that folks were shocked to learn that Buffalo Bill was on the "water wagon." But even if Cody abstained from alcohol, he did not oppose it and still provided visitors to the show the hospitality that people had become acquainted with. Goldie Griffith, a performer with the Wild West during this period, remembered that on cold and rainy days, Cody invited the performers to his tent to warm up with hot toddies, which he mixed in a silver punch bowl given to him by Queen Victoria.[28]

In 1911 Buffalo Bill headed back to the TE Ranch outside Cody after finishing the season. Instead of drinking with friends until the wee hours, he requested that his cook prepare a "Buffalo Bill cocktail." This consisted of two fresh eggs broken into a few ounces of vinegar, topped off with a large dose of Worcestershire sauce, salt, and pepper. The next morning he was up early enough for a big breakfast of ham or bacon, two eggs, and three sourdough pancakes.[29]

In the years after Cody's death, the stories of his drinking were greatly overstated. For example, one story said that the agreement between Cody and Salsbury allowed him one small drink a day while with the show. By 1938 that one drink became a tumbler of whiskey. And in 1976, when Robert Altman's movie *Buffalo Bill and the Indians* came out, the tumbler had grown to a tankard. But there was no truth to any of it. Nellie Snyder Yost discovered some stories about Cody's drinking when she interviewed people

Fig 23. Buffalo Bill and his wife, Louisa, ca. 1915. Cody's enjoyment of alcohol aggravated an already rocky marriage. His
effort to divorce his wife was denied in 1905, but they had
reconciled by the time this photograph was taken. Object
ID#313, Buffalo Bill Museum and Grave, Golden co.

who knew him in North Platte for her book published in 1979, but more were positive than negative. Charlie Whalen said that Cody was everyone's friend and a gentleman, whether he was sober or drunk. Julia Siebold also stated that he was a perfect gentleman, and while he did drink, "Show me the man in those days who didn't!" Mrs. John Dick said similarly, "You couldn't blame Cody. He was no worse than the other men. They all drank."[30]

Other stories told of Cody's drunkenness even after he became a celebrity, but how often did this actually occur? Cody occasionally referred to going on a legendary drunk, but in some cases he was joking or exaggerating for effect. While working on a new autobiography, he wrote to a friend, "I find I have to put in a lot of drunks to liven the book. Who ever heard of anything funny without booze." A good example would be his letter to Nate Salsbury in 1885, in which he remarked that he was going to get really drunk after the disastrous season in New Orleans. There is no evidence he actually followed through on that statement. Many of the accounts compiled by Yost consistently repeated the same incidents, suggesting they were infrequent. And it was stated often during the divorce trial that when he did get drunk, it was rarely to the point where he was incapacitated.[31]

As for his drinking during the show season, Buffalo Bill mostly abstained. Salsbury's health deteriorated around the turn of the century, and he grew bitter, resenting Cody for the fame he felt he deserved. Not long before his death in 1902, Salsbury listed his grievances against Cody. Yet his list contained only around five incidents of drunkenness on the job during eighteen years of partnership, and aspects of those incidents seem to have been embellished because of Salsbury's resentment. In the years after Salsbury's death and Cody's "spiritual awakening," Cody appears to have finally become a teetotaler. Looking at his life in its totality, one can readily say that he drank during most of it, but also that reports of his drunkenness were greatly exaggerated. He was a social drinker who enjoyed alcohol of various kinds, particularly whiskey, and was in control of it, not the other way around. Buffalo Bill was a drinker, but he was not a drunk.[32]

17

The Banquet Ends

Out in the west I have my horses, my buffaloes, my sturdy staunch old Indian friends, my home, my green fields—but I never see them green. When my season is over, the hillsides and meadows have been blighted by a wintry frost and the sear and yellow leaves cover the ground. I want to see nature in its prime, to enjoy a rest from active life; my message to you is one of farewell.

Buffalo Bill, 1911

The first two decades of the twentieth century were marked with significant farewells for Buffalo Bill Cody. He said farewell to his lifelong friendship with alcohol. He also said farewell to his business partner Nate Salsbury, but not before that partner turned on him with bitterness. He bade farewell to his show as it was taken from him. His longed-for farewell to his wife was thwarted but eventually replaced by a reconciliation and farewell to the acrimony that had marked the first forty years of their marriage. And then, after a full life, he took his last bow.

The route cards printed at the beginning of each show season, for use by the employees to plan their year, bore the words "Home Sweet Home" in large letters after the dates of the last performances. Those words also heralded the celebratory farewell banquets that were often held at the end of each season. These dinners were begun in the late nineteenth century, the first a rib roast staged by the Wild West's Indians when the show completed its season at Erastina in 1886. They continued intermittently into the early twentieth century.[1]

The show toured England in December 1902 at the start of a long season that did not conclude until late October 1903. After nearly a full year of performing, the show held a well-deserved farewell dinner at Burton-on-Trent, a town in Staffordshire known for its breweries. Despite such access to beer, the dinner offered only tea and coffee, in keeping with the Wild West's tradition of serving no alcohol to its employees. The banquet featured two menu designs offering identical food selections. One showed a cupid shooting arrows at ducks and chickens, both prominent entrées on the menu in addition to the customary beef and pork. The fish course featured boiled Columbia River salmon in hollandaise sauce. At the conclusion of the meal, Cody gave a brief address to the group, wishing everyone good health and a safe return home and noting that he looked forward to seeing many of their faces back in the arena the following spring. The show returned to England that next spring, and another farewell dinner with similar entrées was held in Staffordshire the following October.[2]

Nate Salsbury, who had accompanied the Wild West throughout most of its earlier European tours, was not present at those farewell dinners. His partnership with Buffalo Bill made him quite wealthy, even if it did not bring him the renown Cody enjoyed. Along with John Burke and his extraordinary marketing ability, the three formed a triumvirate that created an entertainment juggernaut from 1883 to 1900.

During those decades, Salsbury received nearly equal billing with Cody. He appeared on Wild West posters, and the two men were frequently mentioned together in newspaper articles. Salsbury was feted during the trips to Europe and when he was with the show in the United States. His scrapbooks reveal many newspaper articles about him, though fewer than those about Cody. Burke also was often mentioned in the press, but he always deferred to Cody when it came to the spotlight. While Salsbury accompanied the show on its first European tour and occasionally attended it while it was in America, Salsbury does not seem to have been as physically engaged with it as Burke and Cody, who accompanied the Wild West throughout each season. Cody in particular maintained a higher profile with Buffalo Bill's Wild West not only because it bore his name, but also because he was always there, greeting visitors, eating with guests in the dining tent, and spending time with the show's employees. Salsbury was essential to the enterprise, however, coordinating finances, arranging for loans, and even fronting his own money. After his death in 1902, many articles stated that the success of Buffalo Bill's Wild West was due "in no small degree" to Salsbury's hand as its manager.[3]

With the new century, and after nearly twenty successful years, the triumvirate of Cody, Burke, and Salsbury began to fall apart, in large part because of Salsbury's failing health. In the beginning, Nate Salsbury had seemed to relish his role as manager and impresario of Buffalo Bill's Wild West. Just like Cody, he was wined and dined by royalty in Europe and captains of industry in the United States. But Buffalo Bill was always in the spotlight, and as Salsbury, who had been a successful comedian and actor, got older, he began to feel Cody had stolen the limelight from him. Age and ailments made him bitter. Growing stomach problems gave him a great deal of discomfort, and he began to withdraw from his activities with the show. His health was also likely behind a pettiness that disrupted the relationship between the three personalities. He even blamed his illness on his years of working with Buffalo Bill and the show. Perhaps his resentment of Cody had always simmered somewhere below the surface, but after 1900 it emerged full-blown. He began work on a memoir that was not intended to be published but was privately titled "Sixteen Years in Hell with Buffalo Bill." The memoir and correspondence in the Nathan Salsbury Papers in Yale's Beinecke Library reveal a very bitter man. Even minor slights, past and present, were given prominence in his mind. Cody's letters in response to Salsbury's criticism of him, Burke, and other members of the Wild West company had a surprised and injured tone, peppered with occasional apologies. But the public and performers in the show were unaware of this discord until years later, when Salsbury's private papers were revealed.[4]

In "Sixteen Years in Hell with Buffalo Bill." Salsbury claimed that the Wild West was entirely his idea. He also asserted, "I invented every featrure [sic] of the Wild West Show that had had any drawing power." Salsbury furnished no details, and examination of the situations suggests that his claims were greatly exaggerated, if not downright false. He asserted, for example, that the visit to England in 1887 was entirely of his doing; however, this had been Cody's ambition before he even met Salsbury, and it was Cody who initially met with John Whitley to coordinate the show's appearance in London.[5]

Cody had been at least as successful in his career as Salsbury before they met. Both had been the stars of popular stage shows. But it was Buffalo Bill who had the celebrity on which the Wild West was built. As the years went by, it was Cody's celebrity, flamboyance, and vision that drove the show. While Salsbury seemed content to be the businessman behind the show, Cody used his position to address issues that concerned him, something he had begun to do before joining with Salsbury. He spoke out regarding Indians' rights and took tribal members of his show to meet with American presidents. He also supported women's rights, encouraged President Roosevelt's efforts to preserve the American wilderness, pushed for development of the Bighorn Basin, and helped found the town of Cody. In all these things, his ambitions were greater than Salsbury's. But Salsbury excelled in an area where Cody did not: managing money. As often seen in business partnerships, Cody was the better entrepreneur but not a very good manager, while Salsbury was a better manager but not a very good entrepreneur. Salsbury may have placed the order for the popcorn sold in Europe during the 1889–92 tours, but it was probably Buffalo Bill's idea. It is likely that without Cody, Salsbury would have remained a successful but minor impresario, and without Salsbury, Cody would have been a successful actor but would not have achieved the phenomenal show business success that he was able to with a good manager.

As Salsbury's health declined and he gradually withdrew from the Wild West, Cody tried to fill the gap by adding James Bailey, of Barnum and Bailey fame, as a partner. Salsbury was still involved, however, and his resentment did not prevent him from joining Cody, Burke, and others for a steak dinner on May 31, 1902, hosted by a group of New York City businessmen. His health rallied that evening as well. and he happily consumed his share of steak and joined in the after-dinner tale-telling. He was still credited with being the director general and manager of the show that fall. But Salsbury's health took a turn for the worse that winter, and he died on December 24 of a "disease of the stomach." After his death, articles paid tribute to him as a prime mover behind Buffalo Bill's Wild West. Some even claimed it was Salsbury who discovered Buffalo Bill, ignoring the fact that Cody already had a successful career in show business before Buffalo Bill's Wild West. Cody was in London with the show when Salsbury died, so he was unable to attend the funeral. When the show opened on December 26, he ensured that the show's flags were at half-mast and its banners covered with black crepe.[6]

The partnership with Bailey did not last long, as he died four years after Salsbury. Bailey had put together the arrangements for the Wild West's tours of Europe from 1902 until his death in April 1906. Cody received the news of Bailey's death while the show was in Ravenna, Italy, so he could not make it to the funeral, but he sent a large wreath of flowers and his sympathy. Bailey's passing did not interrupt the show, which continued traveling through Europe until fall. It returned to the United States, where it resumed its tours in the spring of 1907. But while it still drew crowds, Buffalo Bill's Wild West was not received as enthusiastically as in the past. After two years of declining attendance, Cody merged Buffalo Bill's Wild West with Pawnee Bill's Far East. Gordon "Pawnee Bill" Lillie had gotten his start in show business with Cody years earlier, in 1883. When he left Buffalo Bill's Wild West, he formed his own show and eventually became Cody's most successful competitor. But both shows had suffered from poor attendance in the new century. By combining rather than competing, they hoped to increase audiences and revenue. The result of their partnership was named Buffalo Bill's Wild West Combined with Pawnee Bill's Great Far East.[7]

The two new partners soon discovered that the heights of the past were no longer reachable. Combining the two shows injected new life into them but represented a larger expense without a commensurate increase in income. Wild West shows no longer excited the public's imagination, and they were experiencing competition from the professional rodeos and western movies they helped stimulate. Cody remarked, "The old show isn't drawing as it used to, and the moving picture reel is responsible for it all." In 1910 they decided to stage a series of farewell shows highlighting the sixty-four-year-old Cody's retirement from show business. It was not the first time he had talked about retiring; eight years earlier, he had announced that he would stop touring when the show returned from Europe. "I have toured the old world and the new and I've given my show in every nook and corner and it's high time now that I am getting out of it." But for reasons known only to him, he did not quit. Now he was going to make it final.[8]

The farewell seasons began in New York City on April 26, 1910, with Cody's retirement announcement made at a Friars banquet honoring entertainer George M. Cohan at the Hotel Astor. (Ten years later, Cohan organized a fundraiser to memorialize him at the Broadway Theater in Denver.) "Buffalo Bill Bids You Goodbye!" trumpeted the headlines as the show crossed the country over the next two years This message was emblazoned on the show's souvenir programs, which also conveyed a "Farewell Salute" from Cody. Crowds turned out in large numbers. In Moline, Illinois, a town the Wild West had not visited before and did not visit again, twenty-six thousand people attended the afternoon and evening shows.[9]

Despite that kind of attendance in some places, when the farewell shows concluded at the end of the 1911 season, the partners discovered the scheme had not been as lucrative as they'd hoped. Cody also had other debts to contend with. He was investing considerable amounts of money in development around his town of Cody and gold mines near Oracle, Arizona. When the show was not performing in 1910–12, he traveled back and forth between the two locations, spending the bulk of the winter months enjoying the warmth in Arizona. While in Tucson, he stayed at the Santa Rita Hotel, often entertaining friends and potential investors at dinner parties there. In 1912 he remained through Christmas, when he dressed as Santa Claus and handed out presents to children whose fathers worked in his mines. It was reported that he "raided the toy shops and sweetmeat stores." After enjoying apples, oranges, popcorn, and raisins, the children consumed "a whooping big dinner." Cody hoped that after he retired, the money from his investments would enable him to live in the lavish manner to which he had become accustomed. Gordon Lillie later remarked that Buffalo Bill spent "like a drunken sailor," staying at the finest hotels and spreading his money around. "Money to him was only made to spend or to aid and make others happy." But his investments did not support that lifestyle; instead, he lost money in both Cody and Oracle. His debts were so high that he was forced to sell Scout's Rest Ranch to Lillie.[10]

With Cody's plans for retirement failing him, he discovered that the show indeed must go on. When Buffalo Bill's Wild West and Pawnee Bill's Great Far East began a new season in 1912, it made no mention of retirement or farewell salutes. The two scouts rode side by side into the arena and onto the cover of the new souvenir program. Audiences who had attended the gala farewell shows were undoubtedly surprised to see Buffalo Bill back in the saddle. They must have been even more surprised when the show ended abruptly in July 1913, a farewell driven by Denver businessman Harry Tammen. By the end of August Buffalo Bill's Wild West and Pawnee Bill's Great Far East was gone, sold on the auction block to meet debts to Tammen and other creditors who, even though their contracts extended to the end of the season, needed to be paid. Along with the show wagons and animals that were sold was a wagon filled with Cracker Jack boxes and peanuts, purchased by the Miller Brothers 101 Ranch Wild West for $165. Employees were laid off and the show dispersed. It was finally farewell for good to Buffalo Bill's Wild West, but no banquet was held in 1913.[11]

Cody still was unable to retire, remarking, "I have to start life over again, with no capital." It appears that Tammen's plan all along had been to force Buffalo Bill to appear in his own show, the Sells Floto Circus. The destruction of the Wild West ensured that Cody would do that, and now Tammen could use his name, calling his show Sells Floto Circus and Buffalo Bill Himself. But Buffalo Bill himself was all that remained of the original show. Cody appeared with Sells Floto for the next two years, promoting the circus and riding around the arena as a celebrity. Perhaps following the Wild West's example, Sells Floto threw a farewell banquet when it closed the season in Fort Worth, Texas, in 1914. The repast included deep sea turtle, baked red snapper, veal sweetbreads, oyster cocktail and patties, suckling pig, turkey, and prime rib. Peach sundae with nuts was a dessert highlight, and claret punch was added to the customary tea and coffee. A poem on the menu ended with the words "Goodbye brother trooper, I'll see you in the spring."[12]

Cody returned to Sells Floto in the spring of 1915. He was finally able to sever the relationship at the end of that year, but only after paying Tammen to be able to use his Buffalo Bill nickname. During the 1916 season Cody appeared with a real Wild West show once again as a featured act with the Miller Brothers, buyers of the wagonload of Cracker Jack and peanuts two years earlier. The show was advertised as Buffalo Bill (Himself) and 101 Ranch Wild West Combined. He confided in Dexter Fellows that he intended to raise enough money to open his own show in 1917. His plans for a new show, however, were never realized.[13]

Bill Cody struggled with ailments of his own, including severe headaches, after the death of Salsbury. To deal with the headaches, he obtained special powders from a cousin in Canada. Because of their potential side effects, including kidney damage, the powders were not allowed to be sold in the United States. They did help with the headaches. As the 1916 season concluded, Cody fell ill with the flu, and his symptoms may have led him to increase the dosage of the powders. After three weeks, he did not feel any better, so he traveled to Glenwood Springs, Colorado, on January 4 in hopes that the hot springs there would provide a cure. It was a trip that many others had taken before him, including Doc Holliday. One of the last photos of Cody reveals a gaunt man, only a shade of his former self, standing in front of the hot springs (fig. 24). After two days with little improvement, he collapsed, and the doctor at the hot springs, W. W. Cook, told him there was no hope for his recovery.[14]

A discouraged Buffalo Bill didn't even try to reach his ranch in Cody but instead went to his sister's home in Denver. Later it was claimed that he stopped for his last drink in Idaho Springs en route, but eating and drinking were probably the last thing on his mind. As he arrived in Denver, word went out across America and the world that the great scout and showman was dying. His wife, Louisa, and daughter Irma rushed to his side. He confided in them that he still wanted to organize a new Wild West. But when a local doctor, J. H. East, examined Buffalo Bill, he reported that Cody's system had broken down, and "the food he partakes of no longer produces life forces." Perhaps that is why no record exists of Buffalo Bill's last meal, as the joys and benefits that eating had once provided him were gone. The Denver doctor's diagnosis was similar to Cook's: Buffalo Bill would not recover. Cody played a last game of cards and began settling his affairs.[15]

William F. "Buffalo Bill" Cody made his final farewell on January 10, 1917. The official cause of death was uremic poisoning as a result of kidney failure. At the time, it was suggested that the kidney failure was aggravated by heart problems or high blood pressure. But it was more likely due to kidney damage caused by the special powders that Cody had been taking.[16]

Like his show had been, Buffalo Bill's funeral in Denver was a spectacle. His body lay in state in the Colorado State Capitol building, while around twenty-five thousand people passed by to give their respects. Then the coffin was put on a caisson and carried to Denver Elks Lodge Number 17. After hundreds of Wild West parades during his lifetime, it was Buffalo Bill's last such appearance, with thousands of spectators lining the streets. Following the service at the lodge, his body was transported back to Olinger's Mortuary. There it stayed under guard until June 3, when he was buried on Lookout Mountain. The burial service, conducted by the Golden City Masonic Lodge, was reported to have been attended by up to twenty thousand people, many of whom filed by his open casket for one last look.[17]

Despite his debts, William Cody did not die a pauper, as some have claimed. On his death, it was announced that his estate was worth between $65,000 and $75,000. It was no small amount of money for the time, but not the millions he once had. As he had said, "I have lost several fortunes in outside ventures." Those ventures, his lavish lifestyle, and his generosity had all contributed to the depletion of his estate.[18]

Attempting to follow through on Cody's last wish, his family immediately organized a new Wild West with the tagline "Let My Show Go On." But it encountered the same competition that had

Fig 24. A gaunt and ailing William Cody in Glenwood Springs on January 4, 1917. He was there to take in the waters and visit a doctor. Told that he had only a few days to live, he continued on to Denver, where he passed away on January 10. Object ID#73.0235, Buffalo Bill Museum and Grave, Golden CO.

kept audiences away from Buffalo Bill's Wild West in its final years. Plus it no longer had Buffalo Bill as a headliner. The show closed before finishing the 1917 season. Although the attempt to begin a new Wild West failed, Buffalo Bill's place in history was already firmly established. William F. Cody lived the West, promoted the West, helped change the West, and left his mark on the West.[19]

18

Still Eating and Drinking with Buffalo Bill

If you don't prepare your dough properly, you can't expect good bread.

Buffalo Bill, 1903

Buffalo Bill's place in history is secure. But he also left a culinary legacy, although it is not as obvious. Today there are many ways, and places, that legacy endures. Near his grave site sits Pahaska Tepee, a café and gift shop begun by his foster son, Johnny Baker, three years after Cody's death. Baker spent most of his life with Buffalo Bill, starting with the Wild West in 1883 as a boy of fourteen. Over the years he grew so close to Bill and Louisa Cody that they regarded him as their foster son, a designation often appearing in posters and other advertising for Buffalo Bill's Wild West. Under Buffalo Bill's tutelage, he became an expert in shooting. Originally billed as the "Cowboy Kid," he became the show's primary sharpshooter after Annie Oakley left in 1901. He eventually rose to be general manager. Baker stayed by Cody's side after the demise of the Wild West in 1913, but when the effort to create another Buffalo Bill's Wild West failed after Cody's death, he had to find a new livelihood.

After thirty years of living with and helping manage one of the biggest food service operations of its time at Buffalo Bill's Wild West, Baker decided to open a catering business in Denver in 1918. Operated by Baker and his wife, Olive, it was called Café Josephine. A ledger of café menus reveals the same gourmet fare that Baker ate with Buffalo Bill. A luncheon for the Denver Press Club included coquille of crabmeat, sirloin of beef, and Parisian potatoes. But by 1920 Baker was looking for a different source of income. He wrote to the City of Denver, offering to operate a museum, gift shop, and café near Buffalo Bill's grave. The city agreed and Pahaska Tepee opened in 1921, combining all three services. It had both a coffee shop and a restaurant, with a joint menu that included breakfast foods, sandwiches, salads, and hot entrées like Rocky Mountain trout. One of the specialties was freshly squeezed orangeade. Non-alcoholic near beer from Coors and Budweiser was served but there were no drinks with alcohol, a practice that has continued through the present day. Today the museum has been moved to a separate building and a café/gift shop operates in the original Pahaska Tepee. The café prolongs the spirit of Buffalo Bill by offering a variety of buffalo entrées.[1]

Buffalo Bill's food legacy took a different turn at the Buckhorn Exchange, opened in 1893 by one of Cody's associates, Henry H. "Shorty Scout" Zietz. It is still Denver's oldest bar. Zietz knew Buffalo Bill from his scouting days, and when Cody visited Denver, he often dropped into the Buckhorn for a visit. Sometime after Cody's death, the bar added a drink to its menu in tribute to him, calling it the Buffalo Bill. A mix of bourbon and sweet cider, it continues to be served at the Buckhorn. According to Zietz's son, it was Buffalo Bill's favorite drink when he visited the tavern on his visits to Denver. This makes sense given Cody's fondness for sweet, rather than hard, cider. For many years the Buckhorn Exchange also served food; a 1930s menu offered a full page of drink choices and a half page of food options. In 1978 the bar was purchased by new owners, who decided to capitalize on its history as an Old West hangout. They expanded the dining menu to match the place's decor of mounted wild game heads, with buffalo being a prominent entrée. With the return of buffalo herds in the late twentieth and early twenty-first centuries, it is now one of Denver's largest purveyors of buffalo meat.[2]

Denver's other major purveyor of buffalo is the Fort restaurant, built in the 1960s by Sam Arnold as a replica of Bent's Fort. With Sam's interest in all things associated with the Santa Fe Trail and the mountain men, it soon became a culinary center for historians interested in foods of the frontier. Sam's daughter, Holly Arnold Kinney, the current owner, continues to promote the culinary history of the Old West. She has produced several cookbooks that facilitate home cooking of Buffalo Bill's favorite foods from his days on the trail and hunting in the Rockies.

Although Buffalo Bill has been promoted through foods in the Denver area because of his grave's location, Buffalo Bill has also been memorialized elsewhere in American foodways in the hundred-plus years since his death. In 1963 a restaurant in Pennsylvania called Longhorn Ranch opened. It pictured Cody in an advertisement for its steaks and other food, all cooked the "Injun Way." It was one of many restaurants capitalizing on the legacy of Buffalo Bill that sprang up throughout the United States and the world. Others included Buffalo Bill's Wild West, "a family adventure in eating out," in Northridge California; the Buffalo Bill Steak Village in Edmonton, Alberta; and Buffalo Bill's Restaurant and Steak House in Kelowna, British Columbia. Some places, like the Sheridan Inn's bar and restaurant in Wyoming and the Buckhorn Exchange in Denver, were actually frequented by Cody and continue to promote that connection in their establishments. Other eating places, like the Longhorn Ranch, used Buffalo Bill for the cachet without any connection.[3]

Whether or not, as the Buckhorn Exchange claims, Buffalo Bill's favorite drink was apple juice and whiskey, his favorite spirit was certainly the latter. It was a drink with which he had long associations. Will Cody's father, Isaac, may even have occasionally patronized Ben Holladay's dram house in Weston in 1854. Today the distillery Holladay established in 1856 continues in operation at its original location and is the oldest operating distillery west of the Mississippi. Renamed McCormick Distilling in 1942, it issued a special decanter in the 1970s depicting Buffalo Bill and his horse. Jim Beam also sold whiskey in a Buffalo Bill decanter in the 1970s.

Buffalo Bill had his encounters with tanglefoot as a young man. Years later he described a "very bad quality of whiskey made in Taos in the early days," which he very well might have imbibed. Made from wheat by illegal stills in that area, it was called "Taos lightning." Just before thirteen-year-old Will Cody went to the Colorado goldfields with a group of other gold seekers, Richens "Uncle Dick" Wootton arrived in the fledgling town of Denver City. It was Christmas Eve 1858, and the earliest prospectors in what came to be called the Pikes Peak Gold Rush were celebrating the holiday. Seeing the miners gathered around a large bonfire, Wootton knocked in the head of a cask of Taos lightning and offered free drinks to anyone who had a cup. According to one witness, drunken miners were soon dancing around the bonfire with abandon. Today a whiskey is sold under the name of Taos Lightning, but it bears little resemblance to the bad whiskey that the miners and frontiersmen like Buffalo Bill consumed.[4]

This was just one of the whiskeys available in the Old West. Sam Arnold said that the traders often watered down their whiskey and used various additives, like red chili, tobacco, or even gunpowder, to give it the taste of full-strength whiskey. Even with its comparatively low percentage of alcohol, this "trader's whiskey" still packed a punch for men who might not have tasted spirits for weeks or months. Among those watered down by the traders was Old Crow, a Kentucky whiskey begun in 1835 and still in production today. In 1957 Old Crow advertisements featured a painting of Buffalo Bill drinking their product at his favorite hotel in New York City, the Hoffman House.[5]

Cody Road Whiskey is "handmade beneath the Iowa sky" in LeClaire. The whiskey was birthed in 2010 by the Mississippi River Distilling Company, 164 years after Will Cody was born in LeClaire. Originally a bourbon bearing Buffalo Bill's name and autograph on its label, it has expanded to nine different flavors, all with Buffalo Bill's profile on their labels.[6]

While Cody Road and Old Crow in no way resemble the tanglefoot or bad whiskey that Buffalo Bill and other men often drank on the frontier, a Buffalo Bill Bourbon of that type emerged several years ago. One reviewer called it "the cheapest rotgut since the Prohibition," stating it had an aftertaste that was metallic, "like sucking a penny. My left eye was involuntarily closed for a full 30 seconds." While the whiskey, with Buffalo Bill's name and a photo of him on the label, is supposedly made in Kentucky, it is of dubious origin. The reviewer noted he acquired the bottle in Cuba, and it appeared to have traveled there from Le Havre, France.[7]

Not to be left out, breweries also use Buffalo Bill's name. In 1983 Californian Bill Owens capitalized on the name with his own brews, although he did not use any images of Cody. In 2011 two Wyoming brewers, both of whom prominently featured Cody on their labels, fought over the right to call their products Buffalo Bill Beer. On one side of the battle were the owners of Irma Hotel in Cody. Begun by Cody and named after his daughter, the hotel has been serving food and drinks ever since its opening in 1902. Located in the center of Buffalo Bill's namesake town, where cowboys still occasionally ride their horses down the main street and there is a daily summer rodeo, the Irma is home to a popular restaurant and the Silver Saddle Saloon. Today it is advertised as a place "where good scouts eat." Also in Cody, the Buffalo Bill Center of the West, with five major museums combined under one roof, celebrates Buffalo Bill throughout, including a cafeteria serving buffalo entrées. The center's cookbook, *The Great Entertainer*, features recipes for wild game and western food favorites and celebrates eating in the spirit of Buffalo Bill.[8]

Elsewhere in Wyoming, the Sheridan Inn and Pahaska Tepee Resort, properties once operated by Buffalo Bill, still promote their connection to him. Buffalo entrées and plenty of whiskey can be obtained at each. North Platte, Buffalo Bill's hometown in Nebraska, celebrates his legacy with Buffalo Bill Days every summer, has a state park that was created around Cody's Scout's Rest Ranch, and sports his visage on its visitors bureau website. But while local menus offer plenty of good Nebraska beef, buffalo entrées are not easy to find.

Moving eastward, most of Buffalo Bill's haunts in New York City have either closed or are so changed that they would be unrecognizable to the old scout. The Hoffman House, his favorite place to stay and dine, has been gone for over a century, closed before Cody's death. One iconic spot that remains is Keen's Steakhouse, opened by Albert Keen in 1885. In addition to serving steaks and mutton chops, Keen's stored and cared for clay churchwarden pipes, used by members of its Pipe Club when they came to dine. Members of the club included Buffalo Bill and his friend Theodore Roosevelt. Today both of their pipes are on exhibit near each other at the restaurant's entrance, along with other pipes used by Keen's famous patrons. The clubby Victorian interior of the steakhouse, with many historic images, nicely complements the same tasty entrées enjoyed by Buffalo Bill over one hundred years ago.[9]

Buffalo Bill's food legacy is just as obvious, perhaps more so, in Europe. The Munich Cowboy Club was inspired by Buffalo Bill's Wild West and the writings of German author Karl May. The club opened in 1913 and, with a brief interruption during World War II, has operated ever since, offering American whiskey in its saloon. Caffè Greco in Rome still proudly shows off images of Cody, as well as a photograph of John Burke and several Lakotas when they were there in 1906. Just up the Mediterranean, France's Buffalo Grill chain offers "Wild West food" and provides souvenir pins with Buffalo Bill's image. In Hungary, a Buffalo Bill western-themed restaurant has Cody's image over its entrance, while in England, Buffalo Bill's café offers Tex-Mex food.[10]

Until the pandemic of 2020, Disneyland Paris staged a Buffalo Bill's Wild West Show as a dinner theater, featuring foods from the American West twice daily and seating two thousand for each show. EuroDisney, later renamed Disneyland Paris, opened Buffalo Bill's Wild West Show in 1992, and it became one of the French Magic Kingdom's most popular attractions. The meal began with corn bread and chili, followed by Texas beef and potato wedges, and finished with an apple dessert. The corn bread was part of Buffalo Bill's legacy in France, where he promoted it during the show's 1889 visit to Paris.[11]

The Martougin chocolate company in Antwerp, a city the Wild West visited in 1891 and 1906, used Buffalo Bill to promote its products during the first half of the twentieth century. Artist Eric Wansart created a series of collector's cards featuring scenes from Cody's life for the company, which closed in the 1960s. Over the years other candy companies in Europe followed suit, with collector's card series issued by Chocolat des Gourmets in France, Great Britain's Anglo Confectionery, and Sweden's Williams Förlags AB. In the United States, the Topps Company issued a Buffalo Bill card with its bubble gum.[12]

Meert, the company that furnished tea and coffee to Buffalo Bill's Wild West when it was in Lille, France, has created a gourmet Buffalo Bill black tea commemorating that 1905 event (fig. 25). The company also has produced small ceramic fèves, little larger than one inch in length or height. A fève is traditionally placed within a cake served at the feast of the Epiphany, also called Three Kings Day, on January 6. The feast celebrates the visit of the three kings to the Christ child, and whoever gets the fève is declared king or queen for the day. Fèves often depict famous people, and the Meert series featured important French and European figures, like Napoleon and Mozart. Only one American is represented in the series—Buffalo Bill.[13]

Buffalo Bill has been commemorated throughout the world as one of the best-known characters in American history. His name has also appeared on eating and drinking establishments throughout the world, ranging from a bar in Denver's Albany Hotel, where he frequently stayed, to a bar in Thailand and a steakhouse in Zimbabwe. These establishments celebrate Buffalo Bill and the Old West, a historic period that was unique to America. They tap into the romance of the Wild West and the life of Buffalo Bill. They also commemorate their culinary connections to William F. "Buffalo Bill" Cody, America's first galloping gourmet.

In 1903 Will Cody wrote to his sister, "If you don't prepare your dough properly, you can't expect good bread." This statement not only used food imagery but also laid out a philosophy he implemented throughout his life. While Cody had his impulsive moments and his failures, his successes show that he prepared his dough properly. And his good bread lasted. Buffalo Bill's Wild West is considered one of the most successful shows of all time, and Buffalo Bill was one of the most famous people of his time, with his name still familiar worldwide. He even made his mark on our culinary history.[14]

Fig 25. Meert Thé des pionniers (Pioneer Tea), featuring Buffalo Bill. The Meert company provided tea and coffee to Buffalo Bill's Wild West when the show was in Lille, France, in 1905. Today the company commemorates that event with this tea. Author's collection.

APPENDIX

Historical Recipes from Buffalo Bill's Life and Times

This appendix contains recipes for a variety of foods eaten by Buffalo Bill, his friends, and the staff of Buffalo Bill's Wild West. The recipes, offered with their historical backgrounds, represent foodways of the late nineteenth and early twentieth centuries. Many are typical of those times, even if they might be unusual to twenty-first-century palates. Most of the ingredients can be found with a little searching. Modern equivalents for ingredients are included when possible. The recipes are listed by the chapters in which they appear. Try some . . . and invite Buffalo Bill into your dining room.

Chapter 1

Corn Bread

Mid-nineteenth-century recipe books included directions for preparation of rye and Indian (corn) bread. Newspapers of the day also contained recipes for corn bread. Corn meal was less expensive than wheat flour, so it was more commonly used for bread than wheat. When a corn bread recipe called for flour, rye flour was often added because it also was less expensive than wheat flour. One writer referred to corn bread as "a sweet and nourishing diet, and generally acceptable to children." It may have been acceptable to Will Cody and his siblings, but after days of eating it on the road, they grew tired of it.[1]

The following corn bread recipe is from an 1853 Glasgow, Missouri, newspaper. On the Missouri River between St. Louis and Weston, Glasgow was a center of commerce and transportation in the 1850s. The Cody family might have passed through the town.

Get your bowl (or pan) ready, with about half a gallon of fine meal: pour over the meal just enough boiling water to make it wet. When it is cool enough, add half a tea-cup-ful of molasses, a teas-sponful of slaaratus, and enough flour to give the dough sufficient adhesive power to form a loaf; don't knead it hard, and when it is light bake it in a well heated oven till it is brown—then you have a loaf of bread worth traveling down the throat of any hungry mortal.[2]

The newspaper incorrectly spelled several things, including the word *saleratus*, an early name for baking soda. While the recipe refers to "fine meal," the corn meal used in the mid-nineteenth century, often ground in a coffee mill, was coarse and more like today's stone-ground corn meal.

Fried Yellow-Legged Chicken

A guide for young cooks published by Mrs. Cornelius in 1859 provided guidelines for choosing chickens for cooking. She stated categorically that "the best are those that have yellow legs." She went on to say that proper cooking of a chicken involved choosing one that was young, with a breast that yielded satisfactorily to being pressed with a finger, and did not have feet and legs that looked "as if they had seen hard service in the world." The chicken could be boiled, broiled, roasted, or fricasseed, but frying seems to have been most popular form of preparation. After being cut up, the chicken was fried in a spider, or three-legged skillet, if cooked on an open hearth. In more established homes with a wood-burning stove, it was cooked in a flat-bottomed iron skillet on the stovetop. A Methodist minister visiting the Cody family would have been welcomed with a meal of fried yellow-legged chicken accompanied by corn bread or biscuits. Mrs. Cody probably made her fried chicken similarly to the following 1853 recipe.[3]

After cutting up the chickens, wash and drain them; season them with salt and pepper; rub each piece in flour, and drop them separately in a frying-pan or dutch-oven of hot lard; when brown, turn the other side to fry; make a thickening of rich milk, flour, a piece of butter, salt, and chopped parsley; take up the chicken on a dish; pour a little water in the pan to keep the gravy from being too thick; put in the thickening, stir it, and let it boil a few minutes; then pour it over the chicken.[4]

Home-fried chicken made in Kansas during the nineteenth century and much of the twentieth changed little. It was fried in a pan, rather than deep-fried, and was cooked in lard. During the twentieth century, Crisco became a popular substitute for lard.

Chapter 2

Hardtack

Hardtack, also called hard bread or pilot bread (Will Cody called it hard tack), was taken along on trips across the Great Plains and figured greatly in any "feast" on the Oregon Trail, including Will Cody's at Fort Laramie. A baker in St. Louis in 1850 advertised he could supply pilot bread that was kiln-dried and guaranteed to keep for two years. While some folks made hardtack themselves, it was readily available at bakers and other merchants. Hardtack dough was a simple mixture of water, salt, and flour cooked for a long time at a low temperature. Thoroughly ridding the bread of moisture during the slow baking process made it less likely to become moldy. The following recipe was collected by Sam Arnold, western historian and restaurateur.[5]

> Knead flour, water, and salt; roll out on greased 12-by-13 inch pan; cut into fifteen pieces; pierce each piece with sixteen holes. Bake for 30 minutes at 425 degrees Fahrenheit, 15 minutes on each side. Reduce temperature to 200 degrees Fahrenheit and bake until all moisture is removed from crackers (approximately 8 to 24 hours. Crackers will not burn in a 200 degree Fahrenheit oven, so may remain in oven almost indefinitely.)[6]

Hardtack was packed in sacks or barrels for transport across the plains. The U.S. Army purchased it by the barrelful to supply to the troops in the West, which is how it came to be part of the meal that Will Cody so relished.

Coffee

Hardtack was usually served with coffee, into which it was dipped. While hardtack was less attractive to insects than other breads, it could become infested with weevils. If soaked for a few minutes in coffee, not only did it soften up, making it easier to eat, but any weevils or other insects that were in the bread would float to the surface. They could then be skimmed off the coffee, which would be consumed with the hard bread.

Mid-nineteenth-century recipe books offered a variety of ways to make coffee, including using substitutes from roasted dry brown bread crusts, rye soaked in rum, and even ground dried peas. Such would have been unacceptable to the soldiers of the U.S. Army, for whom strong coffee was critical for alertness. One cooking manual distributed to the troops stated, "A small roaster, coffee mill, and strainer, should be the first effort of the cook, and the best outlay of the company fund." At Fort Laramie, Will Cody might have had coffee based on a recipe in one such manual. It called for adding three pounds of ground coffee to twelve gallons of boiling water. This was left on the fire for a few minutes, then removed and a half gallon of cold water added. After the dregs dropped to the bottom, about ten minutes, the liquid was poured off and six pounds of sugar were added to sweeten it. This provided one pint of coffee for each of one hundred men. To make a similar coffee in a smaller quantity and more to modern tastes, acquire some Arbuckle Ariosa Coffee. Perfected right after the Civil War, Arbuckle Coffee became popular as an alternative to the tedious process of roasting and grinding one's own coffee beans.[7]

Bacon

Hardtack could also be dipped into hot bacon grease and fried for a few minutes, which softened and flavored it. The bacon used was actually salt pork that was cut into pieces to cook. This pork was so heavily salted, to stay preserved during the trip, that it had to be soaked in water overnight to make it reasonably palatable. Like the hardtack, the salt pork was acquired from suppliers and provided to the troops by the U.S. Army. The army's recipe called for cutting it into pieces of three to four pounds each, soaking the pieces, and then boiling them in water for two to three hours. Then the bacon was either fried in a skillet or added to beans to make soup. If fried, the grease was saved for future cooking purposes; it could even be put in a tin plate with an old piece of cotton for a wick and used for lighting.[8]

Beans

Dried beans were almost ubiquitous on the frontier and were a staple in army rations. They were nutritious, resisted spoilage, and were unattractive to insects. As the Mel Brooks movie *Blazing Saddles* so aptly demonstrated, beans did have side effects. One Oregon Trail emigrant wrote, "Would feel pretty well myself had I not eaten so many beans." Like bacon, beans had to be soaked overnight before they could be cooked. Cooking them also required several hours, as many as 8 hours as directed by one cookbook of the period, so they were best suited to cooking during a long encampment, such as Will Cody's stay at Fort Laramie.[9]

A great diversity of beans was available to mid-nineteenth-century cooks, but recipes only occasionally specified the varieties. Elizabeth Lea referenced dried white beans in her 1853 cookbook. Recipes in the newspapers often called for navy or black beans. The 1887 *White House Cook Book* recommended dried kidney and lima beans, and by 1896, Fannie Farmer's *Boston Cooking-School Cook Book* included recipes for both butter beans and cranberry beans, which resembled cranberries and were common as far back as colonial times. No matter what kind of beans were chosen, *Miss Leslie's Directions for Cookery* from 1851 suggested soaking them overnight, then boiling them for up to 8 hours, straining the liquid, mixing them with butter, and seasoning them with pepper. Fried salt pork, bacon, or ham could also be added. To make bean soup, particularly popular in the army, the liquid was kept, rather than discarded. Meat and seasoning were then added to the liquid.[10]

Chapter 3

Turkey on Toast

At Camp Turkey, Buffalo Bill and his army companions encountered a problem that's still common after Thanksgiving: what to do with all the leftover turkey. In those days, wild turkey was stuffed and roasted, not unlike today. More butter was needed for basting because wild turkeys had less fat than the domestic ones, since they were more active. Marion Harland wrote in her 1871 cookbook, *Common Sense in the Household*, "The dark meat and game flavor proclaim his birthright of lordly freedom." It was an opinion shared with Benjamin Franklin, who felt the wild turkey was a courageous, respectable, and "true original native of America."[11]

Cody was probably joking when he referred to eating "turkey on toast" in his 1879 autobiography. It was a phrase made popular by a humorous story circulating in the newspapers about a man in a restaurant who requested snipe on toast, a common way of presenting the small game bird. Grouse, woodcock, and other small birds were also presented in a similar manner. When the dish was placed before him, the man confronted the waiter, saying he had ordered snipe on toast, not just toast. The waiter replied that this was what was before him, pointing to a tiny black speck on the toast. Stating that he had mistaken the snipe for a fly, the frustrated customer demanded, "Now you take that snipe away and bring me turkey on toast, and darn it, I want a full-sized turkey too!"[12]

By the end of the decade, turkey on toast was being served as an entrée, although cookbooks of the era do not contain recipes for it. It was one way of using up the leftovers from a roasted turkey. One cookbook did provide the following recipe for ragout of turkey, a ragout being bits of meat cooked in a thickened liquid or sauce. Poured over toasted bread, it would have been similar to Buffalo Bill's "turkey on toast."[13]

> Cut the cold turkey from the bones and into bits an inch long with knife and fork, tear as little as possible. Put into a skillet or saucepan the gravy left from the roast, with hot water to dilute it should the quantity be small. Add a lump of butter the size of an egg, a teaspoonful of pungent sauce, a half-teaspoonful of cloves, a large pinch of nutmeg, with a little salt. Let it boil and put in the meat. Stew very slowly for ten minutes—not more—and stir in a tablespoonful of cranberry or currant jelly, another of browned flour which has been wet

with cold water; lastly, a glass of brown sherry or Madeira. Boil up once and serve in a covered dish for breakfast.[14]

Champagne Punch

Punches of various kinds were quite popular in the nineteenth century and earlier. In America, that popularity waned as cocktails grew fashionable. And while some bartenders served punch by the glass, the punch bowl was pretty much confined to parties and celebrations by 1900. Champagne punch was popular in New Orleans but, like other punches, began to wane in popularity elsewhere in the United States by 1871. When Buffalo Bill, General Davies, and their companions celebrated the successful conclusion of their hunting expedition with champagne punch, it was on the decline, like the buffalo they consumed.[15]

In 1862 Jerry Thomas published one of the earliest guides to making cocktails. This pioneering work inspired bartenders throughout the country. In addition to containing a great number of recipes for cocktails, which were on the rise in popularity, it included two champagne punch recipes. One of the recipes used wine rather than champagne but was nevertheless called a champagne punch. The other one, called Rocky Mountain Punch, did contain champagne as well as Jamaican rum. Since the hunting party spared no expense when it came to consumables, it can be assumed that they were adequately equipped with whatever it took to make a fine champagne punch. The maraschino in this recipe is not the juice from maraschino cherries commonly found in supermarkets, but rather a colorless liqueur made from fermented Italian marasca cherries and obtained from liquor stores. This recipe was to be prepared for "a mixed party of twenty."[16]

5 bottles of champagne
1 quart of Jamaican rum
1 pint of maraschino
6 lemons, sliced
Sugar to taste

Mix the above ingredients in a large punch-bowl, then place in the centre of the bowl a large square block of ice, ornamented on top with rock candy, loaf-sugar, sliced lemons or oranges, and fruits in season. This is a splendid punch for New Year's Day.[17]

Chapter 4

Calf's Head en Tortue

Calf's head en tortue was served as one of the entrées at the banquet given for the Grand Duke Alexis at the Spencer House in Niagara Falls. *Tortue* is French for turtle, so "en tortue" means this dish was prepared in the manner one would prepare turtle and refers to the French sauce that was served over stewed turtle or, in this case, calf's head. The head could be prepared and the sauce created in a variety of ways. Most recipes called for white wine boiled with thyme, bay leaf, parsley, sage, basil, rosemary, and sometimes a pinch of cayenne. A few tablespoons of demi-glace and tomato sauce, as well as mushrooms, diced carrots and onions, and even ham, might be added to the sauce. Often it was finished with a bit of Madeira.[18]

The boiled head with sauce was then presented on a platter surrounded by all manner of garnishes: sliced hard-boiled eggs, stuffed olives, mushrooms, fried slices of the calf's brain, and even crayfish. And that is the way this dish, relatively uncommon in the United States, was served—when it was served at all. Even though the dish had a rather elegant-sounding name, strip away the fancy garnishes and it was basically stewed calf's head served in a sauce. The following is one from 1871.

Wash the head in several waters, and taking out the brains, set them by in a cool glass. Tie the head in a floured cloth and boil it two hours in hot water slightly salted. Wash the brains carefully, picking out all the bits of skin and membrane, cleansing them over and over until they are perfectly white. Then stew in just enough water to cover them. Take them out, mash smooth with the back of a wooden spoon, and add gradually, that it may not lump, a small teacupful of the water in which the head is boiled. Season with chopped parsley, a pinch of sage, pepper, salt, and powdered cloves, with a great spoonful of butter. Set it over the fire to simmer in a saucepan until you are ready. When the head is tender, take it up and drain very dry. Score the top, and rub it well over with melted butter; dredge with flour and set in the oven to brown. Or, you can use beaten egg and cracker-crumbs in place of the butter and flour. When you serve the head, pour the gravy over it.[19]

Chapter 5

Boiled Pigs' Feet à la P. T. Barnum

"Pigs' feet, properly cooked, were given me to eat long before I was permitted to partake of any other animal food," P. T. Barnum reminisced in 1881. His recipe was distributed by the wire services and shared in newspapers as far away as Bismarck, North Dakota. The article observed that "housekeepers will be glad to get hold of this new way of cooking pigs' feet" and went on to observe that it would be new only to the everyday cook; the Sturtevant Hotel had been preparing pigs' feet that way for a long time. Since Boiled Pigs' Feet à la P. T. Barnum was a specialty of the Sturtevant House, Buffalo Bill probably had it at least once during his stay there in 1883. Here is Barnum's recipe.[20]

When old and young feet are boiled two and one-half hours, as usual, the old ones are tough and worthless. If they were boiled three and one-half hours the young feet would burst and the gelatine swim away. Now, the secret is to wrap each pig's foot in a cotton bandage wound two or three times around it, and well corded with twine. Then boil them four hours. Let them remain in the bandages till needed to fry, broil, or pickle. The skin will hold together while being cooked, and when you eat it you will find them all tender and delicate as possible.[21]

Chapter 6

Griddle Cakes

Griddle cakes, called pancakes today, were easily made for large numbers of hungry mouths and were standard fare for breakfasts at Buffalo Bill's Wild West. They were cooked on the large, flat frying surface of the stove that was central to the show's range wagon. Eighty pounds of flour were used each day for the griddle cakes, which were smothered with 10 gallons of syrup over the course of a week.[22]

The griddle cakes would have been prepared with a recipe similar to this one, from a book of New England breakfast breads. This quantity is but a fraction of what would have been required for six hundred show personnel. The recipe's daintier subtlety of rolling powdered sugar and butter into the cakes would not have been observed while serving so many people in a limited amount of time.

Two Cups and a Half of Flour
One Teaspoonful of Salt
One Teaspoonful of Soda and Two Teaspoonfuls of Cream
    of Tartar, or Three Teaspoonfuls of Baking Powder
Two Eggs; One Will Do
Three Cups of Milk
Two Even Teaspoonfuls of Butter, Measured Before Melted

Sift the flour with the salt, and the soda and cream of tartar (or baking powder), add the milk gradually, stirring well to be sure it is quite smooth. Then add the butter, melted, and last of all the eggs, which must first be very well beaten. If the milk is very rich, the butter need not be added.

Have the griddle quite hot, and well greased with lard or part butter and part lard, just before frying the cakes. A very pretty way to serve griddle cakes is to melt a tablespoonful of butter, and stir into it, while hot, a tablespoonful of white sugar. Spread over the cakes as soon as they are taken from the grill, and make each into a little roll. In this way they are very nice, and keep very hot.[23]

Fricasseed Chicken

Sundays marked the observation of an old tradition that harked back to Buffalo Bill's early days in Kansas. In 1896 one newspaper reporter noted, "150 chickens are sacrificed to make a Sabbath day feast for the Wild West." No mention was made as to the color of their legs, however. As many as 820 chickens were consumed each week by the cast, although that quantity paled in comparison with the 5,694 pounds of beef eaten on a weekly basis. While beef was served every day, chicken was usually reserved for Sundays and special occasions. During one midweek performance in Sandusky, Ohio, in 1896, the cooks announced that dinner would include a surprise—chicken. Charles Hutchinson, one of the managers of the show, noted, "I think that the singular of the word comes nearer striking it than anything else, for upon investigation it was found that there were only nine small chickens, and the first to arrive at the cook-tent naturally received it all on the staff table." But the cooks usually delivered as promised, and such hollow surprises were rare.[24]

Breast of chicken, prime rib roast, boiled beef, and baked fish were on the dinner menu for June 5, 1899, while the Wild West was in New Jersey, and the main entrée item was fricasseed chicken. This dish was so popular that a recipe for fricasseed chicken, or chicken fricassee, was found in virtually every cookbook of the period. It was easily prepared, as demonstrated in the following 1896 recipe.

> Dress, clean, and cut up a fowl. Put in a kettle, cover with boiling water, and cook slowly until tender, adding salt to water when the chicken is about half done. Remove from water, sprinkled with salt and pepper, dredge with flour, and sauté in butter or pork fat. Arrange chicken on pieces of dry toast placed on a hot platter, having wings and second joints opposite each other, breast in centre of platter, and drumsticks crossed just below second joints. Pour around White or Brown Sauce. Reduce stock to two cups, strain, and remove the fat. Melt three tablespoons butter, add four tablespoons flour, and pour on gradually one and one-half cups stock. Just before serving, add one-half cup cream, and salt and pepper to taste; or make a sauce by browning butter and flour and adding two cups stock, then seasoning with salt and pepper.[25]

Chapter 7

Baking-Powder Biscuits

Biscuits were a quick and easy breakfast item, requiring the sort of "quick oven" that the range wagon supplied. By 1895, when the Wild West began regularly using the range wagon, baking powder was commonly available commercially. This recipe for biscuits was published in 1887 in *The White House Cook Book*, a combination of home recipes and recipes adapted for household use from America's White House, where biscuits and other foods were created for large numbers of guests. In that respect, its cuisine was not too different from that of the Wild West.

> Two pints of flour, butter the size of an egg, three heaping tea-spoonfuls of baking-powder, and one teaspoonful of salt; make a soft dough of sweet milk or water, knead as little as possible, cut out with the usual biscuit-cutter and bake in rather a quick oven.[26]

Roast Sugar-Cured Ham and Madeira Sauce

Sugar-cured ham served with Madeira sauce was not unusual on nineteenth-century menus, although it is less common today. It is a classic French sauce, which would have made the dish seem elegant. Madeira wine, which comes from the Portuguese island of that name, was quite popular during the eighteenth century and was favored by George Washington and the other founding fathers. The unique process used to make the wine, dating back to the fifteenth century, exposes it to excessive heat, which gives it longevity. Subsequent exposure of the wine to heat and even leaving a bottle open for a prolonged time do not negatively affect its flavor, which it can retain for centuries. Thus Madeira would have been a good cooking wine for a traveling show that might visit many climates. It would certainly have held up against the high heat of the Wild West's large range.

Some American cooks served a sweetened Madeira sauce over puddings or other desserts. Ham, however, demands a sauce that combines savory and sweet flavors. A traditional French version of the sauce simply involved adding a few tablespoons of Madeira wine to reduced juices from cooked meat. Heated sugar-cured ham would not have supplied juices as rich as those from beef, so the show's cooks might have used a more complicated recipe.[27]

An 1893 newspaper provided this recipe for a Madeira sauce to be poured around a boiled ham. The cloth napkin would have served to strain the solids from the sauce, making it a clear liquid.

Put a quart of Spanish sauce in a saucepan with a pinch of red pepper, a ladleful of tomato sauce, and a gill of Madeira wine; stir steadily, and briskly for ten minutes; then press through a napkin.[28]

The recipe called for Spanish sauce, which Fannie Farmer included in her cookbook. The brown stock was made from the lean meat, bones, and fat of beef, boiled with vegetables, herbs, and spices until thickened, then strained. For convenience, beef bouillon tablets or cakes, similar to the bouillon found in today's stores, might have been used instead of liquid stock.

2 tablespoons finely chopped lean raw ham
2 tablespoons finely chopped celery
1 tablespoon chopped onion
¼ cup butter
¼ cup flour
1 ½ cups Brown Stock
2/3 cup stewed and strained tomatoes
Salt and pepper[29]

Chapter 8

Tamales

Despite the disparagement of tamales by the reporters in New York City who ate a Mexican breakfast at Buffalo Bill's Wild West, they did become popular. In 1887 the following recipe for tamales was in an article about the subject, distributed by the *Chicago News* and published in other papers throughout the country. It was a year after Buffalo Bill's Wild West introduced the tamale to New York City.

The newest feature of social life in the extreme West is "tamale" parties. The "tamale" is a Mexican invention. The eatable portion is composed of coarsely hashed chicken and a sort of dressing make [sic] of corn meal, raisins, pepper and olives. A small quantity of this mixture—enough to make a roll about the size of an ordinary ear of Indian corn—is then covered with cornmeal batter and rolled up in clean corn shucks. The shucks are firmly tied at each end, and the tamale then looks like a big ear of corn in the husk. A quantity of tamales so constructed are then put into a kettle and boiled. When done it will be found that on opening out the corn-husks the tamale is enveloped in a corn-meal crust and looks like a small pudding boiled in a bag. Most Americans like the dish from the start. When properly made it is very appetizing.[30]

An article that same year in the *Fort Worth Daily Gazette* emphasized the importance of including pepper, although the raisins and olives could be considered optional. This was not the black pepper ordinarily used at the table or for seasoning, but rather dried red chili peppers with the seeds removed. The chilis were crushed and then boiled in water until the pulp was soft. The pulp was strained and the liquid added to the hashed meat.[31]

By 1897 tamales were common enough in the United States, particularly in the West, that one recipe for them in Kansas City included the following warning: "There are three grades of tamales—hot, medium and mild. The hot are so peppery as to be unfit for any stomach, the medium are a degree less so, and the mild are delicious and wholesome." The writer went on to note, "Since learning to make this dish, I have often thought of the convenience and variety it would make for farmers in Iowa, Kansas and other states, where corn husks are so plentiful."[32]

Chapter 9
Doughnuts

Leading suffragist Susan B. Anthony was honored by Buffalo Bill as a guest during the show's appearance in Chicago in 1893. The waifs who were also guests of Buffalo Bill to see his Wild West and Congress of Rough Riders of the World on July 27 were fed sandwiches, doughnuts, pie, and pickles on July 27. The women who prepared their lunches might have followed this recipe for children's doughnuts published a few years earlier in *The Woman Suffrage Cook Book*.

One cup sweet milk, two cups sugar, three eggs, lemon flavoring, three heaping teaspoonfuls baking power. Sift about two quarts flour into mixing pan, making place in the centre for baking powder, sugar, eggs, flavoring, and butter, size of walnut. Add the milk, mixing slowly, and use enough flour to roll without sticking. Roll quite thin; cut in rings, and fry in smoking hot lard. Drain well. Equal parts of lard and beef fat may be used.[33]

Bean Soup

Buffalo Bill said, "You've got to eat bean soup if you live in camp." Certainly, that had been his experience in the army. Thus bean soup was frequently served to Wild West personnel, and it was offered to visitors as a food common in the American West. It also figured in camp dinners served to British dignitaries in both London and Manchester in 1887, when veterans in the Grand Army of the Republic were still holding nostalgic meals of bean soup and even expressing their concern that meals of hardtack and bean soup were disappearing. Many different recipes for bean soup appeared in newspapers that year, as well as in cookbooks of the period. Black or navy beans were frequently used. The following is a rather basic one that probably approximates the bean soup served in the army and at the Wild West.[34]

Soak one quart of beans over night. In the morning add one quart of cold water and set where it will keep warm one hour; add two chopped onions and one pound of salt pork. Cook until the beans are tender, strain and season.[35]

Boston baked pork and beans were also served at the camp meal in Manchester and were often on the menu for Wild West personnel. Leftover Boston baked beans were frequently added to bean soup, something that might have been done by the Wild West's cooks. This recipe for making large quantities of Boston baked beans could very well have been used in the Wild West.[36]

In the Boston bakeries the method of cooking beans is as follows: After being washed clean they are placed in barrels or tubs, and soaked for several hours, after which they are put in large iron kettles and parboiled for half an hour or so. Then they are flooded with cold water to reduce the temperature and put into earthen pots holding ten quarts each, with about five pounds of salt pork sunk to the general level in each pot. At night they are placed in ovens, from under which the fires are drawn and are thus baked slowly ten or twelve hours. The slower the baking the better taste do the beans get.[37]

Chapter 10

Chicken Maryland-Style

When the prince of Wales dined in Buffalo Bill's tent in 1887, he so enjoyed the Maryland-style chicken that he requested the recipe from the show's head cook, William Langan. While it was a dish relatively common in the United States, it clearly was not served with any frequency in Great Britain. The recipe would have been easily prepared for the Wild West troupe and Cody's guests, since the chicken pieces could be baked on trays in the ovens of the range wagon, then served with cream sauce prepared in large quantities on top of the range. Fannie Farmer's 1896 cookbook contained easy recipes for both Maryland chicken and the sauce.

Dress, clean and cut up two chickens. Sprinkle with salt and pepper, dip in flour, egg, and crumbs, place in a well-greased dripping-pan, and bake twenty minutes in a hot oven, basting after first five minutes of cooking with one-third cup melted butter. Arrange on platter and pour over two cups Cream Sauce.[38]

Farmer's cream sauce recipe was made the same way as her recipe for thin white sauce, below, but using cream instead of milk.

2 tablespoons butter
1 ½ tablespoons flour
1 cup scalded milk
¼ teaspoon salt
Few grains pepper

Put butter in saucepan, stir until melted and bubbling; add flour mixed with seasonings, and stir until thoroughly blended. Pour on gradually the milk, adding about one-third at a time, stirring until well mixed, then beating until smooth and glossy. If a wire whisk is used, all the milk may be added at once.[39]

Two American Cocktails

Many of the drinks served at the American bars at the American Exhibition in 1887 were described as "prettily coloured" and sucked "through a straw in orthodox fashion." The British discovered that the sugar in American cocktails accelerated the effects of the alcohol. As a British publication put it at the time, the American cocktail can be "so very nice and so very insidious in its effects, that moderation and cocktails are by no means synonymous terms." The sherry cobbler was one of the more popular drinks at the American Exhibition.[40]

2 Wine-glasses of sherry
1 table-spoonful of sugar
2 or 3 slices of orange

Fill a tumbler with shaved ice, shake well, and ornament with berries in season. Place a straw.[41]

All the drinks at the American bars were available every day, but the bars also had a calendar that promoted a special drink each day, except Sunday, at the American Exhibition. The Exhibition Bosom Caresser was the drink for May 9. Some have erroneously claimed that it was invented in the 1920s in the American bar at London's Savoy Hotel, but it first appeared at the exhibition in 1887 and subsequently was offered elsewhere in London. The bosom-caresser has become a mainstay on some bar menus, perhaps as much because of its racy name as its flavor.[42]

Fill tumbler with chipped ice; put in a teaspoonful of raspberry sirup and a new laid egg; add a liquor glassful of brandy and a little milk; shake well, and strain off into a pony tumbler.[43]

Chapter 11

Chicken Mayonnaise

Chicken mayonnaise, a simple cold salad dressed up with decorative greens and vegetables, was well suited for luncheons. It figured as one of the main entrées served to Count Frederic Chandon de Briailles and other guests when they lunched with Buffalo Bill in Paris in 1889. The following spring, a recipe for cod or chicken mayonnaise was shared on the wire service and published by small-town newspapers throughout the United States.[44]

> Cold boiled cod will do very well removed from the bones and flaked; if cold chicken is used the flesh should be cut into small pieces. For the sauce break the yolks of three eggs into a basin and beat into them, drop by drop, the contents of a half pint flask of salad oil, adding every now and again a teaspoonful of vinegar; beat in a pinch of salt, a dash of cayenne pepper and a few chopped capers. Pile the fish or chicken in the center of the dishes, pour the sauce over and put cut up lettuce round and decorate prettily with chopped beet root and the hard yolks and whites of eggs.[45]

Popcorn Balls

As described by the British newspapers in London in 1887, the popcorn balls sold at Buffalo Bill's Wild West were covered with sugar. Since the popcorn would not stay in a ball shape without some sort of sticky binding, however, it would not have been a handful of popcorn simply rolled in powdered or granulated sugar. One visitor to the show when it was in Germany exclaimed, "Why, it's maize and honey." Although popcorn balls can be made with honey, it does not harden well after cooking and cooling. Recipes from the late nineteenth and early twentieth centuries typically used either sugar or molasses as a binder and sweetener. It is likely that the popcorn balls sold by Buffalo Bill's Wild West also used one of the two, perhaps both. The following 1887 recipe for popcorn balls was made with both molasses and sugar.[46]

> After popping . . . put the nice white popped [corn] in a greased pan. For the candy, take one cup of molasses, one cup of light brown or white sugar, one tablespoonful of vinegar. Boil until it will harden in water. Pour on the corn. Stir with a spoon until thoroughly mixed; then mold into balls with the hand.[47]

Chapter 12

Roman Punch

Roman punch, or Ponch à la Romaine, was reputed to have been popular with the popes in Rome as a refreshing summer drink during the eighteenth century. The recipe was smuggled out of the Vatican to London in the early nineteenth century. From there it spread throughout western Europe and to the United States. By 1862 a recipe for Roman punch was included in Jerry Thomas's *How to Mix Drinks*.[48]

Since its primary ingredients were frozen and many recipes called for Roman punch to be frozen after preparing, it was less of a punch and more of a sorbet. In fact, in 1912 it was served as a palate cleanser between courses on the menu for the *Titanic*'s first-class passengers. At the Fourth of July 1916 banquet, with the menu reading "Buffalo Bill Himself and the 101 Ranch Shows Combined," the punch was served between the soup and the entrées. A variety of recipes have been published for Roman punch. Jerry Thomas's recipe called for lemon juice to be beaten together with eggs to froth, but after the turn of the century most recipes eliminated the eggs. This recipe was published in a 1915 newspaper.[49]

> To one quart of lemon water ice frozen hard, add slowly one-half pint of champagne, one-half pint Jamaica rum, one gill maraschino, one teaspoonful of vanilla; beat well. Put in freezer, pack and cover well, and stand away for four or five hours.[50]

Banana Fritters

Banana fritters were popular as both a banquet item and a home-cooked dessert in 1905. The recipes for the fritters were usually quite similar. They were served simply sprinkled with powdered sugar or with a sauce made from lemon juice, wine, or rum. When served with rum sauce at a ministers' banquet in southern Virginia, they caused quite a scandal among the temperance ladies in that area of the state. They could be a dessert, but when the Wild West cooks served banana fritters in wine sauce during the Fourth of July banquet in Lille, France, they accompanied ox tongue and chicken fricassee.[51]

The following recipe for banana fritters was submitted by Rose Fayette, a member of the Kansan Kooking Klub, and published in *The Kansan Kook Book* in 1905. This may be self-evident, but don't forget to first peel the bananas.

Cut eight bananas in two lengthwise and cut each half in two pieces. Put in a bowl and sprinkle with two teaspoons of sugar, and the juice of half an orange, let stand an hour. Beat two eggs light, and add half cup of milk, pour this mixture gradually over one cup of flour and one half teaspoon of baking powder, add a little melted butter and half teaspoon of salt, beat smooth. With a spoon dip each piece into the batter and drop in boiling fat and fry a light brown, take out and drain, sprinkle with powdered sugar and serve.[52]

This wine sauce recipe from a 1904 newspaper may have been similar to the sauce the Wild West cooks served over their banana fritters.

One-quarter cup butter, ½ cup sugar, 2 tablespoons milk, 2 tablespoons wine. Cream the butter, add gradually the sugar, add the milk and wine very slowly to the first mixture to present separation. Keep in a warm place until served.[53]

Chapter 13

Red Lemonade

On June 28, 1899, in New Haven, Connecticut, hundreds of vendors were stationed outside the Wild West show entrance, all seeking to make some money from the crowd gathered to enter. A local newspaper noted that "the lemonade men were on hand as usual, with gallons of the fluid served in almost any color desired." Red lemonade was the most popular with circus, parade, and Wild West crowds at the turn of the century. Later that summer a Lima, Ohio, newspaper wrote that people were arriving in town "to see Buffalo Bill and drink red lemonade." It appears that the lemonade was sold by independent vendors hanging around the gates and not by the Wild West itself.[54]

Various explanations have been given for how this popular drink got its red color. One newspaper stated that red lemonade was drunk mainly for its color and "makes the prohibitionist fondly dream, for moment, that he is drinking burgundy." It went on to say that the red originally came from "strawberries, or claret, or something good," but "now nobody dares to inquire what it is." A Nebraska newspaper reporter remarked that the Ringling Brothers Circus version of the drink was so superior that he barely noticed the acts, concluding that the red lemonade alone was reason to visit the circus. Perhaps that red lemonade made use of "claret, or something good" for its color. A 1912 newspaper said that both pink and red lemonade originated when cinnamon candies were dropped into lemonade to both color and flavor it. Those candies might have been the "cords of sticks" reported to be immersed in the lemonade in Waterbury. Another article explained that red cinnamon drops were put in the liquid after it was made.[55]

Red lemonade was most closely associated with circuses, and several circus managers claimed they invented it. One asserted that it happened quite by accident, when a red horse blanket fell into a barrel of lemonade and turned it red. More realistically, another newspaper article stated that circuses made red lemonade by adding red food coloring to ordinary lemonade. While some circuses appear to have taken shortcuts with coloring, the best recipes were probably those that added cinnamon or fruit juice. One circus advertised that its lemonade was "made of real lemons and strawberries." A recipe for homemakers specified that either cinnamon or fruit juice could be added to the lemon liquid, noting that "cinnamon drops will make a suspicion of flavor to the lemonade that will only make it more tasty." A different recipe directed that "the nicest red lemonade you ever saw" could be made as follows.[56]

Take a pint of ripe strawberries or raspberries and put them in a clean cheese cloth bag and squeeze all of the juice out of them. Add the juice to about two quarts of lemonade. It takes three lemons to make two quarts of lemonade, and you must squeeze them, not slice them.[57]

Chapter 14

Pommes Parisienne

Pommes Parisienne, also known as pommes à la Parisienne, potatoes Parisienne, or fried potato balls, were common banquet fare in the early 1900s. The size and shape of the potatoes, petite and round, defined them more than the manner in which they were cooked. One recipe directed that they be deep-fried, while another called for them to be boiled. In a more recent recipe from 1985, the potato balls were boiled until tender, then sautéed in butter. All recipes for pommes Parisienne called for them to be served with butter and chopped parsley, and occasionally chives, grated cheese, or meat jelly was added. The following recipe appeared in a newspaper just two years after potatoes Parisienne were served with baked halibut at the 1913 Showmen's League of America banquet.[58]

> Cut potatoes into small round pieces, then cook in salt water until done, pour off water, add lump of table butter, and fine chopped parsley.[59]

Marschino Punch

Punch made with marschino, or maraschino, liqueur was a stylish and unusual palate cleanser popular in the 1890s. At an elegant banquet, like that served in honor of Cody's friend General Nelson Miles, the hollowed-out oranges filled with marschino punch were sure to impress the guests. The following recipe, using the alternative name of maraschino, was published in a Pennsylvania newspaper in 1895.

> Select as many large oranges as the number of guests require, and prepare them by giving each one a transverse cut, about half an inch from the top. The interior, and this sliced part also, are then nicely scooped out, and the pulp is pressed in a sieve, until the juice is all extracted. This is sweetened to taste and weakened with a little water, until a strong orangeade is made. Into this is finally poured a sufficient quantity of Maraschino to flavor the mixture agreeably, and the empty oranges are filled with it. The straws are then prettily tied to the

tops by narrow ribbons drawn through two punctures. These ribbons must match the other decorations of the table, and harmonize as well with the color of the oranges themselves. When the cap is fitted again, they are ready for serving. They may be prevented from upsetting and spilling the contents by being put in paper cases upon small decorated plates. This effect is so charming that, quite apart from the delicious flavor drawn up through the straws, the mere sight of them would inspire a "dying anchorite" to eat.[60]

The "dying anchorite" in the recipe is a reference to Englishman Sydney Smith's early nineteenth-century poem about a salad so delicious that even a secluded religious ascetic would consume it on his deathbed.[61]

Chapter 15
Buffalo Bill's Favorite Beef

When at home in Cody, Wyoming, Buffalo Bill enjoyed good cuts of beef, particularly tenderloin. Harry Wiard, who became cook at the Irma Hotel in 1905, would select a tenderloin at the nearby butcher shop, cut it to five by five inches, then slice it to just over one inch thick. He cooked it to medium rare on a grill, according to Buffalo Bill's specifications. Before serving, he placed the steak on a hot platter in a warming oven with four slices of butter on it. The melted butter was then served with hot biscuits. This technique, allowing the butter to add juiciness and flavor to the steak, is still used at fine restaurants today. Another of Buffalo Bill's favorite meat preparations was something he called "beef à là mode." This began with a good rump roast, which the cook punched full of holes with a sharpening steel. Carrots and parsnips were then cut lengthwise and inserted into the holes. Once cooked, the roast was served with brown gravy and mashed potatoes.[62]

Lobster Newburg

Lobster Newburg was offered for Christmas dinner at the Irma Hotel in 1904. This was a gourmet offering in landlocked Cody, Wyoming. Canned lobster could have been used in the dish, but it would not have been as tasty as a much more desirable freshly boiled lobster. With the Burlington Railroad laying track to Cody in 1901, it was possible to ship fresh lobster by rail by 1904. It would have been expensive but worth it for a fancy Christmas dinner. Different newspapers of the era offered variations on the Newburg sauce recipe. Interestingly enough, it was a Boston newspaper that suggested using canned lobster. This 1902 recipe published in another newspaper may have been the tastiest.[63]

> If possible to procure, only fresh boiled lobster should be used for this preparation. Pick all the meat from the shells of two good-sized, freshly boiled lobsters and cut the solid part into one inch pieces. Put these in a saucepan with an ounce of fresh butter, season with half a teaspoonful of salt and quarter of a salt spoonful of paprika and cook five minutes; add a wine glass of Madeira or four tablespoonfuls of sherry; cook three or four minutes longer and stir in the beaten yolks of three eggs mixed with half a pint of rich cream. Stir gently and cook a few minutes longer, until it becomes thick, then serve at once. This may be made in the chafing dish as well.[64]

Using cream was critical to the success of the dish. One recipe advised never to substitute milk, noting that despite the richness of the cream, the dish was "more easily digested" than if it were made with milk. Another recipe suggested that chicken, duck, or turkey meat could be substituted for the lobster and that Newburg "makes an exceedingly nice dressing for terrapin."[65]

Mint Julep

Buffalo Bill's "fox hunts" for coyotes in the late 1890s departed from Sheridan and often ended at George Beck's ranch to the west. There, everyone enjoyed mint juleps prepared in water buckets. By that time the mint julep was a venerable American drink, with origins in Virginia. Europe already had something called a julep, but these were largely medicinal drinks, herb-based and with little alcohol. It was in America in the eighteenth century that alcohol grew to dominate, and in the early nineteenth century ice was added to juleps. Later in that century bartender Orsamus Willard learned how to make iced juleps from a "Virginia Gentleman," possibly an African American mixologist, and then refined them further at his bar in Washington DC. It was Willard who helped make the iced julep famous. In 1862 Jerry Thomas provided several julep recipes in his book on bartending, including a brandy, a gin, a pineapple, a whiskey, and a mint julep. Twenty years later, in 1882, Harry Johnson's bartender's manual included a whiskey julep, which, like Thomas's whiskey julep, was basically the same as a mint julep. By 1894 the mint julep reigned supreme. Given its origin in Virginia, it was the perfect drink for concluding a western version of a fox hunt.[66]

In 1895 a transplanted southerner wrote an article about the classic mint julep for a Cincinnati newspaper, which was sent out on the wires. It contained the following recipe and musings.

We steep a bunch of the freshest mint in a glass of whisky and brandy, in equal portions, for four hours. This extracts the flavor of the mint without the bitter quality that spoils a julep. Fill a silver pitcher with cracked ice next; we say, pour in the whisky and brandy, with a little water, and send for your friends. When a fine frost settles upon the outside of the pitcher the julep is ripe. Put a dozen springs of fresh mint in a glass, and pack well with cracked ice. Over the top, sprinkle pulverized sugar to the taste; then slowly pour from the pitcher till the glass is filled and the sugar dissolved. Then—drink. Bury your nose in the mist till the delightfully cool scent goes away down to your toes. After one or two of these you will thank the Lord that you are alive. There are other juleps, but this is "The Julep."[67]

Chapter 16

Old-Fashioned

The Old-Fashioned cocktail began as just that. With all the new, and often gimmicky, mixed drinks being invented in the late nineteenth century, some customers began ordering "old-fashioned" drinks like those they had enjoyed in earlier days. Early examples of this preference were the "old-fashioned cocktails" furnished and consumed at a political event in 1880. Two years later a newspaper article said such cocktails were made of "loaf sugar and whisky," preferably rye rather than bourbon. In 1891 a bartender in St. Louis observed, "Old-fashioned whisky cocktails continue to be the favorite with my customers." By 1900 the cocktail had been formally dubbed an Old-Fashioned.[68]

Determining just what the recipe for an Old-Fashioned should be was a good deal more difficult than naming it. Since people had different ideas of what was old-fashioned, the drinks dubbed Old-Fashioned differed considerably. At a meeting of the International Association of Bartenders in 1893, someone remarked that "the old-fashioned cocktail affected by Southern men differs in its composition in various cities." The South was singled out because that was where the cocktail was "found in its mellowest, richest state." Over time the simple old-fashioned drink of sugar, whiskey, and ice became less simple, with bitters and a peel of lemon added.[69]

Buffalo Bill cut his teeth on tanglefoot whiskey on the Great Plains, where there was not much chance of getting fruits to dress it up. For him an Old-Fashioned cocktail meant a drink that was old-fashioned. So the cocktail he served General Fitzhugh Lee probably followed this recipe, originally published in the *New York Sun*.

> The bartender takes an ordinary cube of loaf sugar and places it gently on the bottom of a thin glass. He sends three dashes of bitters upon the sugar and waits until the sugar has assimilated the bitters and turned a deep crimson color. He then seizes a white cedar pestle—it must be cedar, no other wood will answer—and gently crushes the sugar. A piece of ice as big as a thumb nail is added with a small piece of lemon peel. The drinker then pours his stint of rye whiskey into the glass and works his elbow.[70]

Horse's Neck

Buffalo Bill said he accidentally drank a ginger ale highball in 1904, thinking it was a ginger ale horse's neck. A highball typically consisted of ginger ale, soda water, or some other carbonated beverage mixed with alcohol and ice. Since a horse's neck was prepared similarly, but usually without alcohol, such a mistake was indeed possible. When a group gathered in the Merchants Hotel bar in Omaha following Cody's divorce deposition, according to Louisa's attorney, everyone sampled a horse's neck spiked with alcohol. So it is entirely possible Buffalo Bill made that mistake.

The horse's neck originated in Atlantic City and was a popular cooler at the time. Although the drink was nonalcoholic, it was occasionally ordered with a bit of rye whiskey, gin, or even a liqueur. One variation was made with ginger beer, a small bit of lemonade, the peel of an entire lemon, crushed ice, and Benedictine or Chartreuse, both herbal liqueurs. The following recipe from 1905 describes the horse's neck that Buffalo Bill may have expected. It would have been a refreshing summer beverage for any teetotaler.[71]

Peel a lemon in one long spiral, one lemon to each glass. Place two straws in a tall, thin glass and wind the lemon peel arount [sic] to make the spiral the length of the glass. The peel must be as free from tough white skin as possible. After the lemon is arranged fill the glass half full of shaved ice. Add half a bottle of ginger ale and fill the remainder with seltzer water.[72]

Chapter 17

Boiled Columbia River Salmon in Hollandaise Sauce

During the average working day, the members of Buffalo Bill's Wild West ate heartily, with beef and pork entrées as the anchors of every meal. Fresh fish was more difficult to obtain, so it was served less frequently. When a farewell or Fourth of July banquet was held, a fish course was always included, which helped make it a special meal. Serving salmon from Washington State's Columbia River at a farewell banquet in England in 1903 made the experience even more distinctive. The salmon was probably cut into thick pieces before it was boiled (i.e., poached). Salmon was frequently served with hollandaise sauce. This recipe is from a 1903 newspaper.

This is really a warm Mayonnaise, made with butter instead of olive oil. It is the best sauce for serving with salmon or any other boiled fish which is to be served hot. It requires a quarter of a pound of butter, half a lemon, the yolk of two eggs, a little salt, and a half teaspoonful of white pepper. The secret in making it is to preserve an even temperature. The sauce should at no time approach the boiling point, as the eggs would cook and the sauce curdle and be unfit for use. Put the eggs in a small saucepan and add the butter very gradually, stirring constantly with a wooden spoon. It will soon thicken like a Mayonnaise. When the butter is all in, add the salt and pepper, and lastly the lemon juice, stirring until all is well mixed. If the sauce becomes too thick during cooking, add a few drops of water to prevent curdling.[73]

Claret Punch

One of Buffalo Bill's last farewell banquets, while he was with the Sells Floto Circus, ended with claret punch. By then he was steadfastly avoiding alcohol, so he may not have had any. But as one New York newspaper columnist observed, "While the old fashioned prohibitionists may refuse to countenance the punchbowl, its contents may be as innocuous as desired." The writer went on to comment that a combination of fruit juices, sparkling water, iced teas, and even wines allowed the creation of cooling summer punches without the use of spirits, to which prohibitionists were particularly opposed. Claret punch was a long-standing example of that kind of punch. Its recipes were myriad, and every family had its favorite version, though all used lemons, ice, and claret wine. Any number of other ingredients might be added to those basic items. One recipe involved boiling raisins, cinnamon sticks, sugar, and lemon rind, then straining that mixture into lemon juice, orange juice, and claret. Others added components as varied as seltzer, sherry, tea, cloves, or Apollinaris, a sparkling mineral water. The following was the claret punch recipe most commonly published in 1914 newspapers.[74]

> Take the juice of two large lemons and the grated rind, add to this one small glass of sherry and then one quart of claret. For every quart of claret, add one bottle of soda water apollinaris. Pour over the block of ice and decorate with sprigs of geranium or lemon verbena.[75]

NOTES

Abbreviations

AHC American Heritage Center, Laramie, Wyoming

BBCW McCracken Research Library, Buffalo Bill Center of the West, Cody, Wyoming

BBMG Buffalo Bill Museum and Grave, Golden, Colorado

MSY O. C. Marsh Collection, Sterling Library, Yale University

NSBY Nathan Salsbury Papers, Beinecke Library, Yale University

NDSPL Nate Salsbury Scrapbooks, Western History Division, Denver Public Library

Introduction

Epigraph: "A Day with the Wild West," *New York Sunday Tribune*, July 22, 1894.

1. "Annie Oakley Pays Her Tribute to the Last of the Old Scouts," unidentified newspaper clipping, ca. 1917, BBMG.

2. "Buffalo Bill's Bucking Bronchos," *Leamington (ON) Advertiser*, June 18, 1903, NSDPL; *Buffalo (NY) Courier*, March 10, 1895.

3. Alice Schultz, "Buffalo Bill's Favorite," *Cody (WY) Enterprise*, February 26, 1936.

4. Fellows, *This Way*, 93.

5. "Col. Cody Is Reminiscent," *Duluth (MN) Evening Herald*, May 20, 1910, BBMG.

1. Apples, Yellow-Legged Chickens

Epigraph: "Last View of Paris," *Capper's Weekly* (Topeka KS), September 5, 1889.

1. Jonnes, *Eiffel's Tower*, 142.

2. Cody, *Life*, 19.

3. Sizer, "Fruit in Iowa," 81; Nichols, "Apple Varieties," 82, 84.

4. Wetmore, *Last of the Great*, 44–45.

5. Cody, *Life*, 21, 24–25; deposition of William F. Cody for Cody divorce trial, March 23, 1904, https:codyarchive.org.

6. *Kansas Weekly Herald* (Leavenworth), September 22, 1854.

7. William F. Cody, "The Great West That Was: 'Buffalo Bill's' Life Story," serialized in *Hearst's International*, August 1916–July 1917, n.p.; Cody, *Life*, 25; *Western Home Journal*, April 6, 1882.

8. Wetmore, *Last of the Great*, 12; *Kansas Weekly Herald* (Leavenworth), March 30, 1855; "Settlements in Kansas," *Weekly Leavenworth (KS) Herald*, September 22, 1854.

9. Cody, *Life*, 39–40; Paxton, *Annals*, 23, 27, 754; *Weekly Leavenworth (KS) Herald*, October 20, 1954; Monahan, *Golden Elixir*, 28.

10. "Buffalo Bill's Sire," *Quad-City Times* (Davenport IA), September 17, 1879; *Glasgow (MO) Weekly Times*, February 16, September 28, 1854.

11. *Kansas Weekly Herald* (Leavenworth), June 8, 1855.

12. Cody, *Life*, 29; Russell, "Julia Cody Goodman's Memoirs," 464.

13. Cody, *Life*, 38; Russell, "Julia Cody Goodman's Memoirs," 458.

14. *Kansas Weekly Herald* (Leavenworth), June 8, 1855; *Squatter Sovereign* (Atchison KS), March 13, 1855; Cody, *Life*, 28.

15. Russell, "Julia Cody Goodman's Memoirs," 466, 482; Julia Cody Goodman Diary, 156–60, AHC.

16. Russell, "Julia Cody Goodman's Memoirs," 468; Julia Cody Goodman Diary, 41–42, AHC.

17. Russell, "Julia Cody Goodman's Memoirs," 464, 482.

18. Dohner, *Encyclopedia*, 429; Heffron, "Poultry Report," 361.

19. *New England Farmer* (Boston), October 1, 1859; *Topeka (KS) Weekly Commonwealth*, April 11, 1878; *Clay Center (KS) Dispatch*, February 23, 1878; *Kansas Pilot* (Kansas City), March 15, 1879.

20. Wetmore, *Last of the Great*, 45–46.

21. Wetmore, *Last of the Great*, 19; *Squatter Sovereign* (Atchison KS), March 25, 1856; *Kansas Weekly Herald* (Leavenworth), June 13, 1857.

22. "Going West," *Kansas Weekly Herald* (Leavenworth), January 5, 1856; *Weekly Leavenworth (KS) Herald*, March 30, 1855; *Kansas Territorial Register* (Leavenworth), September 22, October 6, November 24, 1855.

23. *Grasshopper* (Grasshopper Falls KS), June 5, 1868; *Jefferson Crescent* (Grasshopper Falls KS), December 25, 1858, January 15, 1959; *Leavenworth (KS) Daily Times*, May 3, 1858.

24. "Delaware Township," *Oskaloosa (KS) Sickle*, December 25, 1880; advertisement, *Kansas Tribune* (Lawrence), July 16, 1856.

25. "Grasshopper Falls," *Leavenworth (KS) Daily Commercial*, May 9, 1873.

26. Russell, *Lives*, 13–14.

27. Cody, *Life*, 40–43; Russell, *Lives*, 14.

28. Russell, "Julia Cody Goodman's Memoirs," 466; Wetmore, *Last of the Great*, 19. Cody, *Life*, 47.

29. Russell, *Lives*, 27; "The Condition and Prospects of our Town," *Grasshopper* (Grasshopper Falls KS), June 5, 1858.

30. Russell, *Lives*, 28; *Leavenworth (KS) Journal*, March 12, 1857, 3; *Kansas Daily Ledger* (Leavenworth), February 2, 1858; *Nebraska Advertiser* (Brownville), March 4, 1858.

2. Hardtack and Wagon Trains

Epigraph: Cody, *Life*, 79.

1. Cody, *Life*, 73; Gould, *Naturalist's Library*, 384–85.
2. Cody, *Life*, 66, 76–77.
3. Cody, *Life*, 77–79; Russell, "Julia Cody Goodman's Memoirs," 483.
4. Russell, "Julia Cody Goodman's Memoirs," 482; Wetmore, *Last of the Great*, 45–46; "Hon. William F. Cody," *Leavenworth Times*, April 8, 1877.
5. Wetmore, *Last of the Great*, 62; Russell, "Julia Cody Goodman's Memoirs," 482–84; Cody, *Life*, 85.
6. Cody, *Life*, 145.
7. *Daily Exchange* (Baltimore), December 29, 1858; Cody, *Life*, 89–90, 93; "Emigration," *St. Joseph (MO) Weekly West*, March 31, 1860; *Leavenworth (KS) Weekly Ledger*, September 12, 1858.
8. Majors, *Seventy Years*, 176–77; Frank Winch, "Chronological History of William Frederick Cody, Buffalo Bill" (unpublished manuscript), BBMG; Warren, *Buffalo Bill's America*, 6–20; Friesen, *Buffalo Bill*, 7–9.
9. Cody, *Life*, 110–18.
10. Majors, *Seventy Years*, 192; *Nebraska Advertiser* (Brownville), March 4, 1858.
11. Monahan, *Golden Elixir*, 24–25.
12. *National Era* (Washington DC), April 15, 1858; Bloss, *Pony Express*, 96.
13. Cody, *Life*, 85–89.
14. *Kansas Weekly Herald*, (Leavenworth), October 13, 1855.
15. *Kansas Herald of Freedom* (Wakarusa), December 5, 1857; Richardson, *Beyond the Mississippi*, 101.
16. Cody, *Life*, 118, 125–27; Buffalo Bill to Frank Winch, October 13, 1910, BBMG; Russell, *Lives*, 58–60; Winch, "Chronological History," BBMG.
17. Cody, *Life*, 135.

3. Becoming a Gourmet

Epigraph: Cody, *Life*, 287.

1. Cody, *Life*, 281–89; Russell, *Lives*, 62, 72.
2. Cody, *Life*, 136, 138; Russell, *Lives*, 67.
3. Russell, *Lives*, 72–75; Paxton, *Annals*, 294.
4. Russell, *Lives*, 74; Cody, *Life*, 142–45.
5. Wetmore, *Last of the Great*, 137–38.
6. Cody, *Life*, 145; Russell, *Lives*, 78, 81.
7. Cody, *Life*, 145, 149–50; Russell, *Lives*, 84; Lt. M. W. Saxton to Lt. J. M. Thompson, August 11, 1867, copy and transcript provided by Jay Burns, Fort Hays Historic Site, Hays KS.
8. Cody, *Life*, 149–51.
9. Russell, *Lives*, 84–85; Cody, *Life*, 154–57.
10. Cody, *Life*, 162, 174; *Daily Kansas Tribune* (Lawrence), January 11, 1868.

11. "Buffalo Hunting in Nebraska," *Fort Wayne (IN) Sentinel*, December 29, 1870; editorial by Buffalo Bill for the *New York Sun*, reprinted in the *Buffalo Weekly Express*, March 8, 1883.

12. Cody, *True Tales*, 67, 77; "Buffalo Hunting in Nebraska," *Fort Wayne (IN) Sentinel*, December 29, 1870; Burke, *Buffalo Bill*, 155; Russell, *Lives*, 93.

13. Friesen, *Buffalo Bill*, 16, 20.

14. "An Indian Camp Surprised," *New York World*, June 9, 1870.

15. Cody, *Life*, 221.

16. Cody, *Life*, 223.

17. King, *Campaigning*, 111; Cody, *Life*, 226.

18. Cody, *Life*, 227–28.

19. Walsh, *Making*, 139; Wikipedia, s.v. "Old Tom Gin," last modified October 10, 2022, https://en.wikipedia.org/wiki/Old_Tom_gin; *St. Joseph (MO) Weekly Union*, March 3, 1870; *Junction City (KS) Weekly Union*, August 14, 1869; *Wyandotte Gazette* (Kansas City KS), July 17, 1874; advertisement, *Columbia (SC) Daily Phoenix*, November 29, 1970; advertisement, *New Orleans Times-Picayune*, February 25, 1881.

20. Danker, *Man of the Plains*, 126, 268; Yost, *Buffalo Bill*, 111; Russell, *Lives*, 157.

21. Danker, *Man of the Plains*, 103.

22. Logan, *Buckskin*, 39, 41; May Cody Bradford, deposition for Cody divorce trial, 1904, https:codyarchive.org; William F. Cody, deposition for Cody divorce trial, March 6, 1904, https:codyarchive.org.

23. Winch, "Chronological History," BBMG; Yost, *Buffalo Bill*, 25–27.

24. William F. Cody, "Famous Hunting Parties of the Plains," *Cosmopolitan* 17, no. 2 (June 1890), 136.

25. Davies, *Ten Days*, 83, 96, 107, 112, 122.

26. *Westminster (MD) Democratic Advocate*, January 20, 1872; "The Buffalo Hunt," *Chicago Tribune*, January 19, 1872.

27. "The Grand Duke's Hunt," *New York Daily Herald*, January 14, 1872; "Our Royal Guest," *Chicago Tribune*, January 15, 1872; Yost, *Buffalo Bill*, 54–55; Cody, *Life*, 302.

28. Cody, *Life*, 305–6.

4. Dining at Delmonico's

Epigraph: Cody, *Life*, 308.

1. Cody, *Life*, 307–8.

2. "Luxury on Wheels," *Topeka (KS) Daily Commonwealth*, August 2, 1872; Hollister, *Dinner*, 10–11; Porterfield, *Dining*, 16–17.

3. *Chicago Tribune*, February 7, 1872.

4. Cody, *Life*, 307.

5. "From the Cleveland Leader," *Chicago Tribune*, February 20, 1872.

6. "Buffalo Bill," *Buffalo Morning Express and Illustrated Buffalo Express*, February 10, 1872; "The Grand Duke," *Buffalo Morning Express and Illustrated Buffalo Express*, December 22, 1871.

7. *Chicago Tribune*, February 13, 1873, 4; *Buffalo Evening Post*, February 10, 1872.

8. Cody, *Life*, 308; "Buffalo Bill," *Rochester (NY) Democrat and Chronicle*, February 12, 1872.

9. Cody, *Life*, 308; Christopher Gray, "Inside the Union Club; Jaws Drop," *New York Times*, February 11, 2007; *New York Daily Herald*, February 14, 1872.

10. *San Francisco Examiner*, March 29, 1872; Cody, *Life*, 309–10.

11. Cody, *Life*, 310; *Charleston Daily News*, February 21, 1872.

12. *Lawrence Daily Kansas Tribune*, March 7, 1872; Thomas Nast cartoon, *Harper's Weekly*, December 4, 1886; *Brooklyn Daily Eagle*, February 21, 1872.

13. "Bowery Theatre: Buffalo Bill," *New York Daily Herald*, February 21, 1872; Cody, *Life*, 311.

14. Cody, *Life*, 311; *New York Daily Herald*, February 24, 1872.

15. *Reading (PA) Times*, March 1, 4, 1872; Chester County Tavern Petitions 1700–1923, Chester County Archives and Record Services, West Chester PA; Cody, *Life*, 312.

16. Cody, *Life*, 311.

17. Cody, *Life*, 320–21.

18. *Chicago Tribune*, December 15, 1872; Cody, *Life*, 322–25.

19. Cody, *Life*, 326–27; *Chicago Tribune*, December 19, 1872; Sagala, *Buffalo Bill on Stage*, 24; Bricklin, *Notorious*, 139.

20. Cody, *Life*, 327–28; *Chicago Tribune*, December 13, 1872; Sagala, *Buffalo Bill on Stage*, 44.

21. Cody, *Life*, 328–29; Sagala, *Buffalo Bill on Stage*, 48.

22. *Rochester (NY) Democrat and Chronicle*, August 16, 1876; Buffalo Bill to James Russell, ca. 1873, BBMG; Sagala, *Buffalo Bill on Stage*, 173.

5. Buffalo Bill Ate Here

Epigraph: *Wilmington (NC) Morning Star*, October 5, 1878.

1. Buffalo Bill to Julia Cody Goodman, May 11, 1873, MS6.0039, BBCW; *Hartford (CT) Courant*, May 28, 1873.

2. Buffalo Bill to Julia Cody Goodman, May 11, 1873, MS6.0039, BBCW.

3. "Personal Gossip," *Hartford (CT) Courant*, May 28, 1873; Sagala, *Buffalo Bill on Stage*, 77–78.

4. Cody, *Life*, 337.

5. Cody, *Life*, 340.

6. "The Indian Campaign" (from a dispatch dated August 3, 1876), *New York Times*, August 17, 1876.

7. Cody, *Life*, 349.

8. Cody, *Life*, 349–50. *Daily Alta California* (San Francisco), September 30, 1876; Cody, "Great West That Was," n.p.

9. Purcell House breakfast menu, 1881, https://digitalcollections.nypl.org; Sagala, *Buffalo Bill on Stage*, 235; Buffalo Bill to Mr. Gardner on United States Hotel letterhead, November 24, 1978, MS6.0046, BBCW; United States Hotel banquet menu, 1881, https://digitalcollections.nypl.org.

10. "Buffalo Bill's Account of Himself," *Woodland (CA) Daily Democrat*, November 6, 1878.

11. *Hartford (CT) Courant*, August 22, 1879; Derek Strahan, "Allyn House, Hartford Connecticut," Lost New England, May 10, 2015, http://lostnewengland.com /2015/05/allyn-house-hartford-connecticut; advertisement, *Hartford (CT) Courant*, June 25, 1880; Allyn House menu, March 5, 1859, Special Collections, University of Houston Libraries, Wikimedia Commons; *Hartford (CT) Courant*, March 4, 1982, August 22, 1879.

12. Sagala, *Buffalo Bill on Stage*, 237; "Amusements," *Nashville Tennessean*, November 25, 1879; "Maxwell House" (guest list), *Tennessean*, November 19, 1879; Buffalo Bill to Capt. Jack Crawford on Maxwell House letterhead, November 25, 1879, MS294.10.14.9, BBCW; "Maxwell House Renovation," *Tennessean*, July 30, 1879; "Nashville," *Cincinnati Enquirer*, October 2, 1879; Ophelia Paine, "Maxwell House Hotel," *Tennessee Encyclopedia*, last updated March 1, 2018, https://tennesseeencyclopedia.net/entries/maxwell-house-hotel/; Maxwell House Christmas menu, December 25, 1879, author's collection.

13. "Buffalo Bill," *Buffalo Morning Express*, May 10, 1880; advertisement, *Buffalo Morning Express*, May 11, 1880; "A Pleasant Gathering," *Buffalo Morning Express*, May 13, 1880; *Buffalo Courier*, December 19, 1877.

14. Sagala, *Buffalo Bill on Stage*, 243; Buffalo Bill to [illegible recipient name] on Combination of Twenty-Four Artists letterhead, January 11, 1883, BBMG; "Old Broadway Landmark to Go," *New York Evening World*, February 20, 1903; Sturtevant House envelope, postmarked January 26, 1882, author's collection; *Brooklyn Union*, March 11, 1882; "Barnum on Pigs' Feet," *New York Times*, March 13, 1881.

15. Sagala, *Buffalo Bill on Stage*, 174, 243; "Interview with Bill," *Lewiston (ME) Sun-Journal*, March 9, 1883.

6. Founding and Feeding the West

Epigraph: "Buffalo Bill Is Here," *Brantford (ON) Courier*, July 15, 1897.

1. Cody, *Story of the Wild West*, 693–94.

2. Estelline Bennett, *Weekly Pioneer Times Mining Review* (Deadwood SD), July 29, 1909; Mark Twain to William Cody, September 10, 1884, Mark Twain Papers, Bancroft Library, University of California–Berkeley.

3. "The Wild West," *Bloomington (IL) Bulletin*, May 24, 1883; Cody, *Story*, 694.

4. Cody, *Story*, 695.

5. Russell, *Lives*, 302–3.

6. Friesen, *Buffalo Bill*, 52–53.

7. Cody and Salsbury, "Origin of the Name 'Rough Riders,'" *Rough Rider*, 1899, BBMG.

8. "An Hour with General Cody," unidentified newspaper clipping, May 29, 1891, George Crager scrapbook, MS6.3772.017.03, BBCW (Cody had been appointed the position of general with the Nebraska National Guard during the Ghost Dance conflict of 1890–91); "Big Show Is Here," *Kansas City (MO) World*, September 21, 1899; "What It Costs to Work the 'Wild West,'" *Tit-Bits*, May 28, 1892, MS6.3778.036.02, BBCW; "Wild West Men Have Gay Sunday," *New York Press*, April 11, 1899, NSDPL; Henry Finn Diary, May 29, July 24, August 5, 1911, BBMG; *New York Tribune*, December 12, 1886; Jonnes, *Eiffel's Tower*, 142.

9. "Buffalo Bill," *Holyoke (MA) Daily Democrat*, May 22, 1897, NSDPL; "Battle of San Juan, Wild West Mimicry like the Real Thing," *Boston Traveler*. June 13. 1899, NSDPL; "Wild West Hotel," *Ottumwa (IA) Courier*, September 17, 1900, NSDPL.

10. *Dayton Enquirer*, August 23, 1897, NSDPL; *New Brunswick (NJ) Home News*, May 19, 1898, NSDPL; "A Motley Group," *Davenport (IA) Times*, August 15, 1898, NSDPL; "Buffalo Bill Is Here," *Brantford (ON) Courier*, July 15, 1897.

11. Glenda Riley, *Life and Legacy*, 33; "Daily Expense of Big Show," *Long Branch (NY) Press*, June 7, 1899, NSDPL; "Buffalo Bill," *Holyoke (MA) Daily Democrat*, May 22, 1897, NSDPL; "This Is High Feeding," *Hamilton (ON) Herald*, July 17, 1897; "Buffalo Bill's Village," *Minneapolis Times*, September 14, 1896; *Columbus (OH) Dispatch*, July 13, 1896; "What It Costs to Work the 'Wild West,'" *Tit-Bits*, May 28, 1892, MS6.3778.036.02, BBCW; "Buffalo Bill's Coffee Pot," *Los Angeles Herald*, April 5, 1896.

12. Charles R. Hutchinson, *Official Souvenir, Buffalo Bill's Wild West and Congress of Rough Riders of the World*, 1896, BBMG; *New Orleans Times-Picayune*, October 29, 1900, 3.

13. Hutchinson, *Official Souvenir*, 1896, BBMG.

14. *Columbus (OH) Dispatch*, July 13, 1896; Wild West expense sheet, July 6–13, 1896, BBMG.

15. "Saved from Famine," *Indianapolis Journal*, April 21, 1901; *Emporia (KS) Gazette*, October 4, 1900.

16. "Hour with General Cody," BBCW; "Wild West's Kitchen," *Chicago Evening Post*, June 6, 1896; "Like Feeding an Army," *New York Recorder Journal*, June 11, 1894, NSDPL; Griffin, *Four Years*, 128.

17. *Idaho Statesman* (Boise City ID), August 18, 1902.

18. *Daily Eastern Argus* (Portland ME), July 13, 1908, Johnny Baker Scrapbook, BBMG; *New York Tribune*, April 20, 1902; "The Wild West,'" *Portsmouth (UK) News*, August 10, 1903; "Wild West Hotel," *Davenport (IA) Times*, September

3, 1900; "History of the World Flashed in the Arena," *Cleveland Plain Dealer,* June 1, 1908.

19. "Buffalo Bill's Boys at Dinner," *Sketch* (London), January 7, 1903.

20. "How the Army Is Fed," *Sioux City (IA) Journal,* August 5, 1901, NSDPL.

21. "The History of Ice Cream," International Dairy Foods Association, accessed October 19, 2022, https://www.idfa.org/news-views/media-kits/ice-cream /the-history-of-ice-cream; "Thousand Employees Dine," *Los Angeles Herald,* October 17, 1910; "Col. Cody Here with Great Show," *Vancouver (BC) Daily World,* September 12, 1910.

22. *Montpelier (VT) Evening Argus,* June 1, 1911; "Thousand Employees Dine"; *San Francisco Examiner,* September 27, 1910; advertisement, *Appleton (WI) Post-Crescent,* August 20, 1912; advertisement, *Chickasha (OK) Daily Express,* September 20, 1912.

23. *Montpelier (VT) Evening Argus,* June 1, 1911; "How Buffalo Bill's Rough Riders of the World Are Fed," *Chicago Evening Post,* June 6, 1896, Buffalo Bill's scrapbook for 1896, BBCW; "Show Day Comes with the Show Train on Time," *Paducah (KY) News-Democrat,* June 18, 1913, 20.

24. Beecher, *Bishop,* 154–55.

25. "How Buffalo Bill's Rough Riders"; Buffalo Bill's scrapbook for 1896, BBCW; Alice Schultz, "Buffalo Bill's Favorite," *Cody Enterprise,* February 26, 1936; "Arrival at Ipswich," *Ipswich (UK) Times,* September 7, 1903, NSDPL; "Buffalo Bill's Big Show," *Philadelphia Times,* August 13, 1888; "Likes the Life," *Butte (MT) Miner,* September 3, 1910; Cody, *Life,* 79.

7. Meals on Wheels

Epigraph: *Knoxville (TN) Daily Journal,* October 11, 1897.

1. Buffalo Bill's Wild West Route Book, 1902, BBMG.

2. Map of the official route of Buffalo Bill's Wild West, 1898, BBMG; "Buffalo Bill," *Dayton Evening News,* July 6, 1896.

3. Map of the official route, BBMG; "Formation of Trains for Buffalo Bill's Wild West" (unpublished manuscript, 1905–6), Buffalo Bill Collection, Western Heritage Center, Laramie WY; "Buffalo Bill's Wild West," *New York Sun,* April 17, 1899, BBCW.

4. Buffalo Bill's Wild West Route Book, 1902, BBMG.

5. Buffalo Bill's Wild West Route Book, 1902, BBMG; Wild West advertisement, *New York Sun,* July 14, 1886, NSDPL; "Buffalo Bill on Tour," *London Answers,* May 9, 1903, NSDPL.

6. "Buffalo Bill," *Dayton Evening News,* July 6, 1896; Henry Finn Diary, May 26, 1911, BBMG.

7. Buffalo Bill's Wild West Route Book, 1902, BBMG; map of Buffalo Bill's Wild West, M56, box 3, Buffalo Bill Collection, BBCW; "A Motley Group," *Davenport (IA) Times,* August 15, 1898, NSDPL.

8. "Buffalo Bill Is Here," *Brantford (ON) Courier*, July 15, 1897; "Buffalo Bill under the Search Light," *Electrical Engineer*, September 12, 1894; photo of Buffalo Bill light plant, BBMG.

9. Sigabette, editor of *La Nazione*, quoted in Urban, "When the 'Wild West,'" 2.

10. "Wild West's Kitchen," *Chicago Evening Post*, June 6, 1896, Buffalo Bill's Scrapbook for 1896, BBCW; "Wild West Hotel," *Davenport (IA) Times*, September 3, 1900; "A Visit to the Grounds at Mealtime," *Columbus (OH) Dispatch*, July 13, 1896, NCDPL; water permit obtained by Buffalo Bill's Wild West from Appleton WI, June 24, 1912, author's collection.

11. "The Wild West," *Portsmouth (UK) News*, August 10, 1903; "Buffalo Bill," *Holyoke (MA) Daily Democrat*, May 22, 1897, NSDPL.

12. "With the Riders," *Lowell (MA) Daily Courier*, July 10, 1899, NSDPL; "Wild West Show," *Akron (OH) Beacon Journal*, July 25, 1899, NSDPL; *Nottingham (UK) Evening News*, October 19, 1903, NSDPL; "Monster Range on Wheels," *Chicago Evening Post*, June 6, 1896, Buffalo Bill's Scrapbook for 1896, BBCW.

13. "Buffalo Bill's Show," *Swindon (UK) Herald*, June 29, 1903, NSDPL.

14. "A Day in the Wild West" and "Odds and Ends," *Dundee (UK) Evening Telegraph*, August 18, 1904.

15. "Wild West's Kitchen," *Chicago Evening Post*, June 6, 1896; "Daily Expense of Big Show," *Long Branch (NY) Press*, June 7, 1899, NSDPL; "Buffalo Bill's Village," *Minneapolis Times*, September 14, 1896; *New York Evening Telegram*, Johnny Baker Scrapbook, 1902–16, BBMG.

16. "Buffalo Bill Here," *Richmond (IN) Evening Item*, May 6, 1899.

17. "How Big Show Gets out of Town," *Decatur (IL) Herald*, August 2, 1910; "Buffalo Bill on Tour," *London Answers*, May 9, 1903, NSDPL.

8. The World at Buffalo Bill's Table

Epigraph: "Big Show Is Here," *Kansas City (MO) World*, September 22, 1898.

1. *Rough Rider Courier*, 1911, BBMG; *Buffalo Bill Wild West Program* for New London CT appearance, June 25, 1899, BBMG; "Buffalo Bill's Wild West," *Bedfordshire (UK) Times and Independent*, September 18, 1903.

2. *Dundee (UK) Courier and Argus*, June 6, 1892; "Buffalo Bill Is in Town," *Utica (NY) Daily Press*, July 17, 1908, BBMG.

3. "Buffalo Bill's Big Family," *Brooklyn Times*, August, 1894, NSDPL; "How the Indians and the Other People of the Show Live," *Baltimore News*, May 12, 1898, NSDPL.

4. "Camp Life in Town," *New York Sun*, December 12, 1886.

5. Wild West Advertisement, *New York Sun*, December 15, 1886, 8; "At a Mexican Breakfast," *New York Sun*, December 19, 1886; "A Mexican Breakfast," *New York Times*, December 19, 1886.

6. "Tamales in New York," *New York Tribune*, February 11, 1894; "Destruction of a Hot Tamale Outfit," *New York Tribune*, June 1, 1894; Arellano, *Taco*, 38–40.

7. "A Unique Dinner," *Monroe (LA) News-Star*, May 6, 1913; "Show Day Comes with the Show Train on Time," *Paducah (KY) News-Democrat*, June 18, 1913.

8. "White Eagle and His Hardy Aggregation of Rough Riders of the World," *Adrian (MI) Times and Exposition*, August 4, 1896; "History of World Flashed in Arena," *Cleveland Plain Dealer*, June 1, 1908, Johnny Baker Scrapbook, BBMG; "The Wild West Camp," *New York Sun*, May 13, 1894, https:codyarchive.org.

9. "Sunday with the Wild West," *Philadelphia Record*, May 2, 1908; "How the Indians and the Other People of the Show Live," *Baltimore News*, May 12, 1898, NSDPL; "Buffalo Bill Is in Town," *Utica (NY) Daily Press*, July 27, 1908, Johnny Baker Scrapbook, BBMG; Frederic Remington, "Buffalo Bill in London," *Harper's Weekly*, September 3, 1892; "The Wild West," *Brooklyn Daily Eagle*, June 24, 1894.

10. Makharadze, *Georgian Trick Riders*, 150.

11. Makharadze, *Georgian Trick Riders*, 17, 93, 110, 111.

12. *Minneapolis Tribune*, August 7, 1898, NSDPL; "The Show Is Here," *Peoria (IL) Transcript*, September 20, 1897, NSDPL; Julian Ralph, "Behind the 'Wild West' Scenes," *Harper's Weekly*, August 18, 1894, NSDPL; "History of the World Flashed in Arena," *Cleveland Plain Dealer*, June 1, 1908, Johnny Baker Scrapbook, BBMG.

13. "White Eagle and His Hardy Aggregation of Rough Riders of the World," *Adrian (MI) Times and Expositor*, August 4, 1896.

14. "Hatchets for Buffalo Bill," *New York Evening World*, July 21, 1890; "Indians Well Treated," *New York Times*, November 16, 1890, https:codyarchive.org; Gallop, *Buffalo Bill's British*, 158.

15. Short Bull manuscript, BBMG; Standing Bear and Brininstool, *My People*, 251, 260–63.

16. "Sioux Indians at Cliff House," *San Francisco Chronicle*, September 14, 1902.

17. "Heart to Heart Talks with the Wild West Indians," *New York Sunday Telegraph*, March 29, 1899, NSDPL; "Camp Life in Town," *New York Sun*, December 12, 1886.

18. "Big Indian, Eat Heap Much," *New York World*, June 17, 1894, NSDPL; "Indians at Breakfast," *New York Morning Telegraph*, April 24, 1900, NSDPL Library; Dobrow, *Pioneers*, 160.

19. "The Sioux Dog Feast," *New York Mail and Express*, July 7, 1886; "Hold Dog Feast," *Hutchinson (KS) News*, May 14, 1910, 3; "Buffalo Bill Starts His Farewell Tour of America," *Leslie's Weekly*, May 26, 1910; "New Indian Styles: No Long Hair, Painted Faces, Ghost Dances, Dog Feasts nor Blankets," *Boston Globe*, January 17, 1902; Frank Whitbeck to Frank Winch, n.d., BBMG.

20. "Buffalo Bill," *Holyoke (MA) Daily Democrat*, May 22, 1897, NSDPL.

9. Rib Roasts and Public Relations

Epigraph: "Red-Skins at a Rib-Roast," *New York Morning Journal*, July 23, 1886.

1. Dobrow, *Pioneers*, 83–86.
2. Dobrow, *Pioneers*, 146.
3. Ingraham, *Buffalo Bill*, 1, 8–9; "In an Indian Encampment," *Omaha Daily News*, June 20, 1884; Walsh, *Making*, 259; "Buffalo Bill Gives a Party," *New York Times*, June 16, 1884.
4. "Initiatory Performance of Buffalo Bill at Beacon Park," *Boston Globe*, August 12, 1884; "A Rib Roast," *Boston Herald*, July 31, 1885, NSDPL; "A Barbecue at Beacon Park," *Boston Daily Globe*, July 31, 1885, NSDPL; "A Dinner Party," *Boston Evening Traveller*, July 31, 1885, NSDPL.
5. "Sitting Bull and Buffalo Bill Entertain in True Frontier Style," *Philadelphia Times*, July 3, 1885.
6. "A Prairie Dinner at Point St. Charles," *Montreal Gazette*, August 14, 1885, NSDPL; "Buffalo Bill," *Montreal Times*, August 13, 1885, NSDPL; "A Wild West Dinner," unidentified newspaper clipping, Montreal, August 13, 1885, NSDPL.
7. "Dining with Buffalo Bill," *Brooklyn Daily Standard*, July 23, 1886, NSDPL; "Red-Skins at a Rib-Roast," *Morning Journal*, July 23, 1886, NSDPL; "Eating Beef with Indians," *World*, July 23, 1886, Julia Cody Goodman Scrapbook, AHC.
8. "Dining with Buffalo Bill," *Brooklyn Daily Standard*, July 23, 1886, NSDPL; "Dining with Buffalo Bill's Indians," unidentified newspaper clipping, n.d., NSDPL.
9. "Red-Skins at a Rib-Roast," *Morning Journal*, July 23, 1886, NSDPL; Walsh, *Making*, 259.
10. *Minneapolis (KS) Messenger*, September 22, 1887; "An Indian 'Rib Roast,'" *Suffolk (UK) East Anglian Daily Times*, August 11, 1887; Indian rib roast menu, August 9, 1887, NSBY; "Buffalo Bill's Barbecue," *Boston Daily Advertiser*, August 11, 1887, https:codyarchive.org; Burke, *Buffalo Bill*, 236–37; *London Referee*, August 14, 1887.
11. "High Jinks at the Wild West," unidentified newspaper clipping, n.d., Pony Bob Haslam Scrapbook, BBMG.
12. "The 'Wild West' Show," *Guardian* (London), January 5, 1888; Cody, *Story*, 758–59.
13. "William Entertains," *Oshkosh (WI) Northwestern*, June 20, 1888; "Bill's Indian Barbecue," *Black Hills Daily Times* (Deadwood SD). June 19, 1888; "Ribs on Stakes," *New York Times*, July 23, 1888, NSDPL; "A Big Wild Indian Roast," *New York Star*, July 23, 1888, NSDPL.
14. "Buffalo Bill Entertains a Prince Regent," *Dundee (UK) Evening Telegraph*, April 25, 1890; *Guardian* (London), April 26, 1890.
15. "Nebraska Art at the Fair," *Sioux City (IA) Journal*, July 1, 1893, 2; *New York Sun*, July 4, 1893.
16. "World's Fair and Waifs," *Chicago Post*, August 12, 1893, NSDPL.

17. "Playday of Waifs," *Chicago Tribune*, July 28, 1893, NSDPL; "Happy Day for Waifs," *Chicago Herald*, July 28, 1893, NSDPL; "Waifs Have a Picnic," *Chicago Journal*, July 28, 1893, NSDPL.

18. "Big Treat for Waifs," *Chicago Post*, July 27, 1893, NSDPL.

19. "Wild West Hospitality," *Chicago Times*, November 1, 1895, NSDPL.

20. "Buffalo Bill's Paris Gift," *New York Times*, June 14, 1889; Friesen, *Buffalo Bill*, 98–99.

21. "The Wild West Show," *Brooklyn Daily Eagle*, April 19, 1894.

22. "Expert Rough Riding," *Brooklyn Daily Eagle*, May 10, 1894.

23. "Guests of Buffalo Bill," *New York Herald*, June 12, 1894, NSDPL; "Buffalo Bill's Luncheon," *New York World*, June 12, 1894; "Buffalo Bill's Luncheon," *Nashville Tennessean*, August 5, 1894; "Women of the Press Dine," *New York Recorder*, June 12, 1894, NSDPL; "Wild West and Beauty," *New York Morning Journal*, June 12, 1894, NSDPL.

24. "Newspaper Men at the Wild West," *New York Times*, July 20, 1894, NSDPL; "Off for the Wild West Show," *Newark (NJ) Advertiser*, June 16, 1894, NSDPL; "Mayor Gilroy at Wild West," *Brooklyn Times*, June 6, 1894, NSDPL.

10. Buffalo Bill's British Invasion

Epigraph: *Bristol (UK) Mercury*, September 29, 1891.

1. Mark Twain to Bill Cody, September 10, 1884, Bancroft Library, University of California–Berkeley; Lowe, *Four National Exhibitions*, 56–57.

2. "Buffalo Bill in Camp," unidentified newspaper clipping, April 23, 1887, https:codyarchive.org; Russell, *Lives*, 327; Cody, *Story*, 709.

3. Cody, *Story*, 712–13.

4. "A Visit to the 'Wild West' and Buffalo Bill," *Staffordshire (UK) Herald*, n.d.

5. Map of the American Exhibition, BBMG; Lowe, *Four National Exhibitions*, 57; "The American Exhibition," *Newcastle (UK) Weekly Courant*, May 13, 1887.

6. Lowe, *Four National Exhibitions*, 76; map of the American Exhibition, BBMG.

7. Cody, *Story*, 722; "Colonel Cody in England," *Omaha Daily Bee*, May 10, 1887.

8. Gallop, *Buffalo Bill's British*, 44.

9. *The American: The Daily Official Programme and Journal of the American Exhibition*, October 77, 1887, author's collection; Traveling Correspondent, "Rambles about Europe," *Wichita (KS) Eagle*, July 6, 1887, https:codyarchive.org; map of the American Exhibition, BBMG; Gallop, *Buffalo Bill's British*, 59; excerpt from *Official Catalog of the American Exhibition*, BBCW; "Buffalo Bill's Bar," *Omaha Daily Bee*, September 1, 1887, https:codyarchive.org; "Gossip of the Day," *Shields Daily Gazette and Shipping Telegraph* (Durham, UK), June 21, 1887; *Yorkshire Post* (Leeds, UK), May 10, 1887; "The Stage and the Ring," *Baltimore Sun*, August 29, 1887, https:codyarchive.org.

10. "The Stage and the Ring," *New York Sun*, August 29, 1887, https:codyarchive .org; "A Royal Visit to the American Exhibition," *London Daily News* article

in *Fort Collins (CO) Courier*, July 14, 1887, https:codyarchive.org; "American Mixed Drinks," *London Pall Mall Gazette*, June 20, 1889.

11. "Sugared Popcorn: Buffalo Bill Claims the Honor of Introducing It in England," *San Jose (CA) Mercury News*, May 2, 1888; *Emporia (KS) Evening News*, July 6, 1887.

12. "Buffalo Bill and Popcorn," *New York Evening World*, May 28, 1888; advertisement, *Lloyd's Weekly Newspaper* (London), September 16, 1888.

13. "The Wild West," *San Francisco Bulletin*, August 17, 1887; "Buffalo Bill and the Princess of Wales," *Dundee (UK) Courier and Argus*, June 4, 1888.

14. "Served Edward VII, Wild West Fare," *Buffalo (NY) Courier*, January 30, 1901.

15. Cody, *Story*, 724; Gallop, *Buffalo Bill's British*, 54; "An American View of 'Buffalo Bill,'" *London Pall Mall Gazette*, July 8, 1887.

16. "The Biggest Man in London," *New York Sun*, May 29, 1887; *San Francisco Examiner*, April 30, 1887; *National Republican* (Washington DC), July 13, 1987.

17. "The Biggest Man in London," *New York Sun*, May 29, 1887; *Derbyshire Courier* (Chesterfield, UK), May 7, 1887; invitation to tea with Mr. and Mrs. Oscar Wilde, BBMG.

18. Warren, *Buffalo Bill's America*, 308–13; Tine Hreno, "The Sublime Society of Beefsteaks," *Writers in London in the 1890s* (blog), September 1, 2013, https:// 1890swriters.blogspot.com/2013/09/the-sublime-society-of-beefsteaks.html.

19. Salsbury memoir, NSBY; "A Wild West Dinner," *Cincinnati Enquirer*, September 4, 1887.

20. Advertisement, *Liverpool (UK) Mercury*, December 21, 1887.

21. Advertisement, *Manchester (UK) Weekly Time and Examiner*, December 24, 1887; Cody, *Story*, 763–64.

22. Short Bull manuscript, BBMG.

23. "Arrival of the Wild West in Sheffield," *Sheffield (UK) Daily Telegraph*, August 10, 1891; "Buffalo Bill in Portsmouth," *Portsmouth (UK) Evening Mail*, October 5,1891, https:codyarchive.org; "Round the Wild West," *Hampshire (UK) Telegraph*, October 10, 1891, https:codyarchive.org.

24. Cunningham, *Your Fathers*, 41–44, 82–83.

25. Cunningham, *Your Fathers*, 46; menu and wine list, uncatalogued scrapbook, Royal Conservatoire of Scotland Archives and Collections, Glasgow.

26. "After the Play," *Glasgow (UK) Evening News*, November 7, 1891; "Mr. Irving and Buffalo Bill," *Glasgow (UK) Evening Citizen*, November 7, 1891.

27. "Banquet to Mr. Henry Irving," *Glasgow (UK) Herald*, November 28, 1891; Tom F. Cunningham, "Pen and Pencil Club Dinner" (unpublished paper), author's collection.

28. Galloway invitation with menu in Wojtowicz, *Buffalo Bill Collector's Guide*, 234; *Glasgow (UK) Evening News*, December 5, 1891.

29. Invitation to 1390 club luncheon, menu and recipe for Argonaut Soup, BBCW.

30. "Buffalo Bill and Indians in Grand Hotel," *North British Daily Mail,* December 23, 1891, https:codyarchive.org.

31. Cunningham, *Your Fathers,* 133–34; "Buffalo Bill," *Bradford Daily Telegraph* (Yorkshire, UK), January 23, 1892; *Glasgow (UK) Herald,* March 5, 1892; "The Approaching Horticultural Exhibition," *London Morning Post,* April 22, 1892; *Sheffield and Rotherham (UK) Independent,* May 9, 1892.

32. *Wilkes-Barre (PA) Times Leader,* June 25, 1892; "Banquet of the International Society at Earl's Court," *Evening News and Post,* May 28, 1892, https:codyarchive .org; Buffalo Bill Scrapbook from 1892, BBMG; "The Fourth in London," *Walnut Valley Times* (El Dorado KS), July 6, 1892; menu in Buffalo Bill scrapbook, 1892, BBMG.

33. *Liverpool Sentinel,* May 21, 1892, https:codyarchive.org; *Music Hall and Theatre Review* (London), July 22, 1892.

34. *London Morning Post,* October 11, 1892; Auction Bill, October 13 and 14, 1892, BBMG; "Final Performances of Buffalo Bill's Show in London," *New York Times,* October 13, 1892.

35. *St. James Gazette,* October 1892, quoted in Sagala, *Buffalo Bill Cody,* 115. "Cham" may be a shortened version of champagne, given its mention with beer.

36. Standing Bear and Brininstool, *My People,* 250–51.

37. "The London Press Club," *London Observer,* January 11, 1903; *Guardian* (London), February 6, 1903.

38. "The Wild West in Cheltenham," unidentified newspaper, June 30, 1903, NSDPL.

39. "Great Wild West Show at Swansea," *Swansea (UK) Leader,* July 14, 1903, NSDPL; "Buffalo Bill at Abergavenny," *Abergavenny Chronicle and Monmouthshire (UK) Advertiser,* July 10, 1903; Griffin, *Four Years,* 33.

40. Griffin, *Four Years,* 51–52.

41. Griffin, *Four Years,* 52; Barkers and Kent Company bowls and plates, ca. 1890, from Longton, UK, BBMG.

42. Griffin, *Four Years,* 56.

11. Introducing American Cuisine

Epigraph: "All around the World," *Sacramento Daily Union,* October 24, 1889.

1. Buffalo Bill's Wild West Menu, SS *Persian Monarch,* May 17, 1888, BBCW.

2. *Brooklyn Daily Eagle,* May 30, 1889; *Buffalo (NY) Morning Express,* June 9, 1889.

3. *New York Times,* May 26, 1889, 9; Burns, *American West in France,* 32–33; *Cecil Whig* (Elkton MD), September 14, 1889; *Manchester (UK) Weekly Times and Examiner,* February 9, 1889; *London Morning Post,* July 26, 1889.

4. *Brooklyn Daily Eagle,* June 9, 1889; map of Buffalo Bill's Wild West, *Buffalo Bill's Wild West Program,* 1889, BBMG; *Brooklyn Daily Eagle,* September 13, 1889.

5. "The Paris Exposition," *Knoxville (TN) Evening Sentinel,* May 6, 1889; *Davenport (IA) Daily Times,* May 20, 1889.

6. Steve Friesen, "Paris Catches Wild West Fever," *True West*, March, 2018, 25; Mathews, "Gauguin."; Mai Britt Guleng, "Edvard Munch: The Narrator" (monograph), Munch Museum, Oslo, Norway; Jonnes, *Eiffel's Tower*, 267; "Little Known Painting," *Delphos (OH) Daily Herald*, May 7, 1900.

7. "Last View of Paris," *Capper's Weekly* (Topeka KS), September 5, 1889; "Buffalo Bill's Social Triumphs," *Salt Lake Herald*, May 30, 1889.

8. "Comments of French Newspapers upon Cody's Popularity," *Rochester (NY) Democrat and Chronicle*, July 14, 1889.

9. *Topeka Daily Capital*, July 21, 1889; *Daily Buffalo Morning Express*, July 30, 1889; *Buffalo (NY) Courier*, May 22, 1889; *Rochester (NY) Democrat and Chronicle*, October 31, 1889; *Lawrence (KS) Daily Journal*, January 4, 1890.

10. William F. Cody to Richard and Mary Winslow, invitation with dinner menu, June 3, 1889, facsimile, author's collection.

11. Menu from Buffalo Bill's Wild West camp, Paris, August 27, 1889, NSBY; "Edison's Exhibit," *Topeka (KS) State Journal*, February 22, 1889; "The Yankee Wizard," *Sioux Falls (SD) Argus-Leader*, November 5, 1889; Jonnes, *Eiffel's Tower*, 227; *Fort Worth Daily Gazette*, September 2, 1889; "A Visit to Paris," *Brooklyn Daily Eagle*, September 13, 1889; *Great Falls (MT) Leader*, October 31, 1889.

12. "The Shah in Paris," unidentified newspaper, n.d., Pony Bob Haslam Scrapbook, BBMG; *Galveston (TX) Daily News*, October 16, 1889.

13. *New York Times*, October 6, 1889; *Aspen (CO) Tribune*, March 31, 1898.

14. *Buffalo Courier*, December 23, 1889; *Nortonville (KS) News*, November 22, 1889; Jonnes, *Eiffel's Tower*, 268.

15. "Buffalo Bill in Italy," *Exeter (UK) Flying Post*, January 25, 1890; *Brooklyn Standard Union*, January 27, 1890, 2; *Wichita (KS) Daily Press*, March 6, 1890.

16. "Buffalo Bill Now in Rome," *Chicago Tribune*, February 21, 1890; "At the Vatican," *Sacramento (CA) Record-Union*, March 5, 1890.

17. Sigabette, editor of *La Nazione*, quoted in Urban, "When the 'Wild West,'" 18; "Buffalo Bill in Italy," *Galignani's Messenger*, Paris, March 17 and 23, 1890, https:codyarchive.org.

18. *Cuba (KS) Daylight*, April 18, 1890; Burke, *Buffalo Bill*, 264; "Cowboys in Old Verona," *New York Times*, May 18, 1890, https:codyarchive.org.

19. "Buffalo Bill Entertains a Prince Regent," *Dundee (UK) Evening Telegraph*, April 25, 1890; "Some Royal Presents," *Pittsburgh Dispatch*, May 8, 1890; "Fred Grant and the Indians," *Spokane Falls Review*, May 13, 1890; Wojtowicz, *Buffalo Bill Collector's Guide*, 118–19; "Buffalo Bill in Berlin," *Das Kleine Journal*, July 24, 1890, https:codyarchive.org.

20. *Winfield (KS) Assembly Herald*, July 5, 1890; "At Buffalo Bill's Wild West," *Deutsches Tageblatt*, Berlin, July 24, 1890, https:codyarchive.org.

21. "At Buffalo Bill's," *Berliner Börsen Courier*, July 23, 1890, https:codyarchive.org.

22. "At Buffalo Bill's"; "An Opening Visit at Buffalo Bill," *Das Kleine Journal*, July 23, 1890, https:codyarchive.org.

23. Burke, *Buffalo Bill*, 266.

24. "The Camp in Charlemagne's City," unidentified newspaper, May 29, 1891, https:codyarchive.org.

25. *Galignani Messenger*, June 7, 1891, https:codyarchive.org.

26. 1889–94 Guestbook, Waterloo Memorial Archives, Braine l'Alleud, Belgium; "Brussels Gossip," *Galignani Messenger*, June 7, 1891, https:codyarchive.org.

27. Burke, *Buffalo Bill*, 284–86.

28. *Lebanon (PA) Daily News*, March 13, 1905.

29. Most of these eastern European countries were part of the Austro-Hungarian Empire at the time. The names listed are their political designations as of the early twenty-first century.

30. Griffin, *Four Years*, 76, 145–48.

31. I visited the Caffè Greco in 2021 and saw the Wild West images proudly displayed there. "The Café Greco and Its Guests," *Rochester (NY) Democrat and Chronicle*, September 21, 1906; "An Ancient Café," *New York Times*, August 21, 1910.

32. William F. Cody, "The Wild West in Europe," *New York Tribune Sunday Magazine*, May 12, 1907, BBMG; *Eau Claire (WI) Leader-Telegram*, May 9, 1906.

33. Griffin, *Four Years*, 90–91; "Pisa Bars Buffalo Bill," *Brooklyn Times Union*, March 19, 1906; "Letter from Italy," *Concord (NC) Times*, April 27, 1906.

34. Griffin, *Four Years*, 111; "After Buffalo Bill," *Leavenworth Post*, July 31, 1906.

35. "Buffalo Bill Is All Right," *David City (NE) Banner-Press*, March 29, 1906; Griffin, *Four Years*, 113–15.

36. Griffin, *Four Years*, 122; *Buffalo Times*, October 14, 1906.

37. Cody, *Story*, 700.

38. Annie Oakley "Buffalo Bill," unidentified newspaper clipping, 1917, BBMG.

39. "Buffalo Bill at Plymouth," *Plymouth (UK) Mercury*, July 21, 1903, NSDPL.

40. *Nashville Tennessean*, October 4, 1897; Burke, *Buffalo Bill*, 205.

12. Fourth of July Feasts

Epigraph: *Columbus (NE) Journal*, July 22, 1903.

1. Friesen, *Buffalo Bill*, 46; Winch, *Thrilling Lives*, 175–77.

2. Yost, *Buffalo Bill*, 118–22.

3. *Wellington (KS) Daily Standard*, July 5, 1887; Wikipedia, s.v. "The Star-Spangled Banner," last modified October 20, 2022, https://en.wikipedia.org/wiki /The_Star-Spangled_Banner.

4. Menu, July 4, 1887, NSBY.

5. Menu, July 4, 1889, NSBY; Jonnes, *Eiffel's Tower*, 171.

6. Unidentified newspaper clipping, 1893, NSDPL; "Frog Legs at the 'Wild West,'" *New York Advertiser*, July 5, 1894.

7. "How the Men Are Fed," *Toronto Globe*, July 5, 1897, NSDPL; Wojtowicz, *Buffalo Bill Collector's Guide*, 238.

8. Menu, July 4, 1900, Syracuse NY, BBMG; "Big Show," *Mount Vernon (OH) Daily Banner*, NSDPL.

9. Menu, July 4, 1903, BBMG.

10. Griffin, *Four Years*, 53; menu, July 4, 1904, BBCW.

11. Menu, July 4, 1905, Cathy and Don Wagner collection, Milwaukee WI; *Daily Eastern Argus* (Portland ME), July 13, 1908, Johnny Baker Scrapbook, BBMG; Meert company records, facsimile provided by Francois Chladiuk, Western Shop, Brussels, Belgium.

12. Griffin, *Four Years*, 113.

13. Griffin, *Four Years*, 113–14; menu, July 4, 1906, BBMG.

14. William F. Cody, "The Wild West in Europe," *New York Tribune Sunday Magazine*, May 12, 1907, BBMG.

15. Menu, July 4, 1907, BBCW.

16. Menu, July 4, 1908, author's collection.

17. Menu, July 4, 1911, Cathy and Don Wagner collection.

18. *Bridgeport (CT) Times and Evening Farmer*, May 1, 1913; Wojtowicz, *Buffalo Bill Collector's Guide*, 255; Friesen, *Buffalo Bill*, 132–35.

19. Menu, July 4, 1914, BBMG.

20. Menu, July 4, 1916, BBCW.

13. Caterers, Cracker Jack

Epigraph: *Buffalo (NY) Courier*, August 21, 1895.

1. "Buffalo Bill," *Lincoln (NE) Journal Star*, May 7, 1883, 4; Barnes, *Great Plains Guide*, 145–46; Shelley Frear, "Buffalo Bill's Columbus Adventure," *True West*, July 1, 2006, https://truewestmagazine.com/article/buffalo-bills-columbus-adventure/.

2. "A Grand Success," *Omaha Daily Bee*, May 21, 1883; "Home Matters," *Fort Collins (CO) Courier*, May 24, 1883.

3. "Buffalo Bill of Leavenworth," *Leavenworth Times*, October 25, 1888; "The Wild West," *San Francisco Bulletin*, September 5, 1887, https:codyarchive.org; William Cody in London to a friend in the United States, 1887, facsimile, author's collection.

4. Advertisement, *Liverpool Mercury*, December 21, 1887; advertisements, *Western Daily Press* (Bristol, UK), October 2, 1891; "The Shah in Paris," unidentified newspaper clipping, 1889, Pony Bob Haslam Scrapbook, BBMG; "At Buffalo Bill's," *Berliner Börsen Courier*, July 23, 1890, https:codyarchive.org.

5. Unidentified newspaper clipping, 1893, NSDPL; invoice from Columbia Pop Corn Works, July 8 and 9, 1893, BBCW; advertisement, *Chicago Inter Ocean*, May 14, 1893.

6. "Buffalo Bill's Camp," *Chicago Times*, July 9, 1893, NSDPL; "Indians Win a Strike," *Chicago Inter Ocean*, July 29, 1893, NSDPL.

7. Maggie Borden, "Food History: The 1893 Columbian Exposition in Chicago," *James Beard Foundation* (blog), September 15, 2014, www.jamesbeard .org/blog/food-history-1893-columbian-exposition-chicago#; Wikipedia, s.v. "Lancaster Caramel Company," last modified October 20, 2022, https://en .wikipedia.org/wiki/Lancaster_Caramel_Company; "History and Legends of Popcorn, Cracker Jacks and Popcorn Balls," What's Cooking America, October 20, 2022, https://whatscookingamerica.net/history/popcornhistory .htm.

8. Wigwam Restaurant Menu, facsimile, author's collection; "At the World's Fair," *Wheeling Register*, March 12, 1893. "Buffalo Bill Will Give Dinner with Show Tickets," *Wheeling Register*, May 6, 1893.

9. Friesen, *Buffalo Bill*, 107; *Ottawa (KS) Herald*, September 22, 1898.

10. *Buffalo Courier*, August 21, 1895; "Colonel Cody's Wild West," *Albany (NY) Argus*, June 15, 1898, NSDPL; "A Monster Crowd," *Nebraska City Daily News*, September 17, 1900, NSDPL; *Bridgeport (CT) Evening Post*, June 26, 1899.

11. Hutchinson, *Official Souvenir*, 1896, BBMG; Expense/Income Statement from Jule Keen, July 6–13, 1896, BBMG.

12. "Fair Women and Long-Haired Scouts," *New York Evening Telegram*, May 8, 1897, NSDPL.

13. "Daily Expense of Big Show," *Long Branch (NJ) Press*, June 7, 1899, NSDPL; *Fall River (MA) Daily Globe*, June 23, 1899, NSDPL; "It Costs for Food," *Fond du Lac (WI) Daily Commonwealth*, August 29, 1899, NSDPL; *Wilmington (NC) Messenger*, October 8, 1895.

14. "To See Buffalo Bill," *Winsted (CT) Citizen*, June 10, 1899, NSDPL; "Were Here," *Austin (MN) Daily Register*, September 26, 1899, NSDPL.

15. "Buffalo Bill Makes Triumphal Entry," *New York Telegraph*, April 1, 1901, NSDPL.

16. *Historical Sketches and Programme*, Buffalo Bill's Wild West and Congress of Rough Riders of the World, 1902, author's collection.

17. *Buffalo Bill's Wild West and Congress of Rough Riders of the World Program*, Boston, June 16, 1902, author's collection.

18. W. F. Cody, Account Book, 1902–3, BBMG; "Buffalo Bill's Wild West Visit to Bedford," *Bedford (UK) Times*, September 18, 1903, NSDPL; Noble, *Around the Coast*, 16.

19. *Buffalo Bill's Wild West and Congress of Rough Riders of the World Program*, Chicago, July 22, 1907, author's collection; *Buffalo Bills Wild West Combined with Pawnee Bill's Great Far East Program*, author's collection.

20. *Magazine and Official Review*, Buffalo Bill's Wild West and Pawnee Bill's Far East, 1911, author's collection; Treasurer, "Season's Statement, 1910, Buffalo Bills Wild West/Pawnee Bill's Far East," BBMG.

21. *The Pioneer Scouts: A Book of Border Life*, 1912, author's collection.

22. Advertisement, *Bisbee (AZ) Daily Press*, October 22, 1908; "Those Who Cook Christmas Dinners for Chicago's Homeless Rich," *Chicago Tribune*, December 20, 1908.

14. Dining Out with Cody and Friends

Epigraph: Roosevelt, *Theodore Roosevelt's Letters*, letter 45, February 19, 1904.

1. "Of Women, by Col. Cody," *New York Sun*, April 3, 1898. Suits were purchased by Cody from Henry Poole and Company in 1892 and 1903; photographs of the company's ledgers are in the author's collection, and the 1903 suit is in the collection of Buffalo Bill Center of the West.

2. Gallop, *Buffalo Bill's British*, 58; "Personal Intelligence," *New York Times*, May 21, 1888; "Of Women, by Col. Cody."

3. "In Honor of Buffalo Bill," *Philadelphia Times*, July 10, 1885; United Arts Club menu, June 25, 1887, NSBY.

4. Souvenir of visit to Buffalo Bill's Wild West, American Newspaper Publishers Association, NSBY; "Feasting and Song," *Chicago Inter Ocean*, May 27, 1893, NSDPL; "Anatomy of a Restaurateur: H. M. Kinsley," *Restaurant-ing through History* (blog), October 29, 2008, https://restaurant-ingthroughhistory.com /2008/10/29/anatomy-of-a-restaurateur-h-m-kinsley/; Melville Stone to W. F. Cody, December 31, 1896, NSBY.

5. "Hon. W. F. Cody Welcomed Home," *North Platte (NE) Telegraph*, October 7, 1886, Julia Cody Goodman Collection, AHS; "Dinner to Gen. Miles," unidentified newspaper clipping, January 31, 1896, BBMG.

6. "Colonel Cody's Plans," *Chicago Tribune*, May 31, 1902; menu, "An Appreciation of the Wild West," May 1, 1902, NSBY.

7. "Showmen Form a League," *Leavenworth Times*, February 20, 1913; "Old Indian Fighter Elected President of Showmen's League of America," *Natrona County Tribune* (Casper WY), March 20, 1913; "All Ready t' Start! Showmen's Banquet," *Chicago Inter Ocean*, March 15, 1913; "Lad-ees and Gentlemun!," *Chicago Tribune*, March 16, 1913; menu, "A Dinner in Honor of Hon. Wm. F. Cody 'Buffalo Bill,'" Showmen's League of America, March 15, 1913, BBMG.

8. Cody, *Life*, 279–80.

9. *New Haven (CT) Morning Journal-Courier*, W. F. Cody to O. C. Marsh, February 23, November 26, 1873, O. C. Marsh Collection, Sterling Library, Yale University; *Boston Globe*, March 1, 1873; *Hartford (CT) Courant*, January 12, 1874; *Burlington (IA) Weekly Hawk-Eye*, January 22, 1874.

10. W. F. Cody to O. C. Marsh, December 22, 1874, O. C. Marsh Collection, Sterling Library, Yale University; *New Haven (CT) Morning Journal-Courier*, June 3, 1902.

11. "Buffalo Bill Enjoys London," *Boston Post*, May 9, 1887; Anderson and Koval, *James McNeill Whistler*, 314; *Brooklyn Daily Eagle*, September 28, 1887.

12. *London Pall Mall Gazette*, August 11, 1892; *New York Times*, August 14, 1892; invitation, guest list, and menu for Moffat Banquet, August 10, 1892, Buffalo Bill's Scrapbook, BBMG.

13. Hassrick, *Albert Bierstadt*, 57.

14. Hassrick, 117; "Account of a Dinner Party Given by Buffalo Bill," *Oshkosh (WI) Northwestern*, June 20, 1888.

15. *Arizona Silver Belt* (Globe AZ), October 27, 1888; Hassrick, 73–77, 117; *Philadelphia Inquirer*, June 4, 1890; Burns, *American West in France*, 64.

16. "Rosa Bonheur and Buffalo Bill," *Westminster Budget* (London), September 27, 1895, 30; "Rosa Bonheur Painted Cody's Picture," *Los Angeles Herald*, May 7, 1900; Burns, *American West in France*, 66–67; *Buffalo (NY) Morning Express*, October 6, 1889; Jonnes, *Eiffel's Tower*, 245.

17. Fry, "Wonders," 19; Burns, "Art, Ethnography," 131–32; Bonner, "'Not an Imaginary Picture," 51; "Impression of an Artist," *Appleton (WI) Post*, August 27, 1896; Frederic Remington to Nate Salsbury, August 21, 1894, NSBY; advertisement, *Chicago Tribune*, December 22, 1897; *Kansas City (MO) Journal*, December 2, 1897.

18. "Battle Scene Draws Crowds," *Chicago Inter Ocean*, August 24, 1899; menu, April 28, 1902, NSBY; "Nate Salsbury Their Host: They Eat among Indian Warwhoops," *New York Tribune*, April 29, 1902; Fry, "Wonders," 25–28, 30, 34.

19. "Cody and His Indians See Themselves at Show," *Brooklyn Daily Eagle*, May 12, 1909; "Rodman Wanamaker Plans to Erect Indian Statue," *Brooklyn Standard Union*, May 13, 1909.

20. "Statute [*sic*] to Indian in New York Harbor," *Daily Oklahoman* (Oklahoma City), March 6, 1910; Wikipedia s.v. "National American Indian Memorial," last modified October 21, 2022, https://en.wikipedia.org/wiki/National _American_Indian_Memorial.

21. "Col. Cody and Gen. King Swap Stories at Press Club," *Milwaukee Journal*, August 22, 1899, NSDPL.

22. "John Chamberlin," *Louisville Courier-Journal*, July 1, 1896; "General Miles Dined," *Philadelphia Times*, January 31, 1896, 4; "A Dinner to General Miles," *Washington (DC) Evening Star*, January 31, 1896.

23. "Dinner to General Miles," unidentified newspaper clipping, n.d., Pony Bob Haslam Scrapbook, BBMG; "Nine Centuries of History," Château du Clos de Vougeot, accessed October 21, 2022, https://www.closdevougeot.fr /en/history; "General Miles Dined," *Philadelphia Times*, January 31, 1896.

24. Jonnes, *Eiffel's Tower*, 195; Roosevelt, *Theodore Roosevelt's Letters*, letter 45, February 19, 1904.

15. Meanwhile, Back at the Ranch

Epigraph: "A Royal Entertainer," *Wilkes-Barre (PA) Times Leader*, November 7, 1893.

1. "Buffalo Bill at Army Post," *Chattanooga Daily Times*, December 26, 1905.

2. Yost, *Buffalo Bill*, 101–2, 104, 155, 356; "The Romantic Wooing and Happy Marriage of Buffalo Bill's Daughter," unidentified newspaper, February, 1903, BBMG.

3. "Buffalo Bill's Coyote Cry," *Western Kansas World* (Wakeeney), October 30, 1886; "A Living Hero," *Pawnee Rock (KS) Leader*, December 31, 1886; "Hon. W. F. Cody Welcomed Home," *North Platte (NE) Telegraph*, October 7, 1886, Julia Cody Goodman Collection, AHC; Yost, *Buffalo Bill*, 175.

4. "Living Hero."

5. Bill of fare, North Platte Greeting to Buffalo Bill, October 6, 1886, BBCW; Yost, *Buffalo Bill*, 175.

6. Yost, *Buffalo Bill*, 176–78.

7. Yost, *Buffalo Bill*, 211, 214–15; "Buffalo Bill in Omaha," *Lincoln (NE) Evening Call*, November 6, 1888; *Weekly Schuyler* (Schuyler NE), November 15, 1888.

8. "Cody's Hospitality," *Wilkes-Barre (PA) Times Leader*, November 7, 1893; Winona Evans Reeves, "Of Interest to Women," *Daily Gate City and Constitution Democrat* (Keokuk IA), June 25, 1918; Yost, *Buffalo Bill*, 442–44.

9. Yost, *Buffalo Bill*, 266–67, 270; "Buffalo Bill's Show," *North Platte (NE) Semi-Weekly Tribune*, Oct. 13, 1896.

10. Fellows, *This Way*, 158–60.

11. Walsh, *Making*, 324.

12. Bonner, *William F. Cody's*, 7; Russell, *Lives*, 426–27.

13. Yost, *Buffalo Bill*, 258.

14. Yost, *Buffalo Bill*, 296.

15. William F. Cody to Julia Cody Goodman, March 23, 1902, https:codyarchive.org; Bonner, *William F. Cody's*, 168; Foote, *Letters*, 97–98; William F. Cody to Julia Cody Goodman, May 22, 1902, https:codyarchive.org; Irma Hotel Christmas dinner menu, 1904, Cathy and Don Wagner collection.

16. Kensel, *Pahaska Tepee*, 14–15, 20–21.

17. Kensel, *Pahaska Tepee*, 43; Russell, *Lives*, 427; "Homes in the Big horn Basin," Shoshone Irrigation advertisement, *Buffalo Bill's Wild West Program*, 1897, BBMG.

18. Foote, *Letters*, 106; William F. Cody to John H. Tait, August 10, 1916, https:codyarchive.org; William F. Cody to William Goodfellow, May 2, 1914, facsimile, author's collection; *Buffalo Bill's TE Ranch*, brochure, 1916, author's collection; Walsh, *Making*, 344.

19. William F. Cody to W. L. Walls, 1915, BBMG; Albright and Schenck, *Creating*, 131–33, 175–76.

20. Frank Winch, *How Buffalo Bill Is to Spend His Time*, brochure, ca. 1911, BBCW; "Western News," *Salida (CO) Record*, November 19, 1909, CHN; Yost, *Buffalo Bill*, 361–62.

21. "Homes in the Big Horn Basin"; "Colonel Cody Leaves Tucson to Attend Housewarming," *Tucson (AZ) Citizen*, December 9, 1910; "Col. Cody, the Modern to-Date Business Man," *Arizona Daily Star* (Tucson), November 7, 1911; "Col. Dyer Describes Trip with Buffalo Bill," *Arizona Daily Star*, March 26, 1911.

22. "Buffalo Bill Here to Hunt," *New York Sun*, October 30, 1904.

23. "Buffalo Bill's Chef," *Iowa City Press-Citizen*, November 20, 1901.

24. Yost, *Buffalo Bill*, 355–59.

25. "Buffalo Bill's Cook Attended Dedication," *Canonsburg (PA) Daily Notes*, August 8, 1932; advertisement, *Parsons (KS) Daily Sun*, January 7, 1905; "Buffalo Bill's Cook," *Decatur (IL) Herald and Review*, October 22, 1923; "Dead at Age of 74," *Ogden (UT) Standard-Examiner*, February 10, 1935.

26. *Billings (MT) Gazette*, February 24, 1946; "The Vic Hugo Days," *Cedar Rapids (IA) Gazette*, September 25, 1945.

27. "Visiting Old Friends of the Show World," *Billings (MT) Weekly Gazette*, December 6, 1912; "Local Man Long Served Scout as His Cook," *Billings (MT) Gazette*, November 25, 1934.

28. "Local Man Long Served"; "Heimer's Tavern Here, Specializes in Dutch Lunches," *Billings (MT) Gazette*, July 30, 1933.

29. Henry Leonard Wiard, *Memoirs of Henry Leonard Wiard*, 1958, 29, 86, BBCW.

30. "Local Man Long Served."

16. Tanglefoot, Ginger Ale

Epigraph: "Buffalo Bill's Wild West," *Joplin (MO) Herald*, September 27, 1898.

1. Monahan, *Golden Elixir*, 24–25.

2. Monahan, *Golden Elixir*, 32; Army Stores advertisement, *Leavenworth Times*, February 7, 1865.

3. Cody, *Life*, 135.

4. *Chicago Tribune*, May 2, 1882; *Kansan* (Jamestown), May 6, 1882.

5. Beach I. Hinman, deposition for Cody divorce trial, February 9, 1905, https:codyarchive.org; W. B. "Bat" Masterson, "A Few Incidents in the Adventurous Career of the Famous Buffalo Bill That Have Passed under My Personal Observation," *Washington Post*, March 8, 1908, https:codyarchive.org; May Cody Bradford testimony at Cody divorce trial, BBCW.

6. Walsh, *Making*, 199.

7. Sagala, *Buffalo Bill on Stage*, 44; Friesen, *Buffalo Bill*, 27; "The Curb and Corridor," *Leadville (CO) Herald Democrat*, May 22, 1892, https://www.coloradohistoricnewspapers.org/; *Inter Ocean*, August 7, 1880; "Buffalo Bill Badly Beaten," *Brooklyn Daily Eagle*, August 18, 1880.

8. *Fort Collins (CO) Courier*, March 2, 1882, CHN.

9. Walsh, *Making*, 229.

10. Russell, *Lives*, 302–3; Buffalo Bill to Nate Salsbury, ca. May 29, 1884, NSBY; Walsh, *Making*, 244; Foote, *Letters*, 44; "A Chat with Buffalo Bill," supplement to *Manchester (UK) Courier*, October 22, 1892.

11. Sagala, *Buffalo Bill on Stage*, 129–30; "Buffalo Bill at Last Stand," *Chicago Tribune*, February 17, 1905; Russell, *Lives*, 157, 360–61.

12. Sorg, *Doctor, Lawyer*, 117; Joan Kent, "Fiction Cloud's Powell's History," *La Crosse (WI) Tribune*, January 5, 1997.

13. Sorg, *Doctor, Lawyer*, 123–24; "Big Coffee Mill," *Wood County Reporter* (Grand Rapids), October 26, 1893; "Cody as a Purveyor," *Chicago Times*, September 23, 1893, NSDPL; Foote, *Letters*, 74, 76.

14. Jule Keen to Buffalo Bill, April, 1887, NSBY.

15. *Salt Lake Tribune*, April 29, 1887; *Ravenna (OH) Democratic Press*, March 25, 1887; *Salt Lake Herald*, February 15, 1887; *Rock Island (IL) Daily Argus*, February 28, 1887; *Columbus (NE) Journal*, May 25, 1887; *Glasgow (UK) Evening News and Star*, June 30, 1887; *Edinburgh (UK) Evening News*, July 2, 1887; "'Buffalo Bill' at Cardiff," *South Wales (UK) Daily News*, September 26, 1891.

16. "Buffalo Bill's Wild West," *Joplin (MO) Herald*, September 27, 1898, NSDPL; Walsh, *Making*, 298; unidentified newspaper clipping, n.d., Pony Bob Haslam Scrapbook, BBMG.

17. Walsh, *Making*, 323–24; William F. Cody to George Beck, September 7, 1895, codyarchive.com.

18. Foote, *Letters*, 41; Pony Bob Haslam testimony at Cody divorce trial, 1905, codyarchive.com.

19. Yost, *Buffalo Bill*, 248–51; Dr. E. B. Warner testimony at Cody divorce trial, February 9, 1905, https:codyarchive.org.

20. Deposition of William F. Cody for divorce trial, March 25, 1904, https:codyarchive.org; Fellows, *This Way*, 90.

21. Fellows, *This Way*, 92, 99.

22. Blackstone, *Business*, 17; depositions of William F. Cody for divorce trial, March 6 and 23, 1904, https:codyarchive.org.; "Spring Fashions in Drinks," *New York Times*, May 8, 1904; "Colonel Cody on Temperance," *Shields (UK) Daily News*, July 25, 1904; "Buffalo Bill in Praise of Temperance," *Lancashire (UK) Northern Daily Telegraph*.

23. *Lincoln (NE) Star*, February 19, 1905; Dr. E. B. Warner testimony at Cody divorce trial, BBCW.

24. William F. Cody to Julia and Al Goodman, September 24, 1883, BBCW; "Buffalo Bill at Last Stand," *Chicago Tribune*, February 17, 1905.

25. "Buffalo Bill at Last Stand," *Chicago Tribune*, February 17, 1905; Yost, *Buffalo Bill*, 323; "They Vindicate Mrs. Cody," *East Oregonian* (Pendleton), February 27, 1905; *Eagle Valley (CO) Enterprise*, April 29, 1904, CHN; "Buffalo Bill and His Wife Both Appear to Poor Advantage," *Lamar (CO) Register*, February 22, 1905, CHN; "Cody Divorce Case," *Colorado Transcript* (Golden), February

23, 1905, CHN; "Buffalo Bill Loses," *Colorado Republican*, March 30, 1905, CHN; *Nashua (IA) Reporter*, April 27, 1905, 7; *San Miguel (CO) Examiner*, July 15, 1905, CHN.

26. William F. Cody to Julia Cody Goodman, June 14, 1904, BBCW; "The Show in Prison," MS006, 1909 Scrapbook, BBCW; Foote, *Letters*, 126.

27. "Domestic Difficulties Are Adjusted through Efforts of Grandson," *Champaign (IL) Daily News*, March 28, 1910; "Grandson of Buffalo Bill as Mediator between Couple," *Tampa Tribune*; unidentified newspaper clipping, n.d., Pony Bob Haslam Scrapbook, BBMG; Yost, *Buffalo Bill*, 368–69; photograph of Cody and Louisa, ca. 1915, BBMG.

28. Beck, *Beckoning Frontiers*, 243; "Buffalo Bill Drinks Only Buttermilk," *Watertown (WI) News*, April 2, 1909; "Gave 'Em a Shock," *Martinsville (IN) Reporter-Times*, March 30, 1909; Yost, *Buffalo Bill*, 382.

29. "Buffalo Bill's Cook," *Billings (MT) Gazette*, January 12, 1964.

30. *Brooklyn Daily Eagle*, August 29, 1938; Yost, *Buffalo Bill*, 438.

31. William F. Cody to Clarence Buell, ca. 1915, https:codyarchive.org.

32. Salsbury memoir, ca. 1902, NSBY.

17. The Banquet Ends

Epigraph: "Buffalo Bill Says Goodbye to 26,000," *Moline (IL) Dispatch*, August 3, 1911.

1. "A Banquet for the Indians," *New York Times*, September 26, 1886, Julia Goodman Scrapbook, AHC; 1898 Farewell Dinner menu, BBMG.

2. 1903 and 1904 Farewell Dinner menus, BBMG; "Colonel Cody's Farewell to His Men," *Burton (UK) Mail*, October 4, 1903, NSDPL.

3. "Buffalo Bill's Show Coming Next Week," *Saint Paul Globe*, July 18, 1902.

4. Burke, *Foursome*, 94; Salsbury memoir, NSBY.

5. Salsbury memoir, NSBY; Warren, *Buffalo Bill's America*, 496; Lowe, *Four National Exhibitions*, 56–57.

6. "A Feast in the Tombs," *Chattanooga News*, May 31, 1902; advertisement, *Spokane Spokesman-Review*, August 17, 1902; advertisement, *Guthrie (OK) Daily Leader*, October 7, 1902; "Death of Nate Salsbury," *Nebraska State Journal* (Lincoln), December 25; *Chicago Tribune*, December 25, 1902; Walsh, *Making*, 329.

7. "James A. Bailey Buried," *Brooklyn Daily Eagle*, April 14, 1906; "Buffalo Bill in Sunny Italy," *Buffalo (NY) Courier*, May 6, 1906.

8. "No More Wild West," *Jackson (MS) Daily News*, May 15, 1910; "Movies Hit Buffalo Bill," *Coffeyville (KS) Daily Journal*, March 19, 1913; "Buffalo Bill's Farewell," *Lincoln (NE) Star*, November 12, 1902.

9. "Cohan Dined by Friars," *New York Times*, April 4, 1910; "Cohan and Harris to Give Big Matinee Here for Cody Fund," *Denver Post*, January 28, 1917; "Buffalo Bill Says Goodbye to 26,000," *Moline (IL) Dispatch*, August 3, 1911.

10. "Buffalo Bill Well Pleased with His Mine," *Arizona Daily Star* (Tucson), December 9, 1910; "Buffalo Bill One of Oldest Elks in World," *Arizona Daily Star*, March 21, 1912; Russell, *Lives*, 435–36; "'Buffalo Bill' Adopts Another Role," *Tucson (AZ) Citizen*, December 22, 1912; Wilson, *Buffalo Bill's Wild West*, 208–9; Yost, *Buffalo Bill*, 380.

11. *Pioneer Scouts Program* for Buffalo Bill's Wild West and Pawnee Bill's Great Far East, Combined, 1913, author's collection; Walsh, *Making*, 341; "Court Is Asked to Order Sale Now of All Wild West Property," *Denver (CO) Post*, August 22, 1913.

12. Walsh, *Making*, 342–43; 1914 Sells Floto Farewell Dinner menu, author's collection.

13. Walsh, *Making*, 355; Fellows, *This Way*, 160.

14. William Cody to his cousin Frank Cody, ca. 1915, facsimile, author's collection; "Col. W. F. Cody Ill at His Hotel Here," *Arizona Daily Star* (Tucson), March 2, 1910; "'Buffalo Bill' Removed to Glenwood Springs CO," *Arkansas Democrat* (Little Rock), January 4, 1917; "Col. W. F. Cody Is Said to Be Dying," *Oregon Daily Journal* (Portland), January 7, 1917.

15. "Buffalo Bill, Dying, Plays Game of High Five," *Wilmington (DE) News Journal*, January 9, 1917.

16. Louisa Cody, *Memories*, 1919, 324; "Buffalo Bill Is Dying," *Pantagraph* (Bloomington IL), January 9, 1917; Friesen, *Buffalo Bill*, 141–42.

17. Friesen, *Buffalo Bill*, 142–46.

18. "Buffalo Bill's Estate $65,000," *St. Louis Post-Dispatch*, January 25, 1917; Walsh, *Making*, 311.

19. Wetmore and Grey, *Last of the Great*, 332.

18. Still Eating and Drinking

Epigraph: Foote, *Letters*, 95.

1. Café Josephine menu ledger, 1918, BBMG; Pahaska Tepee menu, 1931, BBMG.

2. "Mile High Dining," *Denver Post*, July 11, 1975; Monahan, *Golden Elixir*, 67; Buckhorn Exchange menu, ca. 1933, BBMG; Buckhorn Exchange menu, 1978, author's collection.

3. Auction advertisement, *American Swineherd*, ca. 1919, author's collection; Longhorn Ranch advertising card, ca. 1963, author's collection.

4. Arnold, *Frying Pans West*, 33; Steve Friesen, "Denver's First Christmas Party," *Denver Monthly*, December 1979.

5. Kinney, *Shinin' Times*, 56; Old Crow advertisements, author's collection.

6. "Spirits," Mississippi River Distilling Company, accessed October 21, 2022, https://www.mrdistilling.com/spirits/.

7. Buffalo Bill's Brewery, accessed October 21, 2022, http://www .buffalobillsbrewery.com; Martin Kidston, "Buffalo Bill Beer," *Billings (MT) Gazette*, June 20, 2011.

8. Author research visits to the town of Cody and Buffalo Bill Center of the West, 2010, 2011, 2017, 2018, 2022.

9. Author research visit to Keens, New York City, November 29, 2016; "History of Keens," accessed October 21, 2022, https://www.keens.com/historyofkeens.

10. Author research visits to Europe and artifacts in author's collection.

11. Author research visit to Disneyland Paris, France, 2005.

12. Artifacts in author's collection.

13. Artifacts in author's collection.

14. Foote, *Letters*, 95.

Appendix

1. Leslie, *Miss Leslie's Directions*, 377; Hale, *Good Housekeeper, 1841*, 27–28; "To the Quindaro Housewives," *Quindaro (KS) Chindowan*, July 18, 1857.

2. "Corn Bread," *Glasgow (MO) Weekly Times*, May 26, 1853.

3. *Kansas Pilot* (Kansas City), March 15, 1879; Cornelius, *Young Housekeeper's*, 102; *Sterling (KS) Gazette*, June 7, 1877; *Richland County (WI) Observer*, January 5, 1858.

4. Lea, *Domestic Cookery*, 26–27.

5. *St. Louis Western Watchman*, August 8, 1850; Williams, *Wagon Wheel*, 14–16.

6. Arnold, *Eating*, 62.

7. Child, *American Frugal*, 82; Sanderson, *Camp Fires*, 11; Randolph, *Directions for Cooking*, 3; Arnold, *Eating*, 21.

8. Williams, *Wagon Wheel*, 23–25; Sanderson, *Camp Fires*, 9; Randolph, *Directions for Cooking*, 6.

9. Williams, *Wagon Wheel*, 28; Leslie, *Miss Leslie's Directions*, 197–98.

10. Lea, *Domestic Cookery*, 34; Gillette and Ziemann, *White House*, 185; Farmer, *Boston*, 255; Weaver, *Heirloom Vegetable*, 92–93, 106–7; Leslie, *Miss Leslie's Directions*, 197–98.

11. Harland, *Common Sense*, 61; Eighmey, *Stirring the Pot*, 225.

12. "Snipe on Toast," *Leavenworth (KS) Daily Commercial*, November 3, 1872.

13. *Great Bend (KS) Weekly Tribune*, December 3, 1880; Harland, *Common Sense*, 87.

14. Harland, *Common Sense*, 87.

15. Wondrich, *Imbibe!*, 82–85.

16. Thomas, *How to Mix*, 16.

17. Thomas, *How to Mix*, 28.

18. FitzGibbon, *Food*, 482; Lang, *Larousse*, 1090–91.

19. Harland, *Common Sense*, 119.

20. "Barnum on Pigs' Feet," *Bismarck (ND) Tribune*, April 1, 1881.

21. "Barnum on Pigs' Feet."

22. "Wild West's Kitchen," *Chicago Evening Post*, June 4, 1896; "Buffalo Bill's Steward," *New York Times*, August 26, 1894.

23. Swett, *New England Breakfast*, 107–8.
24. "Daily Expense of Big Show," *Long Branch (NY) Press*, June 7, 1899; Hutchinson, *Official Souvenir*, 1896, 102, BBMG.
25. Farmer, *Boston*, 221.
26. Gillette and Ziemann, *White House*, 223.
27. Williams, *Savory Suppers*, 294; Lang, *Larousse*, 642.
28. "Boiled Ham, Madeira Sauce," *Richford (VT) Journal and Gazette*, February 24, 1893.
29. Farmer, *Boston*, 242.
30. "Tamale Parties in the West," *Louisiana Democrat* (Alexandria), May 18, 1887.
31. "What Is a Tamale?," *Fort Worth Daily Gazette*, April 19, 1887.
32. "Hot Tamales," *Kansas City (MO) Journal*, December 4, 1897.
33. Burr, *Woman Suffrage*, 10.
34. "Bean Soup," *Carlisle (PA) Sentinel*, August 30, 1887; *Harrisburg (PA) Telegraph*, September 5, 1887; "Likes the Life," *Butte (MT) Miner*, September 3, 1910.
35. "Bean Soup," *Clarion (PA) Democrat*, April 7, 1887.
36. *Boston Globe*, January 20, 1887, 6.
37. "Boston Baked Beans," *Bismarck (ND) Tribune*, September 2, 1887.
38. Farmer, *Boston*, 223.
39. Farmer, *Boston*, 237.
40. *Newcastle (UK) Weekly Courant*, July 22, 1887; "American Mixed Drinks," *London Pall Mall Gazette*, June 20, 1889.
41. Thomas, *How to Mix*, 47.
42. "Opening of the American Exhibition," *London Daily News*, May 10, 1887.
43. "Tourists Have New Handbook: It Is Filled with Recipes for Making Fancy American Drinks," *Muncie (IN) Star Press*, July 4, 1920.
44. Invitation with dinner menu sent to Richard and Mary Winslow by William F. Cody, June 3, 1889, facsimile author's collection.
45. "Mayonnaise," *Sun and Erie County Independent* (Hamburg NY), May 23, 1890.
46. *Winfield (KS) Assembly Herald*, July 5, 1890; Shillaber, *Practical Guide*, 227–28, 233.
47. Gillette and Ziemann, *White House*, 403.
48. Hill, *Epicure's Almanac*, 128; Thomas, *How to Mix*, 185.
49. Archbold and McCauley, *Last Dinner*, 67, 83; Thomas, *How to Mix*, 185.
50. "Roman Punch," *Buffalo (NY) Evening News*, February 22, 1915.
51. *Decatur (IL) Daily Review*, February 4, 1905; *Weekly Oregon Statesman* (Salem), January 3, 1905; *Kellogg's Wichita (KS) Record*, June 17, 1905.
52. Newton Kansan, *Kansan Kook Book*, 41.
53. "Wine Sauce," *Boston Globe*, June 23, 1905.
54. "Wild West Show in Town," *New Haven (CT) Register*, June 28, 1899, NSDPL; *Lima (OH) News*, August 5, 1899.

55. "This Is Circus Day," *Waterbury (CT) Evening Globe*, June 27, 1899, NSDPL; *Brooklyn Daily Eagle*, July 3, 1895; *Lincoln (NE) Evening Call*, May 4, 1894; "When Lemonade Was Pink," *Montgomery (AL) Advertiser*, October 13, 1912; *Rush Springs (OK) Gazette*, October 5, 1912.

56. "Red Lemonade Is From Horse Blanket," *Appleton (WI) Post-Crescent*, July 9, 1909; *Rush Springs (OK) Gazette*, October 5, 1912; "No Red Lemonade," *Coffeyville (KS) Daily Journal*, July 20, 1908; advertisement, *Waterloo (IA) Courier*, April 30, 1913; "Red Lemonade," *Buffalo (NY) Courier*, August 26, 1915; untitled news item, *Minneapolis Star Tribune*, June 29, 1902.

57. Untitled, *Minneapolis Star Tribune*, June 29, 1902.

58. Herrick, *Consolidated Library*, 3; "Parisienne Potatoes," *Indiana (PA) Gazette*, April 2, 1985.

59. "Potatoes Parisienne," *Lawrence (KS) Daily Gazette*, November 26, 1915.

60. "Valuable Selections for Winter Dinners," *Scranton (PA) Republican*, October 19, 1895.

61. Sydney Smith, "A Recipe for a Salad," accessed October 21, 2022, http://www.foodreference.com/html/recipe-for-a-salad.html.

62. Wiard, *Memoirs*, 86, BBCW.

63. *Boston Globe*, March 15, 1902.

64. "Lobster Newburg," *Topeka (KS) State Journal*, September 3, 1902.

65. "Cream or Milk in Lobster Newburg," *Wichita (KS) Daily Eagle*, May 16, 1902; *Reading (PA) Times*, April 6, 1906.

66. David Wondrich, "The Lost African-American Bartenders Who Created the Cocktail," Daily Beast, accessed October 21, 2022, https://www.thedailybeast.com/the-lost-african-american-bartenders-who-created-the-cocktail; Wondrich, 9, 12–13; Thomas, *How to Mix*; Johnson, 40.

67. "The Mint Julep," *Philadelphia Times*, June 23, 1895.

68. Wondrich, *Imbibe!*, 245; "Most Popular Drink," *St. Louis Post-Dispatch*, April 2, 1891.

69. "Drinks Their Theme," *Chicago Tribune*, May 14, 1893; "Plain and Fancy Drinks," *Chicago Chronicle*, October 6, 1895; "Couldn't Fool Him," *Wyandot Herald* (Kansas City KS), August 10, 1899; Wondrich, *Imbibe!*, 248, 254–55.

70. "Back to Old-Time Ways," *Western Sentinel* (Winston-Salem NC), July 3, 1890.

71. Wondrich, 146; "What to Drink in Summer," *Kansas City (MO) Star*, June 25, 1905.

72. "Some New and Delicious Summer Drinks," *Los Angeles Herald*, July 30, 1905.

73. Farmer, *Boston*, 10; "Sauce Hollandaise," *Philadelphia Inquirer*, July 19, 1903.

74. "Sparkling Punch Club Brews," *New York Sun*, February 15, 1914; "The Cook Says," *Pittsburgh Press*, August 12, 1914; "Claret Punch," *Meriden (CT) Journal*, April 23, 1914; "Lucy Lincoln's Talks," *Buffalo Sunday Morning News*, November 8, 1914.

75. "Claret Punch," *Fresno (CA) Morning Republican*, November 20, 1914.

BIBLIOGRAPHY

Albright, Horace M., and Marion Albright Schenck. *Creating the National Park Service*. Norman: University of Oklahoma Press, 1999.

Anderson, Ronald, and Anne Koval. *James McNeill Whistler: Beyond the Myth*. New York: Carroll and Graf, 1995.

Archbold, Rick, and Dana McCauley. *Last Dinner on the Titanic*. Toronto ON: Madison, 1997.

Arellano, Gustavo. *Taco USA*. New York: Scribner, 2012.

Arnold, Samuel P. *Eating up the Santa Fe Trail*. Niwot: University Press of Colorado, 1990.

———. *Frying Pans West Cookbook*. Morrison CO: Fur Trade, 1969.

Barnes, Jeff. *The Great Plains Guide to Buffalo Bill*. Mechanicsburg PA: Stackpole, 2014.

Beck, George W. T. *Beckoning Frontiers: The Memoir of a Wyoming Entrepreneur*. Edited by Lynn J. Houze and Jeremy M. Johnston. Lincoln: University of Nebraska Press, 2020.

Beecher, George Allen. *A Bishop of the Great Plains*. Philadelphia: Church Historical Society, 1950.

Blackstone, Sarah J. *The Business of Being Buffalo Bill: Selected Letters of William F. Cody*. Westport CT: Praeger, 1988.

Bloss, Roy S. *Pony Express: The Great Gamble*. Berkeley CA: Howell-North, 1959.

Bonner, Robert E. "'Not an Imaginary Picture Altogether, But Parts': The Artistic Legacy of Buffalo Bill Cody." *Montana: The Magazine of Western History* 61, no. 1 (Spring 2011): 40–59.

———. *William F. Cody's Wyoming Empire*. Norman: University of Oklahoma Press, 2007.

Bricklin, Julia. *The Notorious Life of Ned Buntline*. Guilford CT: TwoDot, 2020.

Burke, Carolyn. *Foursome: Alfred Stieglitz, Georgia O'Keeffe, Paul Strand, Rebecca Salsbury*. New York: Vintage, 2020.

Burke, John M. *Buffalo Bill from Prairie to Palace*. 1893. Reprint, Lincoln: University of Nebraska Press, 2012.

Burns, Emily C. *The American West in France*. Norman: University of Oklahoma Press, 2018.

———. "Art, Ethnography, and Politics." In *Albert Bierstadt: Witness to a Changing West*, edited by Peter H. Hassrick, 123–52. Norman: University of Oklahoma Press, 2018.

Burr, Hattie A. *The Woman Suffrage Cook Book*. 1886. Reprint, Carlisle MA: Applewood, 2019.

Child, Lydia Maria. *The American Frugal Housewife*. Boston: Carter, Hendee, 1833.

Cody, Louisa. *Memories of Buffalo Bill*. New York: D. Appleton, 1919.

Cody, William F. *The Life of Hon. William F. Cody, Known as Buffalo Bill, the Famous Hunter, Scout and Guide: An Autobiography*. Hartford CT: Frank E. Bliss, 1879.

———. *Story of the Wild West and Campfire Chats*. Richmond: B. F. Johnson, 1888.

———. *True Tales of the Plains*. New York: Cupples and Leon, 1908.

Cornelius, [Mary Ann Hooker]. *The Young Housekeeper's Friend*. Boston: Tappan Whittemore, & Mason, 1850.

Cunningham, Tom F. *Your Fathers the Ghosts: Buffalo Bill's Wild West in Scotland*. Edinburgh: Black and White, 2007.

Danker, Donald F., ed. *Man of the Plains: Recollections of Luther North, 1856–1882*. Lincoln: University of Nebraska Press, 1961.

Davies, Henry E. *Ten Days on the Plains*. Edited by Paul Andrew Hutton. Dallas: DeGolyer Library, Southern Methodist University Press, 1985.

DeWitt, Dave. *The Founding Foodies: How Washington, Jefferson, and Franklin Revolutionized American Cuisine*. Naperville IL: Sourcebooks, 2010.

Dobrow, Joe. *Pioneers of Promotion*. Norman: University of Oklahoma Press, 2018.

Dohner, Janet Vorwald. *The Encyclopedia of Historic and Endangered Livestock and Poultry Breeds*. New Haven CT: Yale University Press, 2001.

Eighmey, Rae Katherine. *Stirring the Pot with Benjamin Franklin: A Founding Father's Culinary Adventures*. Washington DC: Smithsonian, 2018.

Farmer, Fannie Merritt. *The Boston Cooking-School Cook Book*. 1896. Facsimile of 1st ed., New York: Weathervane, 1973.

Fellows, Dexter. *This Way to the Big Show*. New York: Halcyon House, 1938.

FitzGibbon, Theodora. *The Food of the Western World: An Encyclopedia of Food from North America and Europe*. New York: Quadrangle/New York Times, 1976.

Foote, Stella. *Letters from "Buffalo Bill."* El Segundo CA: Upton and Sons, 1990.

Friesen, Steve. *Buffalo Bill: Scout, Showman, Visionary*. Golden CO: Fulcrum, 2010.

Fry, Laura F. "Wonders from Out-of-the-Way Places." In *Frederic Remington: A Catalogue Raisonné II*, edited by Peter H. Hassrick, 17–41. Norman: University of Oklahoma Press, 2016.

Gallop, Alan. *Buffalo Bill's British Wild West*. Phoenix Mill, UK: Sutton, 2001.

Gillette, F. L., and Hugo Ziemann. *The White House Cook Book*. 1887. Facsimile of 1st ed., Media Solution, 2003.

Gould, A. A. *The Naturalist's Library*. New York: C. Wells, 1833.

Griffin, Charles Eldridge. *Four Years in Europe with Buffalo Bill*. Edited by Chris Dixon. Lincoln: University of Nebraska Press, 1908.

Hale, Sara Josepha. *The Good Housekeeper*. 1841. Facsimile of 1st ed., Mineola NY: Dover, 1996.

Harland, Marion. *Common Sense in the Household*. New York: Charles Scribner, 1871.

Hassrick, Peter H. "Albert Bierstadt." In *Albert Bierstadt: Witness to a Changing West*, edited by Peter H. Hassrick, 29–122. Norman: University of Oklahoma Press, 2018.

Heffron, D. S. "Poultry Report." In *Report of the Commissioner of Agriculture*, 358–72. Washington DC: Government Printing Office, 1862.

Herrick, Christine Terhune. *Consolidated Library of Modern Cooking and Household Recipes*. Vol. 4. New York: R. J. Bodmer, 1904.

Hill, Benson E. *The Epicure's Almanac for 1842*. London: How and Parsons, 1842.

Hollister, Will C. *Dinner in the Diner*. Glendale CA: Trans-Anglo, 1984.

Ingraham, Prentiss. *Buffalo Bill Cody: A Man of the West*. Edited by Sandra K. Sagala. Lawrence: University Press of Kansas, 2019.

Johnson, Harry. *New and Improved Bartender's Manual*. New York: Harry Johnson, 1882.

Jonnes, Jill. *Eiffel's Tower*. New York: Penguin, 2009.

Kensel, W. Hudson. *Pahaska Tepee: Buffalo Bill's Old Hunting Lodge and Hotel, a History, 1901–1946*. Cody WY: Buffalo Bill Historical Center, 1987.

Kerns, Matthew. *Texas Jack: America's First Cowboy Star*. Guilford CT: TwoDot, 2021.

King, Charles. *Campaigning with Crook and Stories of Army Life*. New York: Harper and Brothers, 1980.

Kinney, Holly Arnold. *Shinin' Times at the Fort*. Morrison CO: Fur Trade, 2010.

Lang, Jennifer Harvey, ed. *Larousse Gastronomique*. New York: Crown, 1988.

Lea, Elizabeth E. *Domestic Cookery, Useful Receipts, and Hints to Young Housekeepers*. Baltimore: Cushings and Bailey, 1853.

Leslie, Eliza. *Miss Leslie's Directions for Cookery*. 1851. Reprint, Mineola NY: Dover, 1999.

Logan, Herschel C. *Buckskin and Satin*. Harrisburg PA: Stackpole, 1954.

Lowe, Charles. *Four National Exhibitions in London*. London: T. Fisher Unwin, 1892.

Majors, Alexander. *Seventy Years on the Frontier*. Chicago: Rand, McNally, 1893.

Makharadze, Irakli. *Georgian Trick Riders in American Wild West Shows, 1890s–1920s*. Jefferson NC: MacFarland, 2015.

Mathews, Nancy Mowll. "Gauguin, Buffalo Bill, and the Cowboy Hat." *Transatlantica* (February 2017).

McLeod, Stephen A., ed. *Dining with the Washingtons*. Chapel Hill: Mount Vernon Ladies' Association, 2011.

Monahan, Sherry. *The Golden Elixir of the West: Whiskey and the Shaping of America*. Helena MT: TwoDot, 2018.

Newton Kansan. *The Kansan Kook Book*. Vol. 1. Newton: Newton Kansan, 1905.

Nichols, Harry E. "Apple Varieties Grown in Iowa, 1800–1970." *Annals of Iowa* 43, no. 2 (Fall 1975): 81–102.

Noble, James. *Around the Coast with Buffalo Bill.* East Yorkshire: Hutton, 1999.

Paxton, W. M. *Annals of Platte County, Missouri.* Kansas City MO: Hudson-Kimberly, 1897.

Porterfield, James D. *Dining by Rail.* New York: St. Martin's Griffin, 1993.

Randolph, J. W. *Directions for Cooking by Troops, in Camp and Hospital, Prepared for the Army of Virginia, and Published by Order of the Surgeon General.* Richmond VA: J. W. Randolph, 1861.

Richardson, Albert D. *Beyond the Mississippi.* Newark NJ: Bliss, 1867.

Riley, Glenda. *The Life and Legacy of Annie Oakley.* Norman: University of Oklahoma Press, 1994.

Roosevelt, Theodore. *Theodore Roosevelt's Letters to His Children.* New York: Charles Scribner's Sons, 1919; Bartleby.com, 1998. https://www.bartleby.com/53/.

Russell, Don, ed. "Julia Cody Goodman's Memoirs of Buffalo Bill." *Kansas Historical Quarterly* 28, no. 4 (Winter 1962): 442–96.

———. *The Lives and Legends of Buffalo Bill.* Norman: University of Oklahoma Press, 1960.

Sagala, Sandra K. *Buffalo Bill Cody: A Collection of Poems on the 100th Anniversary of His Death.* Princeton NJ: Red Dashboard, 2017.

———. *Buffalo Bill on Stage.* Albuquerque: University of New Mexico Press, 2008.

Sanderson, James M. *Camp Fires and Camp Cooking, or Culinary Hints for the Soldier.* Washington DC: Government Printing Office, 1862.

Shillaber, Lydia. *Practical Guide for Housekeepers.* New York: Thomas Y. Crowell, 1887.

Sizer, Rosanne. "Fruit in Iowa: A Brief History." *Palimpsest* 63, no. 3 (1981): 80–89.

Sorg, Eric. *Doctor, Lawyer, Indian Chief.* Austin TX: Eakin, 2002.

Standing Bear, Luther, and E. A. Brininstool. *My People the Sioux.* London: Williams and Norgate, 1928.

Swett, Lucia Gray. *New England Breakfast Breads.* Boston: Lee and Shepard, 1890.

Thomas, Jerry. *How to Mix Drinks, or the Bon-Vivant's Companion.* 1862. Reprint, Kansas City: American Antiquarian Society and Andrews McNeel, 2013.

Urban, William. "When the 'Wild West' Went to Florence." *Illinois Quarterly* (Spring 1978): 5–21.

Walsh, Richard J. *The Making of Buffalo Bill.* New York: A. L. Burt, 1928.

Warren, Louis S. *Buffalo Bill's America.* New York: Alfred Knopf, 2005.

Weaver, William Woys. *Heirloom Vegetable Gardening.* Minneapolis: Voyageur, 2018.

Wetmore, Helen Cody. *Last of the Great Scouts: The Life Story of Col. William F. Cody ("Buffalo Bill").* Duluth MN: Duluth, 1899.

Wetmore, Helen Cody, and Zane Grey. *Last of the Great Scouts (Buffalo Bill).* New York: Grosset and Dunlap, 1918.

Williams, Jacqueline. *Wagon Wheel Kitchens.* Lawrence: University Press of Kansas, 1993.

Williams, Susan. *Savory Suppers and Fashionable Feasts.* New York: Pantheon, 1985.

Wilson, R. L. *Buffalo Bill's Wild West: An American Legend.* New York: Random House, 1998.

Winch, Frank. *Thrilling Lives of Buffalo Bill and Pawnee Bill.* New York: S. L. Parsons, 1911.

Wojtowicz, James W. *The W. F. Cody Buffalo Bill Collector's Guide with Values.* Paducah KY: Collector, 1998.

Wondrich, David. *Imbibe!* New York: Perigee, 2015.

Yost, Nellie Snyder. *Buffalo Bill: His Family, Friends, Fame, Failures, and Fortunes.* Chicago: Sage, 1979.

INDEX

divorce trial, 196–99; life on the frontier with, 24, 26, 31, 42

Cody, Mary (mother), 11, 13, 19, 30, 31, 101, 175, 188; death of, 21–22, 24; as hotelier, 16, 25, 42, 175

Cody, Orra (daughter), 42, 196

Cody, William F.: autobiographies of, 51, 188, 201, 226; birth of, 4; as buffalo hunter, xi, 3, 24, 26–28, 31–34, 180, 189; as cattle herder, 14; and Cody family plot, 48, 49; during Civil War, 3, 16, 24; as colonel, xi, xii, xiii, 60–61, 66, 117, 141, 170; as conservationist, 162, 169, 180–81; death and burial of, 210; and divorce trial, 130, 131, 184, 187, 196–99, *200*, 201, 247; "Dr. Jekyll and Mr. Hyde" 156; failing health of, 133, 209–210, *211*; as farmer, 159; as general, xiii, 60–61; grave of, 213, 215; Guillaume de Buffalo, 123; investments by, 60, 100, 176, 180, 207–8; *Le charmant Guillaume*, 123; on Oregon Trail, 14, 15, *18*, 20, 36, 223; as Santa Claus, 207; scouting by, xi, 3, 21, 22, 24–31, *37*, 40–46, *43*, 48–49; spiritual life of, 198; as teamster, 3, 15–16, 19–20, 24–25, 31, 187–88; unsuccessful retirement of, 133, 206–8; and wealth at death, 210

Cody Canal (Wyoming), 180

Cody Day, 99, 175

Cody Enterprise (newspaper), 177

Cody-Powell Coffee Co., 192

Cody WY, xiii, 176–80, *179*, 183–84, 193–94, 216–17, 243–44

coffee, 36, 74, 85, 108, 113, *116*, 117, 124, 141, 165, 168, 203, 209; Arbuckle Ariosa, 224; at Caffè Greco, 88, 131; and hundred-gallon pot, 63, 66; Maxwell House, 51; Meert, 142, 218, *220*; on the frontier, 8, 12, 15–16, 17, 22, 23, 28, 49; Panmalt, 192; quantities of, 63, 65, 67, 70, 77, 81, 89, 142, 155

cognac, 120, 172

Cohan, George M., 207

Colosseum; in Rome, 126; in Verona, 127

Colt firearms, 50

Columbian Exposition (Chicago), 61, 80, 88, 98, 130, 139, 171, 192, 194; food at, 147–49, 158; Waif's Day during, 99–100, 234

Columbus Journal, 136

Columbus OH, 65

Common Sense in the Household (Harland), 226

Comstock, Bill, 27

concession stand, 108, 125, 127, 128, 147–50, *151*

confectionary, 64, 108, 142, 148, 149, 150, *151*, 153–54, 207, 218

Cook, W. W., 209

Cooke, Louis E., 137

Cope, Edward, 160

corn, 8, 13, 70, 96, 115, 124, 135, 138, 140, 142, 144, 150; bread, 4, 11, 96, 103–4, 115, 124, 135, 168–69, 218, 221–22; cake, 88, 135; exports to Europe, 125, 135; field, 13; grits, 50; hominy, 8, 96, 124; husks, 90, 234; Indian, 117, 233; maize, 128, 238; meal, 135, 155, 222, 233; popcorn ball, 108, 128, 238; popcorn, 108, 114, 120, 124–125, 127, 135, 147–50, 154, 205, 207; roasted, 97, 163

Cornelius (*The Young Housekeeper's Friend*), 222

cossacks, 79, *80*, 81, 83–85, 118, 139

egg, 12, 50, 68, 75, 85, 91, 131, 178, 199; quantities of, 63, 70, 77, 89, 112, 127, 150, 155

Eiffel Tower, 121, 130, *132*

electric fan, in Cody's tent, 73

electric lighting (light plant), 71–73, 124

elephant, 61

elevator, 52

elk, 23, 24. 34, 36, 58, 103, 147, 177

England, xii, 30, 62, 87, 95, 96, 117–18, 192, 195, 202, 204–5, 247; Bedford, 153; and "Biggest Man in London," 109–10; Birmingham, 96, 111; Bristol, 103; Burton-on-Trent, 118, 203; Cheltenham, 118; Cornwall, 117, 119; Gainesborough, 153; Gravesend, 103; Land's End, 119; Leeds, 112; Liverpool, 112, 153; Manchester, 96, 111, 112, 118, 191, 235; Penzance, 119; Staffordshire, 119, 203; Stoke-On-Trent, 119. *See also* London, England

English Channel, 111, 122

Epiphany (Kings Day), 218–19

Erastina, Staten Island, 94, 97, 104, 110, 111, 157, 162, 171, 173, 202

farewell dinner, 158, 180, 203

Farewell Salute, 207–8

Fellows, Dexter, xiii, 175, 195, 209

Ferrell, Della, 130

fève, 218–19

Fifth Cavalry, 29, 30

film, 124–25

"fire water," 63

fish, 13, 23, 36, 40, 50, 63, 68–69, 78, 81, 108, 165, 178; anchovy, xiii, 140, 144; baked, 170; blue, 145; cisco, 23; cod, 113; and "fish"

course, 93, 138; flounder, 73; halibut, 138, 159, 242; mackerel, 12, 155; quantities of, 155; red snapper, 208; salmon, 12, 38, 96, 127, 141–43, 162, 203; sea bass, 144; sole, xiii, 13, 124, 140; trout, 48, 51, 124, 140, 214; turbot, 142; white, 12, 158; whiting, 113

flag, 66, 104, 122, 124, 139, 144–45, 175, 206

Flat Iron, 88

flatware, 66, 85, 96, 117, 226

Fleissner, Otto, 182

Fond du Lac WI, 150

Ford, W. F., 182

Forsyth, James W., 28

Fort Collins CO, 190

Fort Ellsworth KS, 25

Fort Fletcher KS, 25

Fort Hays KS, 23–24, 25–26

Fort Laramie WY, 15, 16, 20, 69, 223, 224, 225

Fort Larned KS, 25

Fort McPherson NE, 23, 27, 28–31, 34, 41, 49, 166, 171, 182, 189

Fort Oglethorpe TN, 170

Fort Yates ND, 191

"fox hunt," 176, 244–45

France, 111, 119, 120, 122, 123, 125, 128, 130–31, 139, 163, 173, 218; Chateau de Fontainebleau, 163–64; Le Havre, 216; Lille, 142, 218, 220, 239; Lyon, 125; Marseille, 125, 131–33, 170; Neuilly, 121. *See also* Paris, France

Franco-Prussian War, 129

Franklin, Benjamin, 226

"free-state" advocates, 12

French cuirassier, 83

French, Daniel Chester, 166

frog legs, 127, 139

Hickok, Wild Bill, 16, 24, 25, 29, 35, 45, 160, 189
hide hunters, 27
Hindus, 61, 70
Hinman, Beach, 172
Holladay, Benjamin, 6–7, 24–25
Holladay, David, 6–7
Holladay distillery, 19, 24–25, 188, 215
Hoover, "Water Hoss," 65, 74
horse, 28, 61, 64, 73, 111, 119, 121, 152, 202, 217; bucking, 68, 147; glanders, 131–33; number in show; 71, 72, 74, 100, 103, 117, 118, 126, 141; rumored abuses of, 132–33; thoroughbred, 171
hotel, 4, 16–17, 26, 36, 45–46, 49, 61–63, 120, 156–57, 161, 182, 207; Albany Hotel (Denver), 219; benefits from show, 146, 151, 152; Allyn House (Hartford), 50–51; Brevoort Place (New York City), 39–40; Briggs House (Chicago), 189; Brown Palace Hotel (Denver), 181; Canfield House (Omaha), 176; Chamberlin Hotel (Washington DC), 166–68; Continental Hotel (Buffalo), 38; DeWitt Hotel (Lewiston), 53; Golden Rule House (Salt Creek Valley), 16–17, 25, 42, 175; Granby Hotel (Gainesborough), 153; Grand Hotel Alfred Hauser (Naples), 126; Grand Hotel (Glasgow), 114; Green Tree Hotel (West Chester), 41–42, 47, 176; Hoffman House (New York City), 81–82, 157, 159, 177, 196, 216, 217; Hotel Albemarle (London), 115, *116*; Hotel Astor (New York City), 207; Hôtel Bellevue (Brussels), 129; Hotel de France (Fontainebleau), 163; Hotel La Salle (Chicago), 159; Hôtel du Musée (Waterloo), 130; Hotel Metropole (London), 156, 162; Irma Hotel (Cody), 176–177, 178, 183, 217, 243–44; Mansion House (Buffalo), 51; Maxwell House (Nashville), 51; Merchants Hotel (Omaha), 247; Opera Hotel (New York City), 183; Pacific Hotel (North Platte), 172; Pahaska Tepee (Cody), 177, 178–79, *179*, 217; Purcell House (Wilmington), 46, 49–50; Santa Rita (Tucson), 180, 207; Saratoga Hotel (Chicago), 159; Savoy Hotel (London), 107, 237; Sheridan Inn (Sheridan), 176, 215, 217; Sturtevant House (New York City), 52–53, *52*, 82, 93, 229; Tontine Hotel (New Haven), 160; Union Club (New York City), 35, 39–40; United States Hotel (Portland), 50; Valley Grove House (Salt Creek Valley), 16, 25, 42; Waldorf (New York City), xi, 150; Wapiti Inn (Cody), 177; Wiltcher's Hotel (Brussels), 129; Winchester Hotel (Winsted), 151. *See also* restaurant
Hudson River, xiii
Hughes-Hallett, Francis, 110
Hungary, 130, 133, 142–43, 218
hussars, 83
Hutchinson, Charles, 231

ice. *See* refrigerator wagon
ice cream, 50, 68, 101, 139, 141, 142, 145, 158, 159, 169, 182; bombe, 115, 162; Keliher Ice Cream Parlor, 174; sorbet, 162, 239; sundaes, 208–9; Viennese ices, 128
Idaho Springs CO, 209

Lillie, Gordon "Pawnee Bill," 61, 206–8
Lima OH, 240
Lincoln, Abraham, 95–96, 166
Lincoln Evening Call, 173
Lincoln Memorial, 166
liqueur, 113, 120, 154, 162, 172, 227, 242, 247
Little Bighorn, 48, 100, 154
livestock, 8, 25, 65, 72, 73, 119, 147, 189
loan, 144, 161, 204
London, England, 71, 80, 96, 103–11, 114–17, 118–19, 121, 124, 128, 133–34, 137–38; American cocktails served in, 106, 237; Earl's Court, 104, *107*, 110, 114–15; 1887 American exhibition, 103, *107*; Henry Poole and Co., 156; United Arts Club, 157; with Remington, 164; with Whistler, 161–62
Long Branch NJ, 150
longhorn, 103
Longhorn Ranch PA, 214
Lookout Mountain (Golden CO), 210, 213–14
Los Angeles, 68
Luden's Cough Drops, 154
Luitpold, Prince Regent of Bavaria, 97–98

Macbeth (Shakespeare), 129
Madam X, 123
Majors, Alexander, 14, 18, 175
Mankato MN, 64
Marie Henriette, Queen of Belgium, 129
Marsh, O. C., 160–61, 175, 180
Maryland, 97, 109, 124, 142, 236
Mason City IA, 65

Massachusetts, 72, 139, 140, 143, 145, 150; Boston, 93–94, 96, 101, 152–53, 235, 244
Mather, Stephen, 178–79
"mauviettes á l'Indienne," 129
May, Karl, 218
McCormick Distilling, 215
McKinley, William, 168
McLaughlin, James, 191
"meat on a stick," 93
Medal of Honor, 3, 42
Mediterranean, 125–26, 218
Medley, Thomas, 47–48
Meert confectionary and tea, 142, 218–19, *220*
Memphis TN, 154, 193
Métis, 94
Mexican cafe, xi, 82, 90–91, 102
Mexicans, 84, 104, 233
Mexican vaqueros, 58, 79, *80*, 81, 82, 84,
Miles, Nelson, 100, 118, 129, 166, 191, 242
milk, 9, 20, 24, 57, 63, 70, 78, 85, 155, 178; and Cody, 110, 130, 187, 199
Miller Brothers 101 Ranch Wild West, 208, 209
Milwaukee Journal, 166
Milwaukee WI, 166
mimic army, 61, 128
mine, 180, 207
Minneapolis MN, 64
Mississippi, 24
Mississippi River, xi, 34, 46, 72, 82, 90, 215
Mississippi River Distilling Co., 216
Miss Leslie's Directions for Cookery, 225
Missouri, 4, 5, 6, 7, 19, 20–21, 24, 50, 188, 193, 221; Missourians, 6–7, 20; St. Louis, 7, 12, 18, 24–25, 26, 27, 42, 46, 221, 223, 246; Weston,

Missouri (*cont.*)
4, 5–7, 5, 8, 11, 12, 19, 24–25, 188, 215, 221
Missouri River, 5–8, 12, 14, 50, 221
Mitchell, Peter, 94
moccasin, 88
Moffat, David, 162
Moffat, E. J., 161–62
Moline IL, 207
molasses, 12, 96, 148, 222, 238
Montreal, 94
Montreal Herald, 94
Moran, Thomas, 105
Morlacchi, Mademoiselle, 43, *43,* 45, 92
Mormons, 5–6, 15–16
moss-haired lady, 141
Mount Hope Cemetery (Rochester NY), 48
Moxie cola, 153
mule, 16, 72, 103, 126
Munch, Edvard, 122, 161
music, 38, 40, 51, 52, 101, 113, 114, 160, 173. *See also* cowboy band
mutton, 51, 68, 69, 81, 87, 104, 117, 139, 148, 155, 162; braised sheep's head, 120; chops, 36, 50, 217; cutlets, 113; leg of, 38, 50, 143, 177; roast, 63, 96; saddle of, 168; stew, 67

napkin, 63, 67, 85, 93, 232–33
Napoleon, 61, 130, 168, 219
Nashville TN, 51
Nast, Thomas, 40
Nebraska, 15, 20, 36, 42, 44, 124, 129, 136, 160, 171–75, 180; Columbus, 58, 137, 146–47, 193; exhibit at Columbian Exposition, 98; Lincoln, 194; Oak Grove Ranch, 20; Omaha, 31, 36, 42, 58, 174, 175,

193–94, 195, 247. *See also* North Platte NE
Nebraska Advertiser, 19
Nebraska National Guard, 60–61
New Haven CT, 160, 161, 240
New Orleans LA, 60, 190, 201, 227
newspaperwomen, 101
New York, 32, 34, 35, 36, 46, 47, 49, 53, 63, 70, 71, 108, 150; Brooklyn, 52, 100–101, 139, 165; Buffalo, 38, 51; New Rochelle, 164; Niagara Falls, 38, *39;* Rochester, 38–39, 47, 48–49, 171; Staten Island, 94, 104, 111, 157, 162, 166
New York City, 3, 23, *37,* 39–41, 92–93, 100–102, 155, 159–60, 183, 189, 190, 205; announces farewell tours, 207; Bowery Theater in, 41–42, 160, 169; hotels, 52, 52, 81–82, 157, 177, 196, 216–17; Indian statue in harbor, 165–66; Madison Square Garden, 60, 62, 66–67, 81–83, 150, 152, 157, 165, 171, 173; Mexican food in, 82, 90–91, 233–34; Niblo's Garden, 38; steamship departures and arrivals at, 117, 120, 163, 173
New York Daily Herald (New York Herald), 41
New York Sun, 27, 81, 91, 246
New York Times, 82, 127, 155
Nixon's Amphitheater (Chicago), 42–44
No Neck, 113–14
North Platte NE, 29, 30, 31, 32, 137, 138, 158–59, 175, 179, 198, 217; Cody residences in, 49, 99, 100, 136, 170–74; Cody statue in, 174; drinking in, 29–30, 171–72, 189, 193–94, 199–201, *200;* generosity toward, 100, 173–75; lessened

attention paid to, 175–77; Old Glory Blowout at, 136–37, 145; scouting and hunting near, 27, 29–32, 189; Union Pacific operations in, 30, 172

Northridge CA, 215

nut, 9, 12, 91, 138, 145, 162; peanuts, 120, 124–25, 128, 135, 147, 148, 208, 209

Oakley, Annie, xii, 3, 60, 62, 63, 134, 213

Ogallala man, 84

Ogilvie, W. W., 94

Oklahoma, 68; Oklahoma City, 195

Old Glory Blowout, 135–37, 145

Old Tom Gin, 29–30

Omohundro, John "Texas Jack," 42–45, *43*, 47, 50, 160, 189

opossum, 51

Oregon Trail, 5, 14, 15, *18*, 20, 36, 223–25

Owens, Bill, 216

Owosso MI, 64

pancake. *See* griddle cake

Paris, France, 3, 97, 109, 119–25, 130, *132*, 133, 142, 147, 148, 154, 168–69; artists in, 163–64; Cody's "retreat" to, 198; Disneyland in, 218; Exposition Universelle, 121–25, 133, 138, 163; Independence Day in, 138–39, *140*

pastry, 51, 64, 101, 113, 138, 142, 155, 160; banana fritters, 142, 239–40; tarts, 38, 63

Patterson, A. H., 190

Pawnee Bill's Far East,, 61, 68, 80, 83, 144, 154, 206, 208

Pawnees, 31, 46, 51, 79, 94

Pennsylvania, 97, 171, 176, 215, 242

Perry, Dave, 30, 189

Persians, 70

personal chef, 182–83

Philadelphia Herd of the Beneficial Order of Buffaloes, 157

Piazza D'armi (Rome), 126, 131

piccalilli, 96, 155

The Picture of Dorian Gray (Whistler), 161

pie, 31, 38, 70, 89, 96, 99, 143, 150, 155, 234; apple, 96, 113, 124, 138, 177; custard, 13, 94, 117, 169; lemon, 138, 177; meat, 63; mince, 124; pumpkin, 97, 117, 142, 163; rabbit, 114

pigeon, 162

Pikes Peak Gold Rush, 17, 215

Pinchot, Gifford, 180

Pine Ridge SD, 173

plate, 32, 66, 85, 93, 94, 95, 101, 115, 119, 243; china, 63, 64, 66, 68, 181; graniteware, 64, 66; tin, 85, 92, 96, 225

Platte River, 36

poetry, 96, 123, 144, 209, 243

Poland, 130, 143

polenta, 127

Polk, James K., 50

Pony Express, 18–19, 175

pork, 63, 67, 68, 69, 81, 127, 148, 155, 168, 203, 231, 247; boar's head, 51; chops, 68, 70, 75, 88; lard, 155, 222–23, 230, 235; loin, 76, 170, 177; pig feet, 52, 114, 155, 229; and beans, 96, 124, 138, 235; quantities of, 155; salt, 115, 224, 225, 235–36; suckling pig, 208. *See also* bacon; ham

Portland ME, 50

portrait, 36, 121, 122, 161, 165

poster, 72, 82, 90, 121, 164, 203, 213

vegetable (*cont.*)
  rejected by the Indians, 83, 87,
    117; spinach, 142, 145, 155; squash,
    8; succotash, 155; tomato, 63, 95,
    112, 158, 228, 233; watercress, 155,
    159. *See also* bean; potato
"vegetable parchment," 129
vinegar, 155, 199, 238
Vin Fiz, 154
Virginia, 97, 239, 244–45
Waddell, William, 14
waiter, 32, 63, 66–67, 68, 69, 83, 87,
    117, 226; in circus outfits, 159;
    special one for Cody, 104
Wales, 109, 117, 118, 119, 122, 141, 236
Wallace NE, 173
Walls, W. L., 178
Wanamaker, Rodman, 165
Wanamaker Department Store, 165
Wansart, Eric, 218
Ward, Henry, 38–39
Ward's Natural Science, 38–39
Washington, George, 144, 232
watermen, 64
water tank, 72
water wagon, 74
Webb, W. E., 26
Welcome Wigwam (North Platte),
    171, 174
West Chester PA, 41–42, 46–47,
    171, 176
W. F. Cody Hotel Co., 176
Whalen, Charlie, 201
whiskey, 52, 84, 91, 112, 165, 175, 191,
    199, 201, 215, 217, 218; Buffalo
    Bill Bourbon, 216; Cody as
    "bartender," 195; Cody Road,
    216; and the Combination, 44,
    45, 189; "dew drop," 171; at 1857
    election, 21; Garrick Club, 153;
    Glenlivet, 120; Holladay, 24–25,

188, 215; Old Crow, 153, 216; on
    the frontier, 6–7, 11–12, 19–20, 23,
    26, 29–30, 31, 48–49, 187–89; rec-
    tified whiskey, 188; at rib roasts,
    93, 94; Taos Lightning, 215–16;
    "the whiskey of Mexico," 91; Very
    Old Highland, 113
Whistler, James McNeil, 161–62
White, William Allen, 65
White Beaver's Cough Cream, 191
The White House Cook Book, 225, 232
Whitley, John R., 103–5, 133, 205
Wiard, Harry Leonard, 183, 243
Wilde, Oscar, 3, 110, 134, 161
Wild West programs, 59, 152–54, 164,
    167, 178, 180, 207, 208
Wilhelm, Crown Prince, 109, 128
Wilhelm II, Emperor, 109, 128
Willard, Orsamus, 244–45
Wilmington Morning Star, 46
Wilmington NC, 49, 151
Wilson, Charles, 35
Wilson, Woodrow, 137
Windsor Castle, 111
wine, 38, 40, 51, 84, 85, 101, 111,
    117, 120, 158, 174, 175, 195; Caffè
    Greco, 131; Catawba, 172; Chateau
    du Clos de Vougeot, 168; Chateau
    Leoville wine, 162; claret, 23, 82,
    106, 113, 120, 157, 209, 241, 248;
    Cockburn's Old Bottled Port, 162;
    in Cody's wine cellar, 170, 171; on
    the frontier, 12, 19, 23, 30, 32, 34;
    Johannisberger Riesling Cabinett,
    168; Madeira, 227, 228, 232–33,
    244; Pauillac, 127; Rhine, 157, 162,
    168; sangria, 106
Winona MN, 64
Winsted CT, 151
wire recording, 125
Wisconsin National Guard, 166

Printed in the USA
CPSIA information can be obtained
at www.ICGtesting.com
CBHW022224220424
7386CB00001B/49